A POTPOURRI OF THOUGHTS ON ENGLISH LITERATURE

S.A.

CHOICE RUMINATIONS ON ENGLISH LITERATURE

Shahla Anand

UNIVERSITY PRESS OF AMERICA

LANHAM • NEW YORK • LONDON

University Press of America,™ Inc.

4720 Boston Way
Lanham, MD 20706

3 Henrietta Street
London WC2E 8LU England

Printed in the United States of America

ISBN (Perfect): 0-8191-3284-5
LCN: 83-6611

Published by Vantage Press, Inc., 1975

CONTENTS

Part I

Part II

A Dedication

Literature is heady wine. I dedicate my essays to all who are enamoured of it, and to Isa Charan Sada, linguist, Urdu poet and writer, without whose inspiration this book would not have been possible.

PART I

"THE PARDONER'S TALE" AND MEDIAEVAL DRAMA

"The tragic face behind the satyr's mask."[1]

The scenes of violence on the stage were Senecan, the tragic fall of the protagonist a heritage from the Greek. In the mediaeval tragedy the two elements fused and with the added liturgical dimension gave posterity the drama of the soul. Mediaeval drama was the verbalized soul-searching of man. In the morality plays the protagonist contended with his inner self and with specious and spurious abstractions for salvation in the hereafter. Had Chaucer fashioned "The Pardoner's Tale" as a morality play, it would have met the requirements of the genre. The Pardoner, Kittredge's "lost soul," would have stood out as the protagonist with the Host and the "gentils" his co-actors and audience. His tale would have then become a play within the play; the subplot carrying the three protagonists who, in search of Death's destruction and for salvation from death, ironically succumb to its most virulent barbs. In the tale, as it stands, the Pardoner comes on the stage like the messenger in *Everyman*, and verbally enacts his consummate short story. The tale has an unexpected reversal, and the necessary repartée and movement and spectacle of a forceful narrative. It is well structured, moves progressively forward to the dénouement and catastrophe, and is formulated, to a large extent, in dialogue. The dialogue is pithy and concise and "has an irreducible quality of familiarity. . ."[2] which gives it the texture of a play. Like the morality plays, for its characteriza-

[1] George Lyman Kittredge, *Chaucer and His Poetry* (Cambridge, MA: Harvard University Press, 1927), p. 218.

[2] Charles Muscatine, "The Canterbury Tales: Style of the Man and Style of the Work," *Chaucer and the Chaucerians: Critical Studies in Middle English Literature*, ed. D. S. Brewer (London: Thomas Nelson, Ltd. 1966), p. 91.

tions it uses prototypes of youth and age and personified abstractions. The emaciated Old Man, for instance, could be equated with Death, if not its messenger: "Lo how I vanysshe, flessh, and blood and skyn!"[3] Like the Morality, the story shows the mediaeval preoccupation with the life beyond the grave as it does with death. Carrying the motif of the pilgrimage, "The Pardoner's Tale" becomes the dramatic "quest for the death of death."[4]

"Chaucer, a highly sophisticated literary artist, wrote his tales to be read aloud at the Court or in the Chancery or before the Merchants' Guild."[5] He gave the *Canterbury Tales* all the highlights of a good performance. In the hands of Chaucer "The Pardoner's Tale," an exemplum, takes on the flavour of a play. His choice of words and expressions reflect the dramatic situation and the emotional content of the story, and give it an aura that makes it palpably real and highly dramatic.

The story itself is coloured by the Pardoner's personality at its best, that is when the Pardoner approximates closest to "a noble ecclesiaste," "a gentil Pardoner." The Pardoner, as the narrator of the tale, occupies a key position on the stage. He is as spectacular as any actor. The audience has already seen him process along with the Reeve, the Miller, the Summoner, the Maunciple, and Chaucer himself in the General Prologue, and anticipates a ribald tale from him, for Chaucer's "portraits work deeply into the themes and plots of his narrative. . . [and he uses] strategy as well as decorativeness in [his] descriptions."[6] As an individual the Pardoner is an oddity for he is neither a "geldyng [n]or a mare." His falsetto, "Com hider, love, to me!"[7] marks him as quaint. He has been at the papal court, but instead of a metaphoric halo, he carries his yellow hair hung in strands "oon and oon"; almost symbolic of the tarnished gold of a wilted halo. He fancies himself "of the newe jet" set, and brazenly flaunts his ware, but his bravado is a mask to cover his pathetic abnormality and inadequacy. If the Pardoner is singled out, it is not for his quaintness alone; he stands out because he is an actor. He is well

[3] F. N. Robinson, ed., "The Pardoner's Tale," *The Works of Geoffrey Chaucer*, 2nd ed. (Boston: Houghton Mifflin, 1961), p. 152, 1. 732.

[4] D.W. Robertson, *A Preface to Chaucer* (Princeton: Princeton University Press, 1969), p. 374.

[5] John H. Fisher, lecture at N.Y. University.

[6] Muscatine, *op. cit.*, pp. 98, 99.

[7] Robinson, *op. cit.*, p. 23, ls. 691 and 672.

aware that he is a master of his profession, unmatched between "Berwyk" and "Ware." Like many others of his trade he has all the customary tricks of extracting money from the gullible crowds, though Chaucer concedes that at his work the Pardoner is good. He has the histrionics of the lay preacher, a liturgist, a story teller, and a cantor, and can make his falsetto "ryinge it out as round as gooth a belle."[8] He himself says that his gestures and contortions in the pulpit are specious[8] enough to vie with those of any actor; and his rhetoric can equal the best of Oxenford.

With an actor such as the Pardoner in the forefront, Chaucer sets the stage for the drama. The lachrymose tale of the Physician has just ended. It has incensed the Host, and he calls on the Pardoner, "Thou, beel amy"[8] to regale them with a jolly tale. The pilgrims expect a bawdy tale from a man of the Pardoner's appearance, and protest:

> Nay lat hym telle us of no ribaudye,
> Tell us som moral thyng, that we may leere.[8]

The Pardoner promises to do both, entertain them and tell them an "Honest" tale, but only after reinforcing himself with a drink. The audience settles down to see the Pardoner take the forefront of the stage, and in the fashion of the Morality, open his drama to view with his monologue.

In his prologue the Pardoner shows himself the prototype of the corrupt churchman. Through his frank confession he reveals himself as an ecclesiast well on his way to damnation. Like Jean de Meun's False Seeming he seems to have been engendered by Fraud and Hypocrisy.[9] Also like False Seeming he frequents both the "cloister. . .[and a] secular abode."[9] His bags are filled with coins and he has little use for the poor and for poverty and can use his rhetoric for his own profit, "a prominent failing of pardoners."[10] Both he and False Seeming were in positions to dispense pardons, to give absolutions, and also to become wealthy unscrupulously. They knew their failings as temporal strength. The Pardoner gives an account of his deceitful ways in the same guise as False Seeming[9] and lards his speech with an exhibition of his relics. He confesses he has little use

[8] *Ibid.*, p. 148, ls. 331, 395-6, 318, 324, 325.

[9] C. W. Dunn, ed., *The Romance of the Rose* (New York: Dutton, 1962), pp. 222-231.

[10] Muriel Bowden, *A Reader's Guide to Geoffrey Chaucer* (New York: Farrar, Straus, and Giroux, 1969), p. 74.

for manual labour, and advocates slothful ease like Milton's Belial. The Pardoner, as False Seeming, characterizes some of the blatant abuses in the mediaeval Church. Both the Pardoner and False Seeming are well versed in the scriptures and the early Church Fathers, and like the Wife of Bath quote the scriptures and philosophize only to illustrate their arguments; at times distorting the interpretation to suit their purpose. Chaucer's Pardoner knew his *Geoffrey of Vinsauf*, and his *ars poetica*: he was a rhetorician.

F. N. Robinson points out, as does Carleton Brown, that "The Pardoner's Tale" has the merits of a mediaeval sermon. It has a subject or theme, an exemplum, peroration or application, and a closing formula or benediction.[11] This may have been Chaucer's specific design, for he experimented with all genres. He gives the Pardoner a tone of voice and choice of words and a sensitivity to the dramatic situation that holds his audience spellbound as though listening to mediaeval pulpit oratory. Although his histrionics are not lost on the Pilgrims or his audience through the prologue, the Pardoner still shocks the audience by the catalogue of his rascality. He deliberately lays bare, like False Seeming, the worst frauds that his profession could perpetrate. If he has any nostalgia for a past when he may have been innocent, or a wistfulness for a shriven future, the Pardoner does not show it. The only remorse, if it can be called that, is voiced at the end of the tale:

> Allas! mankynde, how may it bitide
> That to thy creatour, which that thee wroghte,
> And with his precious herte-blood thee boghte,
> Thou art so fals and so unkynde, allas?[12]

Behind the façade of his bravado, is the Pardoner genuinely tormented as Everyman in the Morality; is he indeed Kittredge's "lost soul" anxious to recapture a lost idealism? Or is he just an actor rehearsing his part before a captive audience? The closing notes of his tale belie his wholesale rascality. In his prologue the Pardoner shows himself worse than the actuality perhaps to shock the audience into undivided attention and to let the gift of his rhetoric cover his piteous abnormality. Does the catalogue of his

[11] Robinson, *op. cit.*, p. 729. Carleton Brown, *Chaucer's The Pardoner's Tale* (Oxford: Clarendon Press, 1963 rpt.), p. xii.

[12] Robinson, *op. cit.*, p. 154.

frauds cover "the tragic face behind the satyr's mask"; or, like a confession, does it "reveal his tortuous soul"?[13]

Bringing all his rhetorical innuendoes into play, the Pardoner introduces Chaucer's "play within the play" in the Tale. The mediaeval narrator moves aside to reveal a tableau on the stage; this becomes animated into a dumb show, a pantomime, and then a Dionysian orgy. The riotous scene, in a Flemish tavern, "the deviles temple," can be equated with the Mummer's Plays that ended in orgies. Replete with "harpes, lutes, and gyternes" the fetishly dressed young revelers dance, crowd round the gambling tables, pass the tankards of ale, and enjoy the pageantry of the dancing girls and vendors of fruit and confectionary and other entertainers. This Flemish orgy leads to 180 lines of pure sermonizing on the part of the narrator, the Pardoner, in the wise of the messenger in *Everyman* and of the two Flagbearers in the *Castle of Perseverance*. The homily is in "Chaucer's learned and scholastic style, characterised by logical argument and Latin terminology."[14] In it the Pardoner preaches the tragic consequences of overindulgence in gluttony and drink, gambling and swearing; the philosophic precepts of *Contemptu Mundi*. His monologue has all the charm of an erudite sermon. "The Pardoner is the only pilgrim dramatically given literary powers comparable to those of Chaucer himself."[15] His speech is a curious mixture of the pathetic and the grotesque.[16] References abound in its close packed lines to the Scriptures and the early Church Fathers, St. Paul and mediaeval theology, Seneca and scholastic philosophy, and to political and historical anecdotes. There is also a blend of more mundane things like gourmet cooking and spicy gleanings from history and the Bible and anecdotes of topical interest, as the "rede" wine and the "white wyn of Lepe" sold in "Fysshetrete" or in "Chepe."

After the long tirade in the homiletic manner, the scene moves to the actual story; dramatically the sub-plot of the play. The theme has many analogues. The earliest written source is traced to the Buddhist *Jatakas* of India, dating to the 2nd century B.C. Among the plethora of folk tales handed to children in

[13] G.G. Sedgwick, "The Progress of Chaucer's Pardoner," *Chaucer Criticism*, R.J. Schoeck and J. Taylor, eds. (Indiana: Notre Dame Press. 1960), p. 192.

[14] Muscatine, *op. cit.*, p. 106.

[15] *Ibid.*, p. 112.

[16] *Ibid.*

India, this tale still figures, and with as many variations of it as the tellers of the tale. Its continuing popularity is due to its preoccupation with death, a reality that every Indian faces stoically, in the hopes that death will lead to a better life, *Nirvana*, the celestial state of peace. The mediaeval mind was also deeply engrossed in the mixed blessings of opulence and its near kin, Death; a theme evident in morality plays. Chaucer's use of the story is in the same scheme of thought. In spite of his lighthearted treatment of the Pardoner, the seriousness of the tale's implications remain. The dancing, the dicing, the dining, the drinking are all overshadowed by the reality of death. In his homiletic aside the Pardoner ruminates on the follies of this life as do the sermonizing characters of morality plays. In "fully natural idioms and rhythms of the dramatic monologues"[17] Chaucer gives the Pardoner's searing lament and denunciation like that of Piers the Plowman:

> O glotonye, on thee wel oghte us pleyne!
> . . .
> Allas! the shorts throte, the tendre mouth,
> Maketh that est and west and north and south,
> In erthe, in eir, in water, men to swynke
> To gete a glotoun deyntee mete and drynke!
> . . . , wombe is hir god!
> O wombe! O bely! O stynking cod![18]

The references to delectable dishes and the befuddling wine and the intemperate victors in history, the humorous comments as "sour is thy breath, foul artow to embrace,"[19] all pale before the finality of death. During the harangue, the interplay was between the Pardoner, the characters, and the audience, but now Chaucer sets the stage for the actual play within the play; and the transition is dramatic. "Thise ryotoures three," suddenly arrive on the scene.

The *dramatis personae* of the playlet are the three rioters, a servant boy, a taverner, an Old Man, an apothecary, and the narrator. The characters that appear in the dumb show are the pall

[17] *Ibid.*, p. 104.
[18] Robinson, *op. cit.*, p.150, ls. 512-534.
[19] *Ibid.*, p.150, 1. 545 ff.

bearers and a man with "large botelles thre."[20]

The three rioters are prototypes ot youth and Mankind. Their course, as that of the acquisitive Human Genus in *The Castle of Perseverance* led by Sir Covetyse, leads the rioters to damnation instead of salvation. The three depict all the impetuosity and arrogance of youth. They are individualized as "oon of them," "the proudest of thise riotoures three," "this oother hasardour," "the worst of hem," "the yongeste of hem alle."[21]

The scene opens ere daybreak and the action is over soon after sundown of the same day, for the youngest rioter, as he had planned, was unable to: "For al the nyght he shoop hym to swynke."[22]

The scene shifts from a tavern to a country lane with a stile, denoting symbolically the obstacles in life's plans. From there it moves to a tree in a grove. The fourth shift of locale is a market square with an apothecary's dispensary, a side street showing a shop of bottles; also a wine merchant's store or a tavern. The final action is in the grove where the treasure is.

As in *Everyman* the three rioters or protagonists appear unconcerned of the "morrow"; they are seen drinking, ere prime, in a tavern. The dramatic tinkling of a bell, a mediaeval practice of dirge-chanting priests at the time of death, arouses the three out of their ennui, and creates the macabre atmosphere of the play. In a dumb show a corpse is carried across the stage by pall bearers. Shaken, one of the rioters opens the dialogue by asking his servant to discover the name of the dead man. The boy states that two hours prior to their advent at the tavern, he had learnt of the death of the man. The dead man was a comrade of theirs and had died in his cups. A mysterious abstraction called Death had come stealthily and had cleft their comrade's "herte atwo" with his spear, then left as silently. In true mediaeval fashion the boy warns them against this abstraction, for it was an adversary that had "a thousand slayn"[23] the year ot the plague. And the taverner corroborates his statement, by speaking the one time he does, to say that the abstraction, Death, had killed indiscriminately; and, as the killings of men, women, and children were in

[20] *Ibid.*, p. 154, l. 871.
[21] *Ibid.*, pp. 152 & 154, ls. 666, 712, 751, 776, 804.
[22] *Ibid.*, p. 154, l. 874.
[23] *Ibid.*, p. 152, ls. 677, 679.

the village a little over a mile from the tavern, Death probably lived there.

This leads to immediate action. The three rioters swear eternal brotherhood to each other and challenge Death wherever it is. They fling themselves out of the tavern in drunken rage and with determination; their quest is death.

The meeting with the sinister and shadowy Old Man near the stile is unexpected and has all the evil portent of the Dance Macabre. His humility, his staid speech, his garb, all irk the rioters. In contrast to the youth he appears an aged philosopher, a contemplative monk sheathed in his cowl and habit. The fact that this gaunt spectre of a man has "walked" all over and been to the farthest point, "Ynde," to seek death for himself and not found it, nor has he been able to change his state for that of youth, though he has solicited many for it, makes him supernatural and shrouds him in the mystery of death. Except for his face, like Donne's effigy, he is already shrouded in a winding sheet. His philosophic and ethical dialogue makes Robinson say of him, "And the Old Man, the Messenger of Death, in his mystery and moral sublimity is one of the most impressive apparitions in poetry."[24] He is uncannily impressive, but is the Old Man "Death" itself? His knocking at the door of the earth, his mother, is of no avail, for she too is afraid to let him in and be annihilated. Like the aging Chinese he keeps his coffin in his chamber. Perhaps Chaucer had in mind the wrought *sarcophagi* that many of the medieval nobles had sculptured for themselves in their life-time as a constant *Memento Mori*. Had the youth attempted to oust this spectre at this juncture as they had threatened to do, they might have escaped their folly and sinister murders. The ambiguity of the situation makes this mediaeval tale more dramatic, the suspense more powerful.

Fascinating though in itself, the rest of the story follows a stock pattern, with stock actions. On finding the eight bushels of florins, "the very fulness of life" instead of death, the master mind, "The worste of hem," becomes the director and the instigator of their crime. Ironically the golden glitter of the hoard is the dénouement of the play. The search for Death is forgotten, "Fellowship" deserts each of them and the horrifying triple murder brings the subplot to a close. There is "a dramatic conflict

[24] *Ibid.*, p. 11.

between . . . Death and the worldly humanity in which riches incite and fellowship conspires in crime and murder. [Similarly] in *Everyman* Fellowship vaingloriously proclaims:

> But and thou will murder, or any man kill,
> In that I will help thee with a good will."[25]

The rioters' sworn brotherhood cannot withstand cupidity nor crime linked to it. The Pardoner points that cupidity and crime lead to isolation and finally death. In the prologue the Pardoner had brazenly proclaimed that avarice was his worst failing. He had hinted at other faults in himself, and like False Seeming, gloried in practically all the seven deadly sins, but cupidity and its handmaid, fraud, he had revelled in most. Paradoxically he uses his vicious tale of avarice to sell his goods to his terrified audiences, to grant them absolution and to receive gifts from them; one of the most unethical abuses of the mediaeval ecclesiasts. Ostensibly the Pardoner uses his tale to instil the fear of death in his pulpit audiences, a laudable precept of the mediaeval church and one of the reasons for the morality play; in reality his concern is not with man's soul, but his own coffers. Likewise the three rioters start idealistically to avenge their slain comrade, but the sight of gold slows them, makes them sober, calculating, practical and grasping. Chaucer achieves this with consummate skill. The characterisation of "The worste of hem" is striking. His wit is sharp and he thinks of the pros and cons of the situation. He suggests that they remove the hoard to his place and do it at night when it is safe, or "for oure ownene tresor doon us honge." It is a realistic picture of plausible plotting. When the lot falls on the youngest and he goes off the stage, "The [worste] oon of hem" subtly remarks on their gain if the gold ". . .departed were among us two." The third rioter agrees, but he can not conceive how; he lacks the criminal mind of "The worste of hem." But once the evil thought sinks in, psychologically he is prepared to collaborate wholeheartedly in plotting the mode of assassination. Artistically Chaucer portrays the whole gory incident in detail well before the actual murder. When the youngest re-enters the stage, all that the narrator says is:

[25] V. F. Hopper and G. B. Lahey, eds. *Medieval Mysteries and and Moralities and Interludes* (New York: Barron's, 1962), p. 53.

For right as they hadde cast his death bifoore,
Right so they han hym slayn, and that anon.[26]

The youngest rioter in the subplot is given some of the most delightful lines in the drama. Before the mediaeval Riches become the bane of his life, he revels in contemplating them:

Ful ofte in herte he rolleth up and doun,
The beautee of thise floryns newe and brighte.[26]

Even in his worst plotting, the youngest man's mind works within the mediaeval theological pattern, where God is at the top of the hierarchy seated on a throne. He soliloquizes that had he all that wealth, he would be the merriest man under God's throne! And he has no intent of ever repenting, adds the Pardoner. Next he is seen buying poison of the apothecary. Chaucer uses more stock images; the usual excuses with their double meaning for the purchase of poison figure: "that he myghte his rattes quelle" and kill the "polcat" who destroyed his capons.[26]

The apothecary's dramatic answer is that he can have the poison; and that the concoction was strong enough to kill any creature. From another man the youngest rioter borrows three bottles, and after poisoning two of them, fills them with wine at the tapster's in the market square.

"That oon," after the horrible killing, sits back to enjoy the drink and then bury the dead. The catastrophe is a result of premeditated evil, as forceful as the machinations of Iago. The dramatic irony lies in the fact that death, an elusive abstraction, is found unsought, and the pilgrimage in quest of death is over. "The quiet, rapid, relentless march of the resolution:- ten verses, with a six-line epilogue"[27] brings this highly dramatic story to a close.

The narrator alone occupies the centre of the stage as he laments the tragedy. The Pardoner's epilogue is almost a benediction. Apparently he has been affected by his own narrative and invention. With an upsurge of emotion he condemns all sins and especially homicide, pointing that "the roots [of morality plays] lie in the sermons of mediaeval preachers."[28] And as in the morality

[26] Robinson, *op. cit.*, p. 153, ls. 812, 880, 838, 854.
[27] Kittredge, *op. cit.*, p. 20.
[28] Edgar T. Schell and J. D. Shuchter, eds. *English Morality Plays and Moral Interludes* (New York: Holt, Rinehart & Winston, 1969), p. vii.

play, this seems the moment of the protagonist's contrition. The mood does not last long; soon the Pardoner is again himself. According to Marchette Chute, "He knows he is a damned soul, and admits it with the sardonic detachment of a man who has ceased to care."[29] Does he really not care or is he just putting on a front? How tragic is the tragic face behind the mask? In the "two dramatized versions of the story. . . the *Rappresentazione di San Antonio,* an Italian miracle play of the fifteenth century . . . [and] *Der Dot im Stok,* a German play by Hans Sachs . . . there is a description of the dying agonies of the poisoned robbers. . . . "[30] In Chaucer, the psychological agony is the lot of the Pardoner. He has suffered with the three dead. His last effort to please has to be as valiant and brazen as his prologue, for now the Host and his audience are back on the stage with him, and he has to re-assert himself as a rascal.

Himself again, and with a twinkle in his "glaringe eyen," he turns to the audience and offers them pardons and his fraudulent relics. Here comes the visual element of mediaeval low comedy.[31] The Pardoner is in full command of his histrionics again; an actor, who with the utmost economy yet eloquence, will give a well-rounded tale of himself. A master of rhetoric, he had shown in the Wife of Bath's prologue that he could appreciate that gift in others; he knew the joys of a well-told tale. He has no illusions about the Pilgrims, and knows that his prologue and tale have not made his image much better, though he is recognized as a skilled story teller and actor. Like False Seeming, he is an honest hypocrite. His oratory and manners are haughty in the pulpit, friendly on a holiday trip; but whenever required of him, he can tell a gripping tale, worthy of a Shakespeare. And he knows the eloquence of silence.

In the Pardoner's prologue and tale Chaucer created a mediaeval morality play plus a tragi-comedy, and made his tragic androgyne transcend his frustrations and emerge triumphant from "behind the satyr's mask."

[29] Marchette Chute, *Geoffrey Chaucer of England* (New York: Dutton, 1946), p. 291.

[30] Carleton Brown, *op. cit.*, pp. xxvi, xxvii.

[31] G. B. Tennyson, *An Introduction to Drama* (New York: Holt, Rinehart and Winston, 1967), p. 74.

BIBLIOGRAPHY

Bowden, Muriel. *A Commentary on the General Prologue to the Canterbury Tales*. New York: The Macmillan Company, 1966.

———. *A Reader's Guide to Geoffrey Chaucer*. New York: Farrar, Straus and Giroux, 1969.

Brown, Carleton. *The Pardoner's Tale*. Oxford: Clarendon Press, 1963.

Browne, E. Martin. *Religious Drama 2*. New York: Meridian Books, 1958.

Burrow, J.A., ed. *Geoffrey Chaucer*. Baltimore: Penguin Books, 1969.

Chute, Marchette. *Geoffrey Chaucer of England*. New York: E. P. Dutton & Co. Inc., 1946.

Fansler, Dean Spruill. *Chaucer and the Roman de La Rose*. Massachusetts: Peter Smith, 1965.

Green, Richard, ed. & trans. *Boethius: The Consolation of Philosophy*. New York: Bob-Merrill, Inc., 1962.

Hopper, V. F., and Lahey, G. B., eds. *Medieval Mysteries and Moralities and Interludes*. New York: Barron's. 1962

Huppe, Bernard F. A. *Reading of the Canterbury Tales*. Albany: State University of New York, 1967.

Kittredge, George Lyman. *Chaucer and His Poetry*. Cambridge, MA: Harvard University Press, 1927.

de Lorris, Guillaume, and de Meum, Jean. *The Romance of the Rose*. Ed. Charles W. Dunn. New York: Dutton, 1962.

Muscatine, Charles. *Chaucer and the French Tradition*. California: University of California Press, 1969.

———."The Canterbury Tales: Style of the Man and Style of the Work." *Chaucer and the Chaucerians, Critical Studies in Middle English Literature*, ed. D. S. Brewer. London: Thomas Nelson, 1966.

Parks, E. W., and Beatty, R. C., eds. *The English Drama: An Anthology 900-1642*. New York: W. W. Norton, 1963.

Robertson, D. W. *A Preface to Chaucer*. Princeton: Princeton University Press, 1969.

Robinson, F. N. *The Works of Geoffrey Chaucer*, 2nd ed. Boston: Houghton Mifflin, 1961.

Schell, T., and Schuchter, J. D., eds. *English Morality Plays and Moral Interludes*. New York: Holt, Rinehart & Winston, 1968.

Schoeck, R.J., AND Taylor, J., eds. *Chaucer Criticism: The Canterbury Tales*. Indiana: Notre Dame Press, 1960.

Tennyson, G. B. *An Introduction to Drama*. New York: Holt, Rinehart and Winston, 1967.

Wimsatt, James I. *Allegory and Mirror*. New York: Pegasus, 1970.

SHAKESPEARE'S "RICHARD LOVES RICHARD"[1]

Whether Thomas More had an erroneous account of Richard III from Morton, Bishop of Ely; and Halle and Holinshed followed suit in describing Richard, it is evident in Shakespeare's treatment of the politico-historic tragedy that his suave and engaging protagonist was a manipulating politician.

Shakespeare may have based his play on More's biography of Richard (1513) or on the homiletic chronicles of Edward Halle (1548) and Raphael Holinshed (1550) or on Polydore Vergil's 1555 *Historia Angliae;* or he may have used for his source the manuscript of the Latin trilogy *Richardus Tertius* performed at St. John's in 1579 and written by Thomas Legge, Master of Caius.[2] Since the defeat and death of the king at Bosworth Field in 1485, Richard had been a fascinating subject for chronicler and playwright. Another of the early plays performed in 1594, *The True Tragedy of Richard III*, records the historic and dramatically charged events, using some of the stock figures of the Moralities, as Truth and Poetry and the Ghost of Clarence.[3] *Richard III* deals with "the conflict of powers—within a constituted society, and with the relation of political exigencies to the personal life of those caught up in them;"[4] and with Richard at the hub of the power politics.

Shakespeare deals with the span of Richard's reign by com-

[1] Mark Eccles, ed., *The Tragedy of Richard the Third* (New York: New American Library, 1964), p. 167.

[2] F. P. Wilson, *Shakespearian and Other Studies*, ed., Helen Gardner (Oxford: Clarendon Press, 1969), p. 9.

[3] E. M. W. Tillyard, *Shakespeare's History Plays* (London: Chatto & Windus, 1964), p. 99.

[4] L. C. Knights, *Shakespeare: The Histories* (London: Longmans, Green, 1962, 1965), p. 16.

pressing "the events of fourteen years into eleven days. . ."[5] and makes Richard an archetypal and demonic monarch and contriver; Machiavellian, scintillating with wit and cynicism and brilliance which is unequalled in all but the Renaissance theatre.

The play opens with the advent of Richard "solus" on the stage and his remarkable soliloquy; a soliloquy that augurs Richard's self-imposed villainy as it extols the peace following victory to the house of York. His verbalised thoughts center round himself. Envious of his brother, Edward, both for his position as king and his allure for the opposite sex, Richard bemoans his own physical handicap:

> But I, that am not shaped for sportive tricks
> Nor made to court an amorous looking glass;
> . . . scarce half made up,
> . . . that dogs bark at me as I halt. . .[6]

but in such deft and urbane a language that it takes on a note of triumph, a kind of catharsis to further advancement, almost therapeutic in its effect. Recalling his physical defects, he promises himself the downfall of his brother, Clarence, who is already at variance with the king; and more especially as Clarence is next in line of succession to the throne. This soliloquy is the first step in a gamut of political intrigues that make the ambitious Richard absolute monarch ere his heroic death. Yet in his life the game of statecraft had to be manoeuvred subtly. Shakespeare makes Richard play his supreme role, that of an actor. He play-acts as he converses; first with Clarence who enters guarded then with his other victims. But all of Richard's play-acting exceeds that needed for political intrigue. Well spoken and sophisticated in his address, he feigns surprise to see Clarence on his way to the Tower and imprisonment. In his colloquy, Richard is scurrilous in his attacks on the Queen, "the jealous o'erworn widow,"[7] whom without any apparent provocation he accuses of intrigue, in continuation of Clarence's naïve statement that Jane Shore, Edward's mistress, sways the king. Richard, having sized the situation with greater intelligence, brings into focus the Queen, a more potent

[5] Lily B. Campbell, *Shakespeare's "Histories" Mirrors of Elizabethan Policy* (San Marino, CA: The Huntington Library, 1947, 1968), p. 318.

[6] Eccles, *op. cit.*, p. 34.

[7] *Ibid.*, p. 36.

danger to his own advancement, and slanders her along with Mistress Shore. Later in the play he accuses the two of witchcraft against himself. There is pleasantry and ribald humour as he bandies words with his brother and Brakenbury, but the sardonic aside:

> Simple plain Clarence, I do love thee so
> That I will shortly send thy soul to heaven[8]

comes as a shock belying his brotherly, though double-edged, solicitations:

> I will deliver you, or else lie for you.[8]

Richard's duplicity in having Clarence murdered by countermanding the king's late decree before the ailing king dies is another rung in Richard's self-advancement. He unflinchingly unveils his villainy as did the Mediaeval Vice. In his asides he tells the audience of his histrionic dissembling as part of the political intrigue in which he deliberately embroils himself:

> But then I sigh, and with a piece of Scripture
> Tell them that God bids us do good for evil;
> And thus I clothe my naked villainy. . .
> And seem a saint when most I play the devil.[9]

Conversant with the Scriptures like the Mediaeval Vice, he uses them for his purpose. To the murderers he suggests the sudden execution of Clarence, not through compassion for the suffering of his brother, but fearing that his pleas may soften his executioners.

His candour is disarming, as the super-Machiavelli he sees himself a utopian head of an ordered state. His forte is his mastery of speech. In spite of his villainy, he talks his way to the throne. His sparkling knack of speech is his best weapon. Even when commiserating his own handicap, he uses it to further a special end, for he is a contriver par excellence. *The Prince* had set the stage for several of the characters in Elizabethan drama;

[8] *Ibid.*, p. 37.
[9] *Ibid.*, p. 61.

some of the prime examples are *The Jew of Malta* and *Sejanus*; but *Richard III* is one of the prime.

Clarence is the first obstacle to be removed, then come in quick succession the removal of Rivers, Grey and Vaughan, all kinsmen of the Queen and a potential danger to his own schemes. Richard found the Queen's brother, Rivers, unpalatable. When apprehensive of the future, during Edward's illness, Elizabeth had predicted of Richard that his regency would portend only harm for her brother and her son, Grey, for Richard was "A man that loves not me, nor none of you,"[10] Rivers had questioned Richard's appointment as Regent. Richard coming on the stage at the moment, with Hastings, and seeing the courtiers around Queen Elizabeth, gave another of his forthright and eloquent harangues, saying that just because he had no flattering graces of a courtier, he was accused of intrigue; and he unmincingly labeled Grey both *gauche* and dishonest. Richard mimics Rivers in disgust when the latter interferes, rather inanely, in his conversation with Elizabeth. The Tudor Queen, Margaret, entering on the scene does not help matters when she puts Rivers in his place. In fear of their role and irritation at their mundane intelligence, and over all, because he has already made his allies, Derby, Hastings and Buckingham, believe that the Queen's henchmen together with her were responsible for Clarence's imprisonment, does he send the trio to Pomfret Castle for execution. Yet looking at it objectively, all the beheaded except the two young princes deserved their fate,[11] not to help accelerate Richard's kingship, but because of their own part in intrigue and murder which they acknowledge in the words of Grey when he exclaims that they were witnesses to the stabbing of Henry VI.[12] When young Edward enquired about his other uncles on his way to his coronation and the Tower, all Richard said in answer was done to poison the lad's mind subtly.[13] Lord Hastings, the liberated courtier, and an ally of Richard is not spared when he wishes to uphold the Divine Right of Kings, and keep Richard from the throne in favour of the young Edward;[14] yet Hastings admires Richard and pays him the tribute of being the epitome of candour:

[10] *Ibid.*, p. 49.
[11] Campbell, *op. cit.*, p. 320.
[12] Eccles, *op. cit.*, p. 104.
[13] *Ibid.*, p. 90.
[14] *Ibid.*, p. 100.

I think there's never a man in Christendom
Can lesser hide his love or hate than he
For by his face straight shall you know his heart.[15]

Buckingham aids and abets the king, but when faced with regicide, he is horrified. None of his boasting avails: his words become a farce:

Tut, I can counterfeit the deep tragedian.[16]

Richard's play-acting had exceeded his role in statecraft, when he made Buckingham feel that he was the king maker, and that Richard had acceded to his wish in accepting the Crown. Buckingham is gulled for a moment, but he cannot palate the colloquy when Richard says, "I wish the bastards dead."[17] Regicide was beyond Buckingham, he is appalled and leaves—but he is quickly replaced; the impoverished Tyrrel comes in the picture, ready to assassinate the princes. Buckingham relents and perhaps would have done the king's bidding, Machiavellian as he was, but Richard's distance towards him and hedging of the promise to give Buckingham the earldom of Hereford, make the latter take arms against Richard. Buckingham is the last to be executed, as his ghost announces to Richard in his hallucination. Before his execution he had sued for an interview with Richard, but was denied it. Every time Richard was through with the usefulness of a person, he was relegated to oblivion.

The women in the play are also used by Richard in his political ambitions. The only one whom he tolerates is his mother, the Duchess of York. His wooing of Anne is dramatic and spectacular and in very bad taste. He professes love when perhaps he feels none, and at a most inauspicious time—the re-interment of Henry VI. Symbolically, therefore, in life he presages death or the sterility and death of their future relationship as husband and wife. The wooing scene is unusually provocative. In stichomythia Anne spurns and rejects his suit, but is not warned enough by the bleeding wounds of the corpse. In her search for security, she listens to the man she erstwhile called "the devil," "the black magician," "the dreadful minister of hell."[18] But in spite of her

[15] *Ibid.*, p. 106.
[16] *Ibid.*, p. 109.
[17] *Ibid.*, p. 127.
[18] *Ibid.*, p. 40.

abusive language, he never loses his couth. When Anne says of Edward that "he was gentle, mild and virtuous," Richard sardonically replies: "The better for the King of heaven that hath him."[19] Richard is eloquent and persuasive through the wooing scene, and employs spectacular histrionics when he offers her the sword and his bare breast. Anne softens and relents and is won, and that is her downfall. "I'll have her, but I will not keep her long,"[20] says Richard as he pays tribute to Anne's dead husband. Later Anne is to bewail ". . .my woman's heart grossly grew captive to his honey words . . . For never yet one hour in his bed did I enjoy the 'golden dew of sleep.' "[21] Next one hears that Anne is "grievous sick"[22] and then that Anne "hath bid this world good night."[23] When her ghost appears it prays for the success of Richmond, Richard's enemy.

Richard then becomes "a jolly thriving wooer,"[23] to young Elizabeth, contemplating another marriage of state, and especially as Richmond is a candidate for Elizabeth's hand. He approaches the dowager Queen Elizabeth for her daughter's hand, professing love as great as he had done to Anne, "Then know that from my soul I love thy daughter,"[24] but also bringing in the expediency of the alliance, "Infer fair England's peace by this alliance."[25] Yet there is a genuineness about Richard that evokes empathy as it savours of repentance, "Plead not my deserts, but what I will deserve."[26] After all the blame and counterblame given antiphonically, Queen Elizabeth, like Anne, succumbs to Richard's sophistries; and then he gives the aside:

> Relenting fool, and shallow, changing woman![26]

The women in the play, like T. S. Eliot's chorus of women in *Murder in the Cathedral* are used for musical lamentations. Shakespeare has used stichomythia, repetition, puns, lyrically antiphonic cadences, to give their lament. Queens Elizabeth and

[19] *Ibid.*, p. 43.
[20] *Ibid.*, p. 47.
[21] *Ibid.*, p. 125.
[22] *Ibid.*, p. 126.
[23] *Ibid.*, p. 133.
[24] *Ibid.*, p. 143.
[25] *Ibid.*, p. 146.
[26] *Ibid.*, p. 150.

Margaret and Anne, and the Duchess of York give "the symphonic words and anguish of spirit. . . . Everything against Richard is musically massed and the women carry the burden,"[27] and serve as a device to keep Richard's crimes constantly in sight.

If Richard loves himself, it is no wonder, for his intelligence and wit far exceed the others in the play. Early in the drama when Clarence bemoans that he is named George, Richard replies:

> Alack, my lord, that fault is none of yours;
> He should for that commit your godfathers.[28]

And when Anne accepts his ring, he scornfully asks:

> Was ever woman in this humor wooed?
> Was ever woman in this humor won?[29]

To Rivers commenting on his sister, Queen Elizabeth, conferring special favours on him, Richard says:

> She may help you to many fair preferments
> And then deny her aiding hand therein
> And lay those honors on your high desert.[30]

When Queen Margaret wants to "make the period" to her curse, Richard says, " 'Tis done by me, and ends in 'Margaret.' "[31] And when he visits Edward on his death bed, Richard wishes him "a happy time of day!" dissembling with words such as

> 'Tis death to me to be at enmity,
> I hate it, and desire all good men's love. . .
> I do not know that Englishman alive
> With whom my soul is any jot at odd.[32]

[27] Dr. Leonard F. Dean's lecture at New York University, 1972.
[28] Eccles, *op. cit.*, p. 35.
[29] *Ibid.*, p. 47.
[30] *Ibid.*, p. 52.
[31] *Ibid.*, p. 57.
[32] *Ibid.*, p. 75.

To Buckingham he says, "Tut, tut, thou art all ice, thy kindness freezes."[33] Few know Richard as well as the Duchess of York, his mother:

> Ah, that deceit should steal such gentle shape
> And with a virtuous visor hide deep vice![34]

She calls Richard "one false glass." In spite of it she blesses her son. Richard says a loud "Amen" to it, and then adds in an aside, "And make me die a good old man!"[35] At his worst, Richard is exhilarating and attractive and his wit always entertaining.

The gulling of the citizens was another of Richard's practical jokes though in line with statecraft; and can be accounted political virtue. Miss Campbell points out that there is a "distinction between private and political virtue."[36] Richard appears exemplary in public life. To be acceptable to the commonality, he has to descend to a "holy descant."[37] All through the scene, Richard dissembles piously. He is chary of accepting "the golden yoke of sovereignty" that they would "impose" on him.[38] After vehemently declaring that he cannot accept the throne, says that he is not made of stone, and though against his conscience, their entreaties make him accede to their behest. "Buckingham 'the deep revolving, witty Buckingham,' who plays his part as Richard's 'other self' with something of his master's swagger;"[39] is as involved in this game of power politics as the Duke of Gloucester.

But Richard is never more serious than at the scene of battle on Bosworth Field. His very words are a premonition of impending doom:

> Up with my tent! Here will I lie tonight;
> But where tomorrow?[40]
>
> Give me a bowl of wine

[33] *Ibid.*, p. 127.
[34] *Ibid.*, p. 79.
[35] *Ibid.*, p. 82.
[36] Campbell, *op. cit.*, p. 307.
[37] Eccles, *op. cit.*, p. 115.
[38] *Ibid.*, p. 118.
[39] Knight, *op. cit.*, p. 18.
[40] Eccles, *op. cit.*, p. 160.

I have not that alacrity of spirit
Nor cheer of mind that I was wont to have.[41]

His sleep that night has all the horrors of a nightmare. His eleven victims appear one by one and lacerate his spirit with their accusations, and by calling blessings on Richmond. Like Faustus, Richard sues for mercy on waking, and then realises that the apparitions were an unsubstantial dream. The soliloquy that follows epitomizes him. His introspection yields:

Richard loves Richard: that is, I am I.
Is there a murderer here? No. Yes, I am.
Then fly. What, from myself? Great reason why!
Lest I revenge. What, myself upon myself?
Alack, I love myself. . .
There is no creature loves me;
And if I die, no soul will pity me.
Nay, wherefore should they, since that I myself
Find in myself no pity to myself?[42]

Was Richard repenting his diabolical statecraft? Like Milton's Satan in the Garden of Eden, to assuage his fears he demeans himself by eavesdropping at Richmond's tent. Once he is affrighted by the supernatural, even in the louring skies he sees disaster. Yet he is not in the doldrums for long. He has his battle manoeuvres in mind. His speech to the soldiers, as compared to Richmond's oration, is reminiscent of his early acrimonious and sophisticated vulgarity. Catesby reports Richard's valour in the field of battle in spite of his having been unhorsed. Richard the manipulator dies a hero. Historically, Richard Plantagenet "was accepted as a Machiavellian;"[43] he may have had the "greedy desire to conquer others [and the] mortal malice to destroy"[44] his own soul, but Shakespeare's Richard loved Richard too well to die a coward.

[41] *Ibid.*, p. 162.
[42] *Ibid.*, p. 167.
[43] Campbell, *op. cit.*, p. 332.
[44] Wilson, *op. cit.*, p. 6.

BIBLIOGRAPHY

Calderwood, J. L., and Toliver, H. E., eds. *Essays in Shakespeare Criticism*. Englewood Cliffs, NJ: Prentice-Hall, 1970.

Campbell, Lily B. *Shakespeare's "Histories" Mirrors of Elizabethan Policy*. San Marino, CA: The Huntington Library, 1947, 1968.

Dean, Leonard F., ed. *Shakespeare, Modern Essays in Criticism*. New York: Oxford University Press, 1957, 1969.

Eccles, Mark, ed. *William Shakespeare, The Tragedy of Richard the Third*. New York: New American Library, 1964.

Knights, L. C. *Shakespeare: The Histories*. London: Longmans, Green, 1962, 1965.

Leech, Clifford. *Shakespeare: The Chronicles*. London: Longmans, Green, 1962, 1964.

Ridler, Ann, ed. *Shakespeare Criticism 1935-60*. London: Oxford University Press, 1963, 1965.

Tillyard, E. M. W. *Shakespeare's History Plays*. London: Chatto and Windus, 1964.

Waith, Eugene M., ed. *Shakespeare, The Histories*. Englewood Cliffs, NJ: Prentice-Hall, 1965.

Wilson, F. P. *Shakespearian and Other Studies*. Ed. Helen Gardner, Oxford: Clarendon Press, 1969.

SHAKESPEARE'S ISIS, GODDESS AND VOTARY

Cleopatra, the last of the Ptolemies[1] and the reigning queen, was the prototype of Isis. The origin of Isis is obscure, but she was an independent goddess of Abydos and Busiris in mythology. She later became one of the trinity with Osiris and Horus, and had a temple erected to her at Philae on the Nile. In her sculptures she often appears as the Mother Goddess with Horus at her breast and the solar disc, a symbol of fertility, a part of her regalia. In sculptures with Osiris, she has an arm round his waist to signify her equality and dynastic partnership with him. A legend recalls her as a mortal and a magician before the Sun God, Ra, deifies her. As a deity she retains her magical power, and her special mission becomes the protection of children. Along with this she was the patroness of sailors, which made her one of the most popular deities of the Egyptian pantheon. Later the Greek and Romans incorporated her cult, and identified her with Athena and Demeter.[2]

Is it a wonder then that Shakespeare's Isis, the goddess incarnate, emulates her counterpart? Twice in the play she is reported as impersonating Isis: on the Cydnus when the marketplace was emptied of all but Antony, to watch her floating goddess-like on her barge; and when she and Antony parceled out the eastern part of the farflung Roman empire, according to Octavius' unhappy comment at the Council in Rome (III.vi.16). She visually appears as Isis a third time when she is ready to meet Antony in the Elysian Fields.

[1] John Dover Wilson, ed., *Antony and Cleopatra* (Cambridge: University Printing House, 1964), p. xi.

[2] Maria Leach and Jerome Fried, eds., *Standard Dictionary of Folklore, Mythology, Legend*, Vol. A-I (New York: Funk and Wagnalls, 1949), p. 529.

If Cleopatra is a goddess, it is in her "infinite variety" and versatility. In her innuendoes and laughter and playful wrangling and teasing and chiding and tears and vivacity and sports, her caprice and fabrications and fickleness, and her ambiguity and unpredictability and complexity she carries the magic of bewitchment. And this magic makes for both tragedy and comedy. Octavia, Antony gallantly states, has the beauty of springtime in her tears (III.ii.43), but the very first sight of Cleopatra "purse[s] up his heart" (II.ii.192). Cleopatra knows all the histrionics to keep Antony enthralled. She "is perhaps the most effective of Antony's satirists"[3] and uses even satire theatrically to charm. As a deity and an empress she had enjoyed the ardour of the greatest men of the era; her brother-husband and emperor-god, Ptolemy-Osiris, Pompey the Great, Julius Caesar; and being a pastmaster in the strategy of love and adept in eroticism, could enmesh "the triple pillar of the world" (I.i.11). Antony could not withstand the onslaught of the charisma of Isis, and became the "noble ruin of her magic" (III.x.18). But this magic of Isis, unlike her other traits, had the single-minded ardour of constancy. Phyllis Rackin's admirable article states, "Cleopatra's incredible parade of shifting moods and strategems, together with Shakespeare's notorious reticence about her motives, has led even her admirers to conclude that her one salient quality is, paradoxically, her lack of one—the magnificent inconstancy that Enobarbus calls 'infinite variety.' "[4] The statement does not quite agree with this thesis. Cleopatra is changeable and surprising in all she does except her love for Antony. Where Antony is concerned her personality changes from that of deity to devotee. This is barely perceptible until she possesses him fully.

Cleopatra suffers her own disasters and mortifications many a time in their turbulent love. She had seen Antony sobered beyond recall by a "Roman thought," (I.ii.84) and by the news of Fulvia's death. She also saw an Antony, who not to be disturbed while with her, say impatiently to a messenger the cryptic, "Grates me! The sum" (I.i.18), give a well-weighed and coolheaded excuse to leave her with, "The strong necessity of time

[3] Matthew N. Proser, *The Heroic Image in Four Shakespearean Tragedies* (Princeton: Princeton University Press, 1965), p. 178.

[4] Phyllis Rackin, "Shakespeare's Boy Cleopatra, the Decorum of Nature, and the Golden World of Poetry," *Publications of the Modern Language Association of America*, 87, No. 2 (March 1972), p. 203.

commands / Our services awhile" (I.iii.43). He had decided to break those "strong Egyptian fetters" (I.ii.118).

Enobarbus with an uncanny understanding of female psychology knew that Antony's departure would be soul-searing for Cleopatra (I.ii.143), but Antony chose to be obtuse. Her words, "Your honor calls you hence / Therefore be deaf to my unpitied folly" (I.iii.98), seem another of her caustic jests, yet they have poignancy. Like a devotee Shakespeare's Cleopatra lives only for Antony. While he is in Rome and Athens, her waking thoughts are reminiscences of their love life. Life apart from him she wishes to drown in mandragora, and in quick diversions as music and billiards and fishing; yet each diversion brings further memories of her "man of men" (I.iv.72). The worst blow is the news of his marriage to Octavia. On learning of it, Cleopatra who could "hop forty paces through the public street" (II.ii.235) has to beg her maids, "Lead me from hence" (II.v.109). This is no theatricality; the impact of the news kills even Cleopatra's buoyancy.

Cleopatra suffers with Antony in his defeat at Actium. Fear had made her turn round, apparently with no knowledge that Antony would follow suit and that the episode would signal the loss of "The greater cantl of the world" (III.x.6). The bitterness of Antony's reproach of her and himself makes her empathize with him, which he at first misses. Her state of mind can be seen in her response to his poetic railing; in the short meaningless, "O, my pardon!" "Pardon, pardon!" (III.xi.62 and 68). He is the rebuking god, she the disturbed and penitent suppliant.

Antony never quite understands her devotion. His rhetoric no doubt is beautiful, and as early as their first appearance in the play, he gives cosmic magnitude to his love for her, in which they are the "peerless pair" (I.i.34) and thus have already reached godhead. His rhetoric envisages a new heaven and new earth for his unfathomable love, and Egypt, the domain of the goddess, becomes his "space." Cleopatra's words on the other hand "whether satiric or eloquent, seldom fail to distract our attention from Antony."[5] However much she declares that "Eternity was in our lips and eyes / . . .none our parts so poor / But was a race of heaven;" (I.iii.35-37) the depth and intensity of her love are lost on Antony. He can leave her, speak of her in Rome as a physical

[5] Proser, *op. cit.*, p. 189.

necessity and an unavoidable diversion, and disregarding her, "I am not married, Caesar" (II.ii.128), contract a marriage of convenience to keep the peace of the triumvirate intact. "Everytime Antony steps outside [of Egypt] into the world of Time and Roman thoughts, its charm evaporates."[6] While Cleopatra languishes for him, sends missives and messengers coursing after him, he decides on a tour in Athens with his new bride. His tawny-fronted strumpet, the lustful gypsy, the foul Egyptian, whom he found "a morsel cold upon / Dead Caesar's trencher" (III.xiii.116) remains steadfast in her devotion. Her constancy keeps elevating her to godlike stature, while Antony is dwarfing himself to a pitiable mortal. Antony is drawn to her by a force beyond his control, but he doubts her fidelity. When he has Thidias whipped for offering her his homage, Cleopatra's simple yet pregnant, "Not know me yet?" brings an absolutely irrelevant counter-question from him, "Cold-hearted towards me?" Antony cannot fathom the psychology of a mystical obsession like hers. He has grandiose verbiage but is mundane, for at core, like Othello, he is simple and forthright and a great soldier.

Cleopatra's coquetry becomes less and less obtrusive as Antony's political and military career is on the wane. His defeats are hers, his joys and successes her moments of brightness. She does not lose her couth, and her wit is as sharp and beguiling as when deflating Antony's rhetorical bombast was an ecstatic game with her, and she was dazzling in "her wild effort to personalize all of life and . . . vivify the world by her beauty and her passions."[7] Like a votary she offers him libations and herself. She caters to his changing moods. When he is dejected she bides by him, when he tries to rekindle his dying enthusiasm she encourages feasting and festivity. When he identifies himself with his humble servants, she is anxious regarding the portent of his words (IV.ii.24). Her scintillating beauty for the time seems to be hidden behind a veil of self-effacement. She takes on Eros' chores to humour him. Still the worshipper, she is progressing towards divinity rightfully hers, for she is Egypt's Isis.

Antony loves Cleopatra, but his love for her and his inordinate preoccupation with his public image and reputation coalesce.

[6] Rackin, *op. cit.*, p. 207.

[7] Julian Markels, *The Pillar of the World* (Columbus: Ohio State University Press, 1968), p. 48.

His two defeats at sea and his single victory over Caesar colour his attitudes and moods. Like Isis the patron of sailors, Cleopatra's medium was water. Her fleets were her strength, but Antony's naval battle was not triggered by her. His pride made him accept Octavius' challenge to fight by sea. Along with the disasters of the sea ventures, the false news of her death, sent so capriciously and insensitively by Cleopatra, at the moment when she is no goddess, destroyed Antony and resulted in his abortive suicide. The tension in the play mounts with the emotionally charged scene of Eros' self-sacrifice; and so Antony's attempted suicide comes near an anti-climax and bathos. The tension abates further when Antony is hauled through a casement in her mausoleum by Cleopatra and her maids: their efforts lightened by her witty quip, "Here's sport indeed! How heavy weighs my lord!" (IV.xv.32). Cleopatra had already said her poignant lament: "O sun / Burn the great sphere thou mov'st in: darkling stand / The varying shore o'th' world!" (IV.xv.9). And now there is no room for tears. The short time left to them has to be spent in stoic reticence and in frank and friendly talk. This is no time for sorrow, for her Antony has redeemed himself—none other but he has conquered Antony and is on his way to godhead.

Antony's magnanimity is at the fore; he is no longer self-centred; his concern is Cleopatra; he has "added . . . [a] capacity for devotion and self-forgetfulness, which he pitifully lacked before."[8] He projects his dying mind to the inevitable confrontation of Cleopatra and young Caesar, and is anxious for her. Cleopatra is resolute. Antony's impending death is giving her a fortitude that will lead to her own immortality. His precaution of all but Proculeius goes unheeded: "My resolution and my hands I'll trust,/ None about Caesar." (IV.xv.49)—words bold and prophetic for a sovereign who was apparently uninterested in statecraft. North's Plutarch's "Life of Marcus Antonius" mentions that besides her brilliant and mellifluous speech and unmatched beauty and grace, Cleopatra was a linguist and also a diplomat in all her foreign relations, unlike many of her predecessors.[9] In the play Shakespeare gives her a statesman's understanding of the

[8] R. H. Case, "Introduction," *The Arden Edition of the Works of William Shakespeare: Antony and Cleopatra*, ed. M.R. Ridley (Cambridge, MA: Harvard University Press, 1956), p. xxxiv.

[9] Barbara Everett, ed., *Antony and Cleopatra* (New York: New American Library, 1964), p. 196.

situation. She is ready for the fray once Antony dies. Now that he has redeemed his honour as a god, she too can re-aspire for godhead, though still his worshipper. He truthfully says, "I lived; the greatest prince o' the world. The noblest;" (IV.xv.54), and she is in accord with it.

Cleopatra's high tribute to this god-like man is typical of a devotee; her language hyperbolic, her metaphors cosmic: "The crown o' th' earth doth melt. . . . there is nothing left remarkable / Beneath the visiting moon." (IV.xv.63-68)

In the early scenes Cleopatra appears a specious Isis, but by the end of Act IV she has experienced death, and "Death in Shakespeare's tragedies brings with it an enhanced perception of life."[10] With this new knowledge, she emerges as the Mother Goddess. Shakespeare devotes the last act to his deified heroine. The finale is incomparable in its sweep and eminence.

Cleopatra's opening speech in Scene ii of the last Act, suggests weariness, the aftermath of consummation. She can now think of Caesar's quest for worldly glory in sardonic terms: " 'Tis paltry to be Caesar: / Not being Fortune, he's but Fortune's knave" (V.ii.1-4). Recalled to her predicament by Proculeius' advent, she parleys words with him. Yet her speech has majesty and the sardonic barbs are not missing:

> If your master
> Would have a queen his beggar, you must tell him
> That majesty, to keep decorum, must
> No less beg than a kingdom: if he please
> To give me conquered Egypt for my son,
> He gives me so much of my own as . . .
> I am his fortune's vassal.
>
> (V.ii.15-29)

Ironic; she has already called him "Fortune's knave." Isis-like a protector of children, her concern is very humane; but she is still changeable—the mood turns to the imperious:

> Know, sir, that I
> Will not wait pinioned at your master's court.
>
> (V.ii.52)

[10] L. G. Salinger, "The Elizabethan Literary Renaissance," *The Age of Shakespeare*, ed. Boris Ford (Harmondsworth, England: Penguin Books, 1966), p.106.

Master of the situation again, she can now give the eulogy that makes her Isis: "vast is the scale of her being, and . . . tremendous the force of her passion."[11] Even if she "forges and creates"[12] Antony, she is no longer play-acting when the paean breaks forth. It is a song of triumph from a soul already unfettered and risen to aesthetic heights that only a Shakespeare could voice. Her romantic imagination gives Antony the stature of a god who "bestrid the ocean: . . . [whose] arm crested the world (V.ii.83), whose voice suggested the celestial music of the spheres, and who could emulate Jove in his thunder, and whose bounty gave more than was garnered; and with it she seals her own divinity. "The peerless pair . . . 'stand up against the widest and most splendid panorama Shakespeare, or . . . any poet, ever painted, and are magnified, not dwarfed, by it. . . ."[13]

And when actual death comes to her, Cleopatra meets it fearlessly enthroned as Isis. She woos death and makes the asp of the Nile her confederate in cheating Caesar of his envisaged triumph, and the mechanic slaves and saucy lictors of Rome from seeing her enchained or parodied by "Some squeaking Cleopatra boy" (V.ii.210-221). "Cleopatra has a joyous exuberance, which transfigures death itself;"[14] and gives the play its final mood of triumph and release."[15]

> There is mettle in death,
> which commits some loving act upon her,
> she has such a celerity in dying.
>
> (I.ii.144)

Celerity indeed, for her immortal longings hear Antony call. In death radiant, fascinating, animated "she looks like sleep/ As she would catch another Antony/ In her strong toil of grace" (V.ii.345).

[11] Case, *op. cit.*, p. lii.
[12] Salinger, *op. cit.*, p. 107.
[13] Wilson, *op. cit.*, p. xxiv.
[14] Markels, *op. cit.*, p. 170.
[15] Robert Ornstein, "The Ethic of the Imagination: Love and Art in *Antony and Cleopatra*," *Shakespeare, Modern Essays in Criticism*, ed. Leonard F. Dean (London: Oxford University Press, 1969), p. 389.

The transfigured pair are celestial. Their story inspired litterateurs as Chaucer and Etienne Jodelle and Garnier, the Countess of Pembroke, Samuel Daniel and Dryden; but the aesthetic invention it evoked in Shakespeare made him imbue Cleopatra-Isis with his own divinity and immortality.

BIBLIOGRAPHY

Calderwood, J.L., and Toliver, H.E., eds. *Essays in Shakespeare Criticism.* Englewood Cliffs, New Jersey: Prentice-Hall, 1970.

Dean, Leonard F., ed. *Shakespeare: Modern Essays in Criticism.* London: Oxford University Press, 1969.

Everett, Barbara, ed. *Antony and Cleopatra.* New York;. New American Library, 1964.

Ford, Boris, ed. *The Age of Shakespeare.* Harmondsworth, England: Penguin Books, 1969.

Granville-Barker, Harley. *Prefaces to Shakespeare,* Volume III, *Antony and Cleopatra, Coriolanus.* Princeton: Princeton University Press, 1965.

Leach, Maria, and Fried, Jerome., eds. *Standard Dictionary of Folklore, Mythology, Legend.* Vol. A-I. New York: Funk and Wagnalls, 1949.

Markels, Julian. *The Pillar of the World.* Columbus: Ohio State University Press, 1968.

Proser, Matthew N. *The Heroic Image in Five Shakespearean Tragedies.* Princeton: Princeton University Press, 1965.

Rackin, Phyllis. "Shakespeare's Boy Cleopatra," *Publication of the Modern Language Association of America.* Vol. 87, No. 2 (March, 1972), pp. 210-212.

Ridley, M. R., ed. *The Arden Edition of the Works of William Shakespeare: Antony and Cleopatra.* Cambridge, MA: Harvard University Press, 1956.

Wilson, John Dover, ed. *Antony and Cleopatra.* Cambridge: University Printing House, 1964.

BEATRICE ALLURED: THE CHANGELING

A short appraisal of the relationship of Beatrice-Joanna and De Flores in Thomas Middleton and William Rowley's play, *The Changeling*.

Alsemero first beholds Beatrice-Joanna in the temple and so interprets his attraction to her as sanctified. Yet it is no spiritual beauty that lures him; it is her grace and charm that make the easily blown ". . . temple's vane to turn full in [Alsemero's] face"(I.i.20). Alsemero, a man who was unmoved by all "snares of beauty," whose one lust was travel and the sea, suddenly wishes his seafaring ventures stayed. Beauty such as Beatrice's could draw men as different as Alsemero, Piracquo, and De Flores, and necessarily siren-like lure them to their destruction.

But what draws Beatrice-Joanna, a socialite, the pampered child of a great house, vain, scornful, wilful, an arrogant aristocrat, to a lowly, serving man, such as De Flores?

In her ducal world of flux, where love lights on every new object, at times just to brush it and pass on, De Flores is the one constant entity. His irksome presence dodges Beatrice-Joanna's footsteps from the very start of the play, and never leaves off until he dominates her wholly and completely. Her own inordinate desires make her the ensnared bird, that cannot escape the steadfast gaze of the viper and is drawn nearer and nearer to it, until it is part of the viper's substance. Middleton and Rowley use the metaphor of "flight" when they make De Flores speak the "aside" in their first encounter (I.i.98) suggesting the image of a bird escaping a sinister situation. Yet, at this point, there is nothing evil about De Flores, except for his ugliness, which according to the seventeenth century mores denoted an evil soul. Anything that was not symmetrical and beautiful spelled disease, decay, and disaster:

Are these but warts, and pock-holes in the face
Of th'earth? Thinke so: but yet confesse, in this
The world's proportion disfigured is.[1].

The question is why does the bird fly the basilisk; does it feel threatened of its sanity, and tries to escape it before its hold becomes too tenacious? The lure is there; the lure of ugliness, the flight though determined is weak from the start. Beatrice's fear of De Flores is instinctive as is the hatred. When questioned why she is upset after a surprise encounter with De Flores, Beatrice-Joanna says to Alsemero:

Your pardon, sir, 'tis my infirmity;
Nor can I other reason render you
Than his or hers, of some particular thing
They must abandon as a deadly poison, . . .
Such to mine eyes is that same fellow there,
The same that report speaks of the basilisk.

(I. i. 105 ff.)

Alsemero tells her if such is the case, De Flores:

. . .does ill to tempt your sight, . . .

(I. i. 127)

In this innuendo Middleton has brought out the moot question, double-edged as it is, that De Flores' presence is strangely moving and tempting for Beatrice-Joanna. She can not but be aware of her attraction for De Flores:

He can not be ignorant of that, sir;
I have not spar'd to tell him so, and I want
To help myself, since he's a gentleman

(I. i. 128 ff.)

It is the eve of Beatrice-Joanna's marriage to Alonzo de Piracquo, a suitor who answers to everything desired by Vermandero of a courtly son-in-law (I. i. 208). Till Beatrice sees Alsem-

[1] J. T. Shawcross, ed. "An Anatomy of the World: The First Anniversary," *The Complete Poetry of John Donne* (New York: Anchor Books, 1967), p. 281, line 301.

ero, her mind is fixed on this marriage, the wind vane has not changed to make her affections light on another handsome face. But no sooner it does, the latent evil in her meteoric character becomes a conscious force. She is determined that her will will supersede that of her father. The wanton lust for Alsemero leads to thoughts of intrigue in her mind. On learning that she is affianced to another, Alsemero ominously changes his tune from courting her to a concern for himself:

> How shall I dare to venture in his castle
> When he discharges murderers at the gate?
>
> (I. i. 219)

The affection of this new lover is not too deep; he too is changeable.

All this time De Flores has not been too far from the scene. Beatrice is the first to note his presence:

> Not this serpent gone yet?
>
> (I. i. 221)

The serpent will never go, for it is a part of her, and now more so, as her playful, innocent flirtation is changing into a determined and inordinate desire for Alsemero, an appetite that will soon turn Beatrice into a criminal.

Middleton uses the glove scene with great felicity. Unconsciously the fallen and rejected glove becomes a token of future favours:

> Take 'em and draw thine own skin off with 'em.
>
> (I. i. 226)

The sadistic callousness of the statement is prophetic of the complete harmony of the hand-in-glove nature of Beatrice and De Flores' final relationship. The gloves here are not only a reluctant favour given by a lady to her knight, but are a symbol of the consummation of De Flores' love for Beatrice and her acquiescence.

De Flores himself can not understand his intense and steadfast love for Beatrice-Joanna, unless it is that she herself baits him, hating him yet unable to rid herself of his repelling fascination:

. . . for she baits me still
Everytime worse than other, . .

(II. i. 32)

and

She turns her blessed eye upon me now,
And I'll endure all storms before I part with't.

(II. i. 50)

Beatrice acknowledges his uncanny fascination:

This ominous ill-fac'd fellow more disturbs me
Than all my other passions.

(II. i. 52)

De Flores is becoming an obsession with Beatrice as Beatrice is with De Flores, and she can not account for this sinister attraction. She uses epithets as "a standing toad-pool," "a dallying, trifling torment," "the thing most loath'd" for De Flores, and wishes him out of her sight. She complains to herself:

I never see this fellow but I think
Of some harm towards me; danger's in my mind still,
I scarce leave trembling of an hour after
. . . Oh, I was
Lost in this small disturbance and forgot
Affliction's fiercer torrent that now comes
To bear down all my comforts.

(II. i. 89 ff.)

Was De Flores one of those "comforts"? De Flores' presence has been so overpowering that the *philos-aphilos* theme has overwhelmed her entire consciousness. The possession of Alsemero is Beatrice-Joanna's immediate concern, and yet in De Flores' presence it is completely obliterated; only after De Flores leaves the stage is she recalled back to Alsemero.

Beatrice-Joanna asks for a little respite before her marriage to Alonzo is solemnized, and in his magnanimity Alonzo agrees to it. Alonzo's brother, Tomazo, sees through Beatrice's hypocrisy; through the "changeling" affections of this scheming young woman, but Alonzo is blind to it, and hurt by his brother's suspicions. This allows for Beatrice to meet Alsemero clandestinely, worried as she is about the forthcoming marriage. In the courtly love tradition, Alsemero offers to contest for her hand in a duel with Alonzo, but Beatrice-Joanna shies at it. She knows it will become a mortal combat for one or the other of them. She is still innocent of crime; wilful, imperious, imprudent, irresponsible, improvident, scheming, but still chary of bloodshed. Yet in the thought of the duel her alert mind finds the escape she desires, and the heinous idea of removing her betrothed is born simultaneously with thoughts of De Flores:

> Blood guiltiness becomes a fouler visage,
> And now I think on one—
>
> (II. ii. 40)

With the plan and De Flores in mind, Alsemero is relegated to the past—at least for the moment, and Alsemero says, "Lady, you hear not me" (II. ii. 48). Beatrice-Joanna is heading towards the basilisk that will consume her; the intimate relationship that will follow will bring desire and destruction. Beatrice-Joanna seems deliberately unaware of De Flores' motive in shadowing her, yet she is quick to use it as a tool to further her plans, and buy her own damnation as well as his. Her hypocrisy, so delectable to De Flores, for it makes her do all he has longed for, wins him to her cause, and catapults her into a situation from which she will never extricate herself. Like Bel Imperia she feigns friendship when the only tie is revenge in the case of Bel Imperia and murder in hers. Bel Imperia's love is tranferred to Horatio with Andrea's ghost still hovering on the periphery, Beatrice-Joanna is paying the price of murder, hoping that it will free her, but she gets more embroiled and sells herself in the bargain. Like Tennessee Williams' Blanche Du Bois they do not realise that their desires will destroy them; that virtue will prove a thin veneer when faced with overpowering evil. Or were their appetites stronger than themselves? Blanche is a creature of circumstances; Beatrice-Joanna enmeshes herself in her own toils. Bel Imperia is party to the slaying of her brother and dispatches Balthazar herself, for hers is the ire of a trapped woman, who hates the authors of her dual sorrow. Beatrice-Joanna destroys herself for her acquisitive desires. Their frailty is their inordinate appetite. Even the virtuous Isabella, the foil to Beatrice-Joanna in the parallel subplot of *The Changeling*, suffers from the malady.[1] She is moved by the adoration of the Changeling, Antonio, and of Franciscus and Lollio, but has the strength to be recalled to sanity ere she succumbs. Kyd, Middleton, Williams have given realistic situations of lust and crime and the consequences that follow: intellectual and moral death.

Until the moment of Beatrice's appeal to De Flores for the murder, De Flores' crime was his ugliness and his desire to be near Beatrice. Now he is faced with a criminal whom he loves, and with the ugliness of her soul. His steadfast love for Beatrice is a mortal disease; he cannot sever himself from her, though he knows it will lead to his spiritual death:

> The errant wilderness of a woman's face,
> Where men can not get out, . . . though they know
> That adders lie a-swimming in their smiles,
> That basilisks drink their poison from their eyes.[2]

His love moves in eternity. And from the time Beatrice-Joanna turns to De Flores for help, her capitulation is complete. On first addressing him, the words she says deal with his physical person:

> . . .you were not wont
> To look so amorously.
>
> (II. ii. 74)

Had she just discovered that, or had his amorous desires always attracted her? She touches him, though he was loathsome "scarce an hour ago" (II. ii. 77). The physical contact, the kind words are hypocritical, but would they have been there, if m'lady had not known that the man desired her?

> When w'are us'd
> To a hard face, 'tis not so unpleasing.
> It mends still in opinion, hourly mends,
> I see it by experience
>
> (II. ii. 86 ff.)

[2] George Chapman, *Bussy D'Ambois*, ed. M. Evans (New York: Hill and Wang, 1968), V. i. 76-80.

Perhaps Beatrice was being true to herself at this juncture, and no hypocrite. She is succumbing to the lure, and with Montsurry it can be said, " 'Tis horrible to think with what monsters women's imaginations engross them when they are once enamoured."[3] She sighs as she speaks to him and for a time forgets what she is after (II. ii. 100-101). His ardour is already overwhelming her. She recollects herself and offers him money:

> Thy reward shall be precious
>
> (II. ii. 129)

De Flores assures her that it will be, and the thought of it ravishes him. When he consents to murder Piracquo for her, she unthinkingly says:

> How lovely now dost thou appear to me!
>
> (II. ii. 136)

Her union with him is consummated no sooner they are mentally one:

> Why, are not both our lives upon the cast?
> Then I throw all my fears upon thy service.
>
> (II. ii. 140-41)

Consciously Beatrice still deludes herself that she will be free of De Flores once the murder is committed.

Beatrice-Joanna is repelled at the deadman's finger with her ring still on it, and quickly shifts the responsibility of contact with it as she did with the glove. She lets her champion keep it as a reward. He accepts it gracelessly and dispassionately, for the issue now is much larger than a paltry largesse. It is the actuality of De Flores' demand that reveals Beatrice-Joanna to herself. No longer can she live a life of lies as far as he is concerned. They are one in crime:

> Look but into your conscience, read me there;
>
> (III. iv. 133)

[3] *Ibid.*, III, ii. 281 ff.

Her pride of birth and arrogance cannot rescue her from a union so distant from her mind, in spite of the long-present and sinister bond between her and De Flores. Spiritually she is his, loathsome as it seems:

> Murder, I see, is followed by more sins.
>
> (III. iv. 164)

In the wake of the murder and their promiscuity follow all the ordinal sins and with no respite. Beatrice-Joanna suffers all the pangs of unconsummated love for Alsemero, paradoxically for whom she had turned a criminal and an adulteress. On account of jealousy and fear of discovery on the bridal night when Diaphanta is bought to take her place by her husband's side (a repetition of the story of Iseult and King Mark) she stoops to lies which are discovered and win her the scorn of those who mattered most to her, Alsemero and her shocked father, Vermandero.

During this passage of time De Flores alone remains constant to her. His distant adulation turns into a companionship and then possession of Beatrice. Compeers in crime, he is her superior in steadfastness. His love for her never diminishes even when he is exposing her hypocrisy to herself and to her husband and father. He has the dispassionate contentment of a "mission accomplished"—Beatrice is his for all time. In him has Beatrice also found the end of her emotional quest?

> A wondrous necessary man, . . .
>
> (V. i. 91)

Middleton has no condemnation for his characters. If they are base, they acknowledge their own unworthiness; frailty sees itself as frailty. Beatrice-Joanna is lured to her serving man, because he is the only pivotal part of her emotional existence. He becomes necessary to her; the only anchor in her meteoric environment. Even in her worst sin he is by her side, and sacrifices himself with her. Like Milton's Adam he erred and suffered volitionally:

> . . . his love
> Had so enobl'd, as of choice t'incurr
> Divine displeasure, for her sake, or Death.[4]

[4] J. T. Shawcross, ed., *The Complete Poetry of John Milton* (New York: Anchor Books, 1963), IX. 991 ff.

With his allure for her, Beatrice is lured to death.

> I love what most I loathe and can not live
> Unless I compass that which holds my death.[5]

T.S. Eliot calls *The Changeling*, ". . .a dispassionate exposure of fundamental passions of any time and any place [which lead to] the tragedy of the not naturally bad but irresponsible and undeveloped nature."[6] But in their elemental passions Beatrice and De Flores are as Machiaveleian as Iago. Not naturally bad conceded, but lust and intrigue and manœuverings mark them for their doom and degeneration. Their machinations are no less developed than those of Iago. In the Diaphanta story, it is no mere irresponsibility that leads to deliberate homicide; neither is it in the murder of Piracquo. Like Iago, Beatrice is caught in her own toils; she has no more control of the situation than had Iago; once the diabolical plan has come to fruition, the infernal engines roll to their destruction. Except that in Beatrice the theme of revenge takes on a new Dimension, self-destruction. The lure of the flesh and the lure of death take their toll; Beatrice-Joanna is the victim. Like their predecessors and many of their contemporaries, Middleton and Rowley are preoccupied with death, but not with revenge. Revenge takes the shape of retribution. The tragedy is a tragedy of false values and misplaced emotions, where lust and death level all differences. The versatile aristocrat and the single-minded servant are intrinsically alike; each desires the other to the point of no return.

[5] Chapman, *op. cit.*, II. ii. 172-73.

[6] T. S. Eliot, *Essays on Elizabethan Drama* (New York: Harcourt, Brace and Company, Inc., 1956), pp. 85, 86.

BIBLIOGRAPHY

Bluestone, M., and Rabkin, N., eds. *Shakespeare's Contemporaries.* Englewood Cliffs, New Jersey: Prentice-Hall, 1970.

Boas, F. S. *An Introduction to Tudor Drama.* Oxford: Oxford University Press, 1933.

Bowers, Fredson. *Elizabethan Revenge Tragedy.* Princeton: Princeton University Press, 1966.

Chapman, George. *Bussy D'Ambois* Ed. Maurice Evans. New York: Hill and Wang, 1966.

Eliot, T. S. *Essays on Elizabethan Drama.* New York: Harcourt Brace and Company, 1956.

Ford, Boris, ed. *The Age of Shakespeare.* Harmondsworth, England: Penguin Books, 1966.

Huston, J. D., and Kernan, A. B. *Classics of the Renaissance Theater.* New York: Harcourt Brace and World. Inc.. 1969.

Middleton, T., and Rowley, Wm. *The Changeling,* Ed. G. W Williams. Lincoln: University of Nebraska Press, 1968.

Shawcross, J. T., ed. *The Complete Poetry of John Donne.* New York: Anchor Books, 1967.

———. *The Complete English Poetry of John Milton.* New York: Anchor Books, 1963.

Wine, M. L., ed. *Drama of the English Renaissance.* New York: Random House, 1969.

JOHN DONNE—AN ARTICLE IN ENCYCLOPEDIA STYLE

DONNE, John (1572-1631), English poet, satirist and divine of the Elizabethan and Jacobean era, was born between January 24th and June 16th, 1572, in Bread Street, Cheapside, within the parish of St. Nicholas Olave, London. His father, John Donne, a Roman Catholic of Welsh ancestry and a prosperous merchant, was the warden of the Ironmongers' Company in 1573. His mother, Elizabeth, was the daughter of John Heywood, a singer, a musician, an author of comedies and interludes, and an epigrammatist; and of Elizabeth Rastell. As a Roman Catholic, John Heywood was a loyal servant of Queen Mary, and upon her death left England for a life of exile in Malines, Antwerp and Lorraine. Elizabeth, Donne's maternal grandmother, was the daughter of the playwright, John Rastell, noted for his *Interlude in Four Elements*, and the great-niece, through John's sister, of Sir Thomas More. Donne was raised in this essentially Roman Catholic and highly cultured home.

Donne's father died on January 16th, 1576; the probate to his will was granted on February 8th. Sometime between May 18th and July 17th of that year, Donne's mother married John Syminges, a widower and a doctor of physics at Oxford, and the President of the Royal College of Physicians; and the family with Donne's four sisters and a brother, and Dr. Syminges' son (—his two older daughters already being married), moved to Little Trinity Lane. Donne's maternal uncles were also ardent Roman Catholics and intellectuals; Jasper Heywood translated the Senecan plays, and both he and his brother, Ellis, being Jesuit priests left England and died in exile. In May 1593, Henry, the nineteen-year-old brother of Donne, was imprisoned in Newgate for sheltering William Harrington, a Roman Catholic seminarian and priest; Henry died of a fever while still in prison.

In 1583 Donne's family had moved to St. Bartholomew the Less. In October of the following year, at the age of twelve, Donne matriculated at Hart Hall, Oxford, and was there until 1587. Being a Roman Catholic Donne was unable to subscribe to the Thirty-Nine Articles of the Anglican Church and thus to acknowledge the Queen as the Supreme Head of the Church. This debarred him from being granted a degree at Oxford. From 1587-90 Donne's movements are obscure; though it is conjectured that he was with the army in the Lowlands. (If Izaak Walton is correct Donne may have been at Cambridge in 1588-89, and travelled abroad in 1589-91.)

Donne's stepfather died on July 7th, 1588, and his mother moved to the parish of St. Saviours in Southwark. Three years later his mother married Richard Rainsford. This was the year when Donne's famous portrait in a military(?) uniform was painted by William Marshall; the picture is inscribed with a Spanish quotation. At this period Donne entered Thavies Inn, London, as a pre-law student, but on May 6th of 1592, was admitted to Lincoln's Inn, and remained there until 1595 or '96. Sir Richard Baker, a contemporary of Donne's, remembered Donne at the Inns of Court as "very neat, a great visitor of ladies, a great frequenter of playes, a great writer of conceited verses."[1] Donne was Master of Revels at the Inn in 1593 and was elected Christmas Steward in 1594. Izaak Walton, Donne's earliest biographer, mentions that in London Donne rose at 4:00 A.M. and worked until 10:00 A.M., and that at nineteen he was so preoccuped with religion that he made the differences and the theological controversies of the Roman and the evangelical churches his special study. These statements may be conjectures on the part of Walton. At the age of twenty-one Donne inherited a considerable amount of his father's property, and in April of the following year came in possession of his brother's estate.

At this period Donne was instructing young students, of whom one was a fifteen-year-old Yorkshire boy, Thomas, the son of Christopher Danby. Apparently for non-payment of living expenses for him, Donne sued his natural brother, Christopher, in 1598.

The poems ascribed to Donne during the period of his resi-

[1] Helen Gardner, ed., *John Donne: The Elegies and the Songs and Sonnets* (Oxford; Clarendon Press, 1965), p. xxiii, n. 3.

dence at the Inns of Court range from the songs and sonnets, lyrics and elegies to the satires. Helen Gardner, a twentieth-century Donne scholar, suggests that Donne's "Book of Elegies." comprising fourteen elegies, could be dated between the years 1593 and 1596; Professor Herbert J. C. Grierson, earlier in this century, had ascribed twenty elegies to these years. Helen Gardner in her sequence has followed the early Westmoreland manuscript, except that she has inserted the poem, "Love's Progress," as the ninth elegy in her compilation, for they are "a homogeneous collection of poems, unified in style . . . and inspired in the main by two literary models, the classical love elegy, particularly the *Amores* of Ovid, and the Italian Paradox."[2]

Donne is acknowledged as the greatest metaphysical poet of the seventeenth century. His elegies as well as his lyrics and satires are a blend of the ornate and the plain, the mellifluous and the abruptly colloquial, of fantasy and urbane reality; as though a combination of Spenser and Wyatt. Donne uses conceits and paradoxes that are startling yet strangely relevant; oblique and hyperbolic but wittily appealing. He uses the question-and-answer technique; poses problems and resolves them; gives geometrical and graphic images as well as unusual thoughts; indulges in sensuous and palpable reflections and incorporates intellectual and metaphoric concepts. The elegies and satires are long poems, the lyrics shorter. Thematically each poem deals with one subject, as in "The Bracelet," "The Perfume," "Loves Warre," "The Anagram," "The Autumnal"; it is the surprising combination of images and thoughts that makes the works remarkable and adds to the theatricality of many a situation and experience embedded in the poems. The *persona* in each poem is vibrant; his impassioned monologue seems addressed to a live person or a live group. At times it seems like banter, often it reflects a grave and serious mood.

In 1596 Donne went on the Earl of Essex's Cadiz expedition, and was on board the *Repulse* at the time of the June 11th victory. From July to October 1597, Donne was with Essex in the Island voyages to the Azores. Donne's verse letters, "The Storme" and "The Calm," are ascribed to his experiences at sea during the Azore voyages, and are examples of Donnian poetic journalism. "The Storme," as originally printed by Donne's son, is addressed

[2] *Ibid.*, p. xxiii.

to "Sr. Basil Brooke," but apparently it was addressed to Christopher Brooke, a close friend of Donne's from his student days at the Inns of Court, where Donne had shared rooms with Brooke. Christopher Brooke rose to be Bencher and Treasurer of Lincoln's Inn (1610-1623), and between 1604 and 1626 was elected six times to the Parliament. It was he who gave away the bride at Donne's wedding. "The Storme" describes the storm that overtook Essex's fleet on July 5, 1597. Lord Thomas Howard, as the Vice-Admiral, and Sir Walter Raleigh, the Rear-Admiral, were also on the expedition. Donne seems to have been on Raleigh's ship. Their battered ships had to return to Plymouth for repairs before they could sail again on August 17th. Donne's poem to Brooke was probably sent from Plymouth. A calm overtook their ships on leaving Plymouth and after they had passed "the Ile called Tercera," according to Georges who was with Raleigh's ships. This mishap may have been the inspiration for Donne's other poem, "The Calm," probably written for Christopher Brooke though not addressed to him.

From late 1597 or early 1598 to 1602 Donne was Secretary to Sir Thomas Eggerton, the Lord Keeper and later Lord Chancellor Ellesmere, at York House, in the Strand, London. The poem *Metempsychosis*, "the progresse of a deathlesse soul," is dated 16th August 1601. It is a long poem of Donne's written in stanzaic form, and has fifty-two verses. It deals with the transmigration of the soul, giving a poetic evaluation of how the soul passes successively from meaner forms of life to the higher species until it passes into Themach, the sister-wife of Cain. During the years at York House, Donne met other eminent men such as Sir Francis Wooley, Sir Henry Wotten, Rowland Woodward, George Gerrard, and Sir Henry Goodyer, who must have been greatly impressed by the genius of this thinker-poet, for they remained his friends. On October 27th, 1601, Donne was elected to the Parliament from Brackley, Northampton, and served for the session that ended December 19th of that year.

While at York House, Donne fell in love with the fifteen-year-old Anne More, niece by marriage of Sir Thomas Egerton, and married her clandestinely and perhaps with an ulterior motive, Anne being the heiress of Sir George More, Chancellor of the Garter, in December 1601. The incensed Sir George had Donne dismissed from York House and brought his political career to an end. Donne moved from York House to a place near Savoy, but the irate father still unhappy about the marriage of his minor daughter, had Donne imprisoned in February 1602. Donne was in the Fleet prison until April 27th, when he was released, his marriage having been ratified by the Archbishop of Canterbury. Anne's cousin, Sir Francis Wooley, asked them to his country house at Pyrford, and they remained there until 1604; their first child, Constance, was born at Pyrford, probably in 1603.

Some of Donne's songs and sonnets, like "The Ecstasy," are thought to be addressed to Anne Donne. These poems have a tenderness and spirituality about them which is different from the sparring wit of Donne's earlier lyrics and elegies, though they deal with physical love. Their son, John, was born in 1604, and they moved to Mitchum soon after; they also took lodgings in the Strand. George was born the following year. Donne was writing poetry all this while, but because he did not write for publication, his poems cannot be dated accurately. From the many extant copies of his poems in different handwritings, it is evident that his poems were circulated among groups of friends and *literati*, and that he was one of the most popular poets of his times. Donne took stock themes and genres, but his brilliant emphasis and unique variations gave the poems an originality that has seldom been eclipsed; neither has their palpable appeal. Aesthetically his poems belong, with others of his period, to the baroque art, but it is his impassioned ardour and wit that sets him apart; yet strangely enough there is little in the poems that could be termed autobiographical.

By 1605 Donne had accepted the tenets of the Anglican Church and by 1606 had become associated with Thomas Morton, who was consecrated the Bishop of Durham a few years after. It is conjectured that Morton and Donne collaborated in issuing controversial treatises entailing the Roman Catholic Church, but there is no evidence of it. In 1607 when Morton became Dean of Gloucester he tried to lure Donne into the Church by offering him a benefice. Donne rejected the proposal.

Anne and John Donne had four other children between 1605 and 1611: Francis in January 1607, Lucy in August 1608, Bridget in December 1609, and Mary in 1611. Five other children were born to them before the death of Anne.

In 1607 Donne wrote the Prefatory verses to Ben Jonson's *Volpone*. In 1608 Donne suffered a severe illness; this was also a period when he was working on *Biathanatos*, a treatise on suicide. There is a conjecture that his illness may have been the inspiration for the treatise; on the other hand the early seventeenth century had a morbid preoccupation with death and Donne was only following a tradition. *Biathanatos* apparently argues the validity of suicide, though in reality the work is a satire on "scholastic and casuististical reasoning. In [it] he demolishes logic by presenting a problem with no solution . . . [and] leaves a dilemma of choices,"[3] according to Joan Webber, a twentieth-century Donne scholar; this throws a different light on the treatise. *Biathanatos* was published after Donne's death in 1646. By 1606 Sir George More was reconciled to his daughter and Donne, and apportioned a dowry to them which he had long withheld. This stabilized their financial position.

From 1608 to 1610 Donne was a frequent visitor at Twickenham, the seat of Lucy, Countess of Bedford, and met several prominent people of the period, especially as Lady Bedford was closely associated with the Court of King James I and Queen Anne and was herself a poet and a patron of men of letters. Donne celebrated some of his friends and associates in verse letters. Six of his verse letters are addressed to Lady Bedford, and poems like "Twickenham Garden" and "The Nocturnal on St. Lucy's Eve" seem also to be designed for her. Donne wrote elegies on Lady Lucy's friends, Lady Marckham and Mrs. Bulstrode, and on her brother, Lord Harrington. Among Donne's patrons and friends were other high-placed women, such as the Countess of Huntingdon, the Countess of Salisbury, Lady Carey, Mrs. Essex Riche, and Mrs. Magdalen Herbert. Donne had known Lady Huntingdon since his days at York House; she was the youngest stepdaughter of Sir Thomas Egerton. Mrs. Herbert, the mother of Lord Herbert of Cherbury and of George Herbert, was one of Donne's most illustrious friends. To this great woman are dedicated some of his verse letters, lyrics, and sonnets.

On April 17th, 1610, his alma mater, Oxford, honoured him with an honorary degree of Master of Arts, and he was incorporated at Cambridge. His first published work, *The Pseudo-Martyr*, had appeared that year. In it he defended the right of the Roman Catholics to take the oath of allegiance to the throne,

[3] Joan Webber, *Contrary Music* (Madison: University of Wisconsin Press, 1963), pp. 5, 7.

and contended that faith and patriotism can co-exist. In 1611 Donne's next great prose work, a satire on the Jesuits, *Ignatius his Conclave*, was published anonymously in Latin and in English, the latter being entitled a translation from the Latin. He used a pseudonym in the dedicatory epistle, "The Printer to the Reader." The work deals with the journey of the soul and conducts a dialogue in hell. Ignatius Loyola figures in it as the counterpart of Satan; with him are such great innovators as Copernicus, Paracelsus, and Machiavelli. Although the work is fictional, it is topical and satiric. There were two Latin and one English editions of it in 1611.

In 1610 Donne became associated with Sir Robert Drury of Hamstead and with Viscount Rochester, who later became the Earl of Somerset. Rochester was a great favourite of the King, and so a powerful ally. Donne wished a position in court, and wrote a letter to Rochester expressing his interest in the Church, whereas he was anxious to secure a diplomatic post through Rochester. Sir Robert Drury's interest in Donne stemmed from both Donne's literary and diplomatic achievements. On the first death anniversary of Sir Robert Drury's fifteen-year-old daughter, Elizabeth, Donne wrote a complimentary address; the long, philosophical and metaphysical poem, *An Anatomy of the World* (1611). The following year he commemorated the occasion by the second anniversary poem *A Progress of the Soul*. In these hyperbolic panegyrics Donne makes Elizabeth Drury the occasion rather than the subject of the poems. In these two companion pieces Donne exalts the female principle rather than the girl whom he had never known. The poems could be in praise of concepts like Sophia, Astraea, the Virgin Mary, or Queen Elizabeth, who had died in the preceding decade, and could be termed religious exercises in meditation. Donne had intended to write one such poem for each of the death anniversaries of Elizabeth Drury, but did not do it. Sir Robert had both the 1611 and 1612 poems published, and gave Donne and his family an apartment in Drury House.

In 1611-12 Donne accompanied Sir Robert to the continent, and spent time in Paris and the Spa, in Germany, and the Low Countries. While Donne was away, Anne had a still-born child; their eighth. According to Walton, Donne saw a vision of his wife the day their child died. The beautiful, impassioned lyric, "Sweetest love I do not goe," is conjectured to have been written by Donne for his wife on the eve of his departure for France. On his return from the continent Donne wrote an elegy on the death of the Prince of Wales. In 1613 he also celebrated the marriage of Princess Elizabeth in a nuptial song; the princess was married to the Elector Palatine on St. Valentine's Day.

In 1614 Donne was elected to the Parliament from Taunton in Somerset. (He had been Member of Parliament for Brackley in 1601.) This continued to be a time of productivity; he composed funeral pieces and complimentary verse letters and another epithalamiun for the Earl of Somerset and the Countess of Essex. Donne and Anne lost two of their children, Mary and Francis this year; Nicholas had been born the previous year. Donne was getting more involved and interested in the Anglican Church and to the years 1615-1619 belong his *Essays in Divinity*; these were first published by his son in 1651. These essays examine and elucidate Christian doctrines, but do not question the doctrines, and like the Aquinas credo, accept faith before reason. These essays were not written for publication, but are the precursors of the great sermons and can be classified as literature of meditation. Donne had still not given up his idea of a diplomatic career, but King James, who was himself a theologian, and the Bishop of London persuaded Donne to accept Holy Orders in the Church of England. He was first ordained a deacon and then a priest on January 23rd, 1615. Yet he spent considerable time as a judge of the Court of Delegates in 1622, as governor of Charterhouse (1626), and as a member of the Court of High Commission (1627).

Priesthood to Donne became a vocation; on it he bestowed much of his intellectual gifts and energy. Donne had deliberated long before finally accepting the office, but he graced it with his poetic energy as he had his secular youth; the witty Jack Donne passed imperceptibly into the witty and forceful doctor of theology. Most of his ecstatic though studied divine poems as *A Litany* and the linked sonnet sequence *La Corona* (The Crown) belong to this period. The songs and sonnets deal with the purpose of life and death. They are contemplative meditation in pursuit of the grace of God. Aesthetically the poems have just as many conceits and startling convolutions and images, metaphors and a masculine rhythm as the earlier poems, but in spite of their baroque fantasy and often colloquial cadences, there is a seriousness of thought and ardour which places them among the highest religious and devotional literature.

Donne received an honorary degree of Doctor of Divinity from Cambridge after his ordination. Like several other priests of the period he held pluralistic livings; Donne held the living of a country parish as well as that of St. Dunston's-in-the-West, which was a city church and the parish of Izaak Walton. Donne's intellectual propensities and his rhetorical training enriched his ministry. To it he brought his experiences and love of learning as well as his piety and devotion. Along with his other duties, he was vicar of Keyston and Sevenoaks in Kent. Donne's first extant sermon was preached at Greenwich before the Queen. This was the year (1615) when his daughter Margaret was born.

In 1616 Donne became Reader in Divinity to the Benchers of Lincoln's Inn, and held the position until February 1622. His daughter Elizabeth was born in 1616, and it was also the year of the publication of his thirteen problems in Latin translations, *Problematum Miscellaneorum, Antaristotelicorum, centuria dimidiata*. 1617 saw him preach his first sermon at Paul's Cross and at Knole. On August 15th of that year, Donne's wife, Anne, died in childbirth—their twelfth child. Seven of their children survived them. Anne was buried in St. Clement Dane's churchyard

From 1619 to 1620 Donne was abroad as the Chaplain to Viscount Doncaster, who later became Earl of Carlisle, on a diplomatic mission to Germany. A crisis was threatening a war; their mission was to avert it. The Thirty Years' War followed.

In November of 1621 Donne was appointed Dean of St. Paul's Cathedral by the king. That year and the following saw the republication of Donne's *The Anniversaries* and the first publication of some of his sermons. There was a likelihood of Donne being elevated to a bishopric, but a severe illness in the winter of 1623 deterred it. The published sermons were: *A Sermon Upon the xv Verse Of The XX Chapter Of The Book of Judges*, and *A Sermon Upon The viii Verse of the I Chapter of the Acts of The Apostles*, 1622. To this period belong his *Devotions*, which were published in 1624, the *Encaenia* on St. John 10:22, and *Three Sermons Upon Speciall Occasions*.

In 1624 Donne was made the vicar of the church of St. Dunstan's-in-the-West. From his association with the parish, Izaak Walton must have come to know him well enough to attempt writing the first biography extant of Donne. This year two issues of Donne's *Devotions upon Emergent Occasions* were published, and two of the sermons were reprinted: *A Sermon Upon*

. . . *The Acts of the Apostles* and *Three Sermons Upon Speciall Occasions*.

With the outbreak of plague in 1625, Donne and his family took shelter in Chelsea, which was then on the outskirts of the city of London, with Lady Magdalen Herbert Danvers. Other of his sermons were published this year together with the first sermon preached to King Charles at the Church of St. James. Even as a churchman Donne had remained close to the Court. He had been appreciated for his learning and theological views by King James I, and Charles I continued the tradition, though, unlike his father, he was not a scholar. Charles honored Donne by asking him to preach the first sermon after his enthronement. There was a steady demand for the printed word from Donne, and each year saw more of his works in print. In 1626 his satire *Ignatius his Conclave* was reprinted along with some sermons. In 1627, the year he lost his daughter Lucy, the third edition of his *Devotions upon Emergent Occasions* was put into circulation along with the famous funeral sermon he preached commemorating his friend and patron, Magdalen Herbert, Lady Danvers; the sermon was based on II Peter 3:13.

On June 13th, 1628, Donne was appointed a member of the commission of the Canterbury Prerogative Court, and in June of the following year sat on the Commission at Lambeth Palace. By 1630 Donne's health was failing. He made his will and spent some time out of London at Abury Hatch, in Epping Forest, with a widowed daughter, Constance Alleyn. He was unable to preach at the Christmas services that year. Donne returned to London in 1631, and on the first Friday in Lent, a day he had long called his own, he preached before King Charles at Whitehall his famous oratorical sermon, *Deaths Duell*. The date of the sermon was February 25th. Donne died on March 31st, 1631. He was buried in St. Paul's Cathedral. A finely sculptured monument by Nicholas Stone, apparently copied from a portrait that Donne had painted of himself, showing Donne in his winding sheets standing atop an urn, survived the fire of 1666, and can be seen in the Cathedral. His mother survived him by a few months, dying on June 28 of the same year.

"Deaths Duell" was published shortly after Donne's death. Donne had left a legacy of eighty of his sermons to his son. These, prefaced by a biographical sketch of Donne written by

Izaak Walton, were published in 1640. Other sermons were published in 1649 and 1661.

Donne was recognised as a great preacher in his own time. His sermons were long, some covering as much as two to three hours, but were popular. Some of his best sermons were preached on special occasions and feast days at St. Paul's Cathedral and St. Paul's Cross, and, as Joan Webber has aptly said, it was in the pulpit that Donne achieved his fullest artistic expression. For along with all the seriousness of his convictions he brings together images and conceits, repetitions and parallelisms, unique interpretations and arguments, juxtaposition of words and phrases, haunting rhythms of pause and stress, imaginative thought and nuances of meaning that make his sermons poetical prose; some are of sonorous music that could equal Milton's. Often in his sermons he poses metaphysical questions like those that one meets in his poetry, and he takes one through similar labyrinths of baroque art. The rhythm varies; at times it is ecstatic and intense, at others conciliatory as if Donne is pleading for the frailties of man and preaching to himself as well as his congregation. His sermons contain a wide range of subjects and themes and draw on the Old Testament as well as the New. A poet himself, he was enamoured of the psalms and the dramatic episodes as those in Job and the prophets. He was conversant with the Bible to the extent that his works include approximately eight thousand references to it. The two predominant and recurrent themes of his sermons are love and death. One hundred and sixty of his sermons are extant.

Other than the Bible Donne draws on contemporary thought and available literature, both classical and of the period. He quotes the early church Fathers, especially St. Augustine. His Biblical sources were the original Hebrew, the Latin Vulgate, the Coverdale and Geneva Bibles. His quotations are often given in Latin followed by an English translation. At times Donne's works seem overburdened with the melancholic strain so prevalent in the early seventeenth century, but he always has the assurance of grace. Donne makes wide use of symbols in his sermons as in the poems; a recurrent symbol is the circle of perfection; where symmetry makes for perfection; any deviation from it spells disease and decay, and God's grace alone mitigates the latter. At times Donne's prose tends to be tedious, but the poet in him takes over and by the magic of his power turns it into pure gold.

The posthumous publications of his works are: "*Deaths Duell*, 1632, 1633 (three issues). *Poems*, 1633; succeeding editions (augmented) or issues of *Poems* in 1635, 1639, 1649, 1650, 1654, 1669. *Juvenilia: Or Certaine Paradoxes and Problemes*, 1633 (two eds.); *Paradoxes*, Problems, Essays, Characters (with Epigrams), 1652; additional 'Problems' from Bodleian MS Tanner 299, published in *Paradoxes and Problemes*, 1923. *Ignatius his Conclave*, 1634, 1635, 1653. *Devotions Upon Emergent Occasions*, 1634, 1638. *Biathanatos*, c. 1646, 1648. *Essays in Divinity*, 1651. *Six Sermons Upon Several Occasions*, 1634; *Sapienta, Clamimans, Wisdome crying out to Sinners: Of Man's Timely Remembering of his Creator* (sermon three in collection, on Eccles. xii 1), 1638, 1639; LXXX *Sermons*, 1640; *Fifty Sermons*, 1649; XXVI *Sermons*, 1660 (actually twenty-three); additional sermon on Psalms xxxviii 9 from MS in Potter and Simpson, II.6, pp.144 ff. Some letters published with *Poems*, in *Letters to Severall Persons of Honour*, 1651 (reissue 1654), in Walton's *Life of George Herbert*, 1670, in other seventeenth-century collections. . . ."[4] Donne appeared in the eighteenth century in Jacob Tonson's edition in 1719, and then in John Bell's *Poets of Great Britain* in 1779. The life of Donne which Walton had first published in 1640, he revised in 1658, 1670, and 1675. Walton adulates Donne to the extent that he is not always right; but being the earliest biographer, his work is invaluable. The two volumes of Sir Edmund Gosse's *Life and Letters of John Donne* (1899) are valuable; in spite of a plethora of Donne scholarship in the twentieth century, Donne's appeal to the twentieth century cannot be overrated. Yeats and T. S. Eliot were two of his votaries in the earlier part of the century. Some of the critics and scholars that have made Donne's work come alive are: D. C. Allen, E. K. Chambers, Helen Gardner, H. J. C. Grierson, G. R. Potter, Evelyn M. Simpson, E. S. LeComte, J. B. Leishman, J. T. Shawcross, Louis L. Martz, Marjorie H. Nicolson, Theodore Spencer, Joan Webber, R. C. Bald, M. Y. Hughes, J. Sparrow, A. Alvarez, Joan Bennett, Helen C. White, and George Williamson; also Sir Geoffrey Keynes, C. S. Lewis, H. C. Combs, Z. R. Sullens, P. Legouis, Miriam Starkman, C. M. Coffin, Earl Miner, and W. Milgate

[4] John T. Shawcross, *The Complete Poetry of John Donne* (New York: Anchor Books, 1967), p. xvi.

In his lifetime Donne had critics like Ben Jonson and Thomas Carew comment on his work. In the centuries that followed he was studied and criticized by men of letters as John Dryden, Samuel Johnson, Coleridge. Donne, therefore, with his wit and brilliance is for all times.

Donne was well acquainted with the ancient sceptics and the Epicureans, with Ovid and Petrarch, with Juvenal, Horace and Persius. Original though his mode, he used their stock themes and figures, and often their expressions as in the use of the hyperbole of the Petrarchans, the badinage of the satirists. He also made considerable use of mediaeval scholastic theology, at times wittily belabouring a point. For example, in "The Dream" the beloved of the *persona* appears to him as an angel and then becomes the God-principle, for she gleans his thoughts and thus shares with God the power of intuition, which is denied to the angels; they lack the power of telepathy! In this profane banter Donne expressed a mediaeval theological concept. Donne was also well aware of contemporary thought and the new philosophy. He mentions the heliocentric Copernican astronomy and the revolutionary findings of Kepler and Galileo; his fertile mind incorporates their thinking in his work whether to disparage it or to agree with it. Pierre Legouis, a twentieth-century French critic, points out that Donne was a meticulous craftsman, and at times sacrificed his intensity of feeling and originality to fit his thoughts to a stanzaic pattern as in "Love's Alchymie." The banality of some of his verses strike one as forcefully as the originality of others, and at times in the same poem. Donne's poems are structured and follow patterns as does his prose. Often his works start with startling intensity and spontaneity, and then show a fading of zest and a quieter, more deliberate verbal pattern. Yet their appeal is always present. This makes Donne alive to the twentieth century as it did to the metaphysical school, to Carew, who was the first to point out that, unlike the traditionalists, Donne made little use of mythological metaphors and references; to Pope who tried to imitate him; to Dryden and Johnson who were enamoured of him, but could not accept his metaphysical mode; to Coleridge; and to Browning, whose dramatic monologues have the Donnian stamp on them.

Donne has had imitators and adulators, and he continues to stimulate the thinker and delight the scholar.

BIBLIOGRAPHY

Clements, A.L., ed. *John Donne's Poetry*. New York: Norton, 1966.

Coffin, C.M., ed. *The Complete Poetry and Selected Prose of John Donne*. New York: Modern Library, 1952.

"Donne, John," ed. G.Bu., *Chamber's Encyclopedia*, 1967, Vol. 4, p. 603.

Encyclopedia Americana, 1969, s.v. "John Donne."

Encyclopaedia Britannica, 1910, s.v. "John Donne."

Encyclopaedia Britannica, 1970, s.v. "John Donne."

Ferry, Anne Davidson, ed. *Religious Prose of 17th Century England*. New York: Alfred A. Knopf, 1967.

Gardner, Helen, ed. *John Donne: A Collection of Critical Essays*. Englewood Cliffs, NJ: Prentice-Hall, 1962.

———, ed. *The Elegies and the Songs and Sonnets of John Donne*. Oxford: Clarendon Press, 1966.

LeComte, Edward. *Grace to a Witty Sinner*. New York: Walker and Company, 1965.

Legouis, Pierre. *Donne The Craftsman*. New York: Russell & Russell, Inc., 1962.

Milgate, W., ed. *The Satires, Epigrams, and Verse Letters of John Donne*. Oxford: Clarendon Press, 1967.

Miner, Earl. *The Metaphysical Mode from Donne to Cowley*. Princeton: Princeton University Press, 1969.

Shawcross, John T., ed. *The Complete Poetry of John Donne*. New York: Anchor Books, 1967.

Simpson, Evelyn M., ed. *John Donne's Sermons on the Psalms and Gospels*. Berkeley: University of California Press, 1967.

Webber, Joan. *Contrary Music*. Madison: University of Wisconsin Press, 1963.

Williamson, George. *The Donne Tradition*. New York: Noonday, 1958.

———. *Six Metaphysical Poets*. New York: Noonday, 1967.

WOMEN AND DONNE

As in *The Anniversaries* Elizabeth Drury is the occasion for Donne's thesis on the wisdom of the soul, *sapientia creata,* and the idealized female principle, so in the verse letters to the great ladies Donne uses poetic conceits, fantasy, hyperbole, flattery, verbal mazes, along with colloquial directness, to write some of the most astonishing lyrics and essays in English. In these poetic essays he does not eulogize a particular woman alone: he expresses his ideas of womanhood exalted—exalted to the point that the ideas become intellectual concepts. The noble woman is as far removed from reality as is Astraea, the last of the goddesses, who fled the earth because of its baseness; yet the ideal is woman enough to call for Donne's love, whether physical or transcendent.

Donne had been criticized for the use of such hyperbole in his own time, but he explained his position:

> . . . that had been a new weakness in me, to have praised anybody in printed verses, that had not been capable of the best praise that I could give . . . that I could conceive.[1]

With this in mind we approach some of Donne's verse letters and poems.

Three of the letters, two to the Countess of Huntingdon and one to Mrs. Magdalen Herbert, were to women who were both friends and patronesses. The letter beginning "That unripe side of

[1] Sir Edmund Gosse, *The Life and Letters of John Donne,* Vol. I (London: 1899), p. 305.

earth, that heavy clime," to Lady Elizabeth Stanley, Countess of Huntingdon, was written apparently around the year 1605, as it is addressed "To the Countesse of Huntingdon," and Elizabeth Stanley was not elevated to the position until that year. Donne must have known Elizabeth Stanley since she was ten years of age, the time her mother, the dowager Countess of Derby, had married Sir Thomas Egerton, the lord keeper, and moved with her three daughters (Elizabeth being the youngest) into York House in the Strand, London. This was in 1600 when Donne was secretary to Sir Thomas Egerton. Anne More, the future wife of Donne and niece by an earlier marriage of Sir Thomas, was also a resident of York House. Donne was about twenty-eight years of age at the time. Young, handsome, and witty, he had won the friendship of this bevy of girls. In his verse letters to the Countess of Huntingdon, the wife of Sir Henry Hastings, fifth Earl of Huntingdon, there is a playfulness of wit, that points to a genuine, Platonic interest in his young married patroness.

The verse letter that begins with, "The unripe side of earth. . ." sums up the different kinds of love experienced by human beings. If Donne expresses love for Elizabeth Stanley, it is not until line 77 of the 130-line poem. It appears as the courtly and reverential love of a poet for a patroness. The types of love he examines are friendship, mutual respect and admiration, intellectual love, physical love, love disdained, and spiritual love. Donne has no use for the Petrarchan kind of love:

> Yet neither will I vexe your eyes to see
> A sighing Ode, nor crosse-arm'd Elegie.[2]

He can only pity those who sigh for love or converse with nature in the absence of the beloved or allow themselves to wilt away.

His thesis on the pre-lapsarian and pre-connubial love is unique, because he equates it with the chaotic state of nature when nothing was categorized or defined. From line 95 to the end of the poem love and virtue become synonymous. They are the elixir, the gold, the philosopher's stone, the inexhaustible life-giving sun, that regenerate and transubstantiate life into a spiritual reality. He ends the poem with the theological assumption of love, that it is the summation of all virtues:

[2] John T. Shawcross, *The Complete Poetry of John Donne* (New York: Anchor Books, 1967), p. 214, lines 21, 22.

Why love among the vertues is not knowne
Is, that love is all contract in one.[3]

This in general is the pattern of Donne's verse letters to the great ladies. Out of the thirty-six of his verse letters extant, a third were written to women; two to the Countess of Huntingdon, one to Mrs. Magdalen Herbert, seven to the Countess of Bedford, one to the two sisters, Lady Carey and Mrs. Essex Riche, and one to the Countess of Salisbury.

Donne follows the courtly tradition in extolling the ladies and belittling himself, though at no point does he cringe in his letters. He is always the artist in command of his material, witty, dignified, full of conceits, flights of imagination, delectable paradoxes, and developing thought patterns which start with the simple and systematically progress to the complex and the abstract. But beneath all this there is the serious, pious Donne, whose main value and concern is "virtue." Virtue for Donne is almost a religion, integrity itself. His great ladies are virtuous not only in goodness, in their honour, in talents, in physical grace and beauty, but they are virtuous in active goodness. Theirs is no "cloistered virtue" but a militant virtue that acts like the sun's rays and draws others to virtue; the philosopher's stone that transforms as it touches the base metal.

In his poems one notes that often, not only does the *persona* speak, but Donne himself speaks. The song, "Sweetest love, I do not goe" though not addressed to Anne Donne may very well have been written for her in 1611 when Donne was accompanying Sir Robert Drury to France. Although the poem is built point by point like a logician and a rhetorician arguing his thesis, it has a tenderness and emotional quality that could only emanate from deep love and concern. According to Edward LeComte, "The Exstasie" may also have been inspired by Anne More. It has a spiritual quality about it that can be associated with Donne's profound and lasting affection for his young wife.

Mrs. Magdalen Herbert was another of Donne's close and valued friends. In the complimentary letters and verses he wrote to her there is a note of respect, cheerfulness and admiration. The sonnet "To the Lady Magdalen Herbert of St. Mary Magdalen," "The Autumnall," the verse letter addressed to her begin-

[3] *Ibid.*, p. 216, lines 129, 130.

ning, "Mad paper stay and grudge not here to burn," all show a genuine depth of feeling for an older but a remarkable woman. Mrs. Herbert was the mother of Edward, the first Baron Herbert of Cherbury and of George Herbert, two eminent men of letters. Lord Herbert was a metaphysical philosopher, a historian who wrote *The Life of Henry VIII;* and a poet and diplomat. He had received his education at University College, Oxford, and had written one of the first autobiographies. George Herbert, a Cambridge man (Trinity College) was a poet-philosopher. An Anglican priest, he wrote emotionally charged meditational verses; "The Temple" being the best known collection of his religious verse. Mrs. Herbert was the mother of these illustrious sons. According to Grierson, ". . .among the ladies whose virtue Donne celebrated, the highest place is held by Lady Bedford and Mrs. Herbert."[4] Apparently Donne first met Mrs. Herbert at Oxford, where she was stationed after her husband's death;—their estate was in Wales. Walton in his *Life of Herbert* says that Donne's "The Autumnall" was written for Mrs. Herbert, and that "the beauties of her mind and body" were celebrated in the poem. By 1607 Donne and Mrs. Herbert were good friends. Donne was about thirty-five at the time and she forty, and his letters to her point his deep appreciation of her. In the genuinely felt compliments he pays her, one can see the accomplishments of the great lady; it was to his credit that he had won her as a friend and patroness. Donne shared his religious poetry with Mrs. Herbert. The crown of linked sonnets, *La Corona*, accompanied the sonnet on her beautiful name for her perusal. During the epidemic of plague, Mrs. Herbert, now the wife of Sir John Danvers, sheltered the Donnes for several months in her home. On her death in 1627, Donne preached the funeral sermon. In the sermon he praised her beauty, the brilliance of her conversation, her cheerful disposition, her great intelligence, her virtues, her hospitality, her concern for her family's education, her charity and philanthropy, her good taste in clothes and furnishings, her moderation, and her great piety. To show the clarity of her mind and thinking, Donne mentioned that two hours before she died she was repeating the responses to the prayers being read to her from the *Book of Common Prayer*.

[4] Helen Gardner, *The Elegies and the Songs and Sonnets of John Donne* (Oxford: Clarendon Press, 1966), p. 248.

The Countess of Bedford was another close associate of Donne. She was Lucy Harington before she married Edward Russell, the third Earl of Bedford in 1594, and the aunt-in-law of Countess Elizabeth Stanley Huntingdon. Perhaps it was through the offices of Sir Henry Goodyer, Donne's friend and secretary to the Earl, that Donne was introduced to the Bedford household. Lady Bedford was closely associated with the court; first as a lady-in-waiting to Queen Elizabeth, and then as a friend of Queen Anne, the consort of James I. Donne's love poem, "Twickman Garden," was written for her, Twickenham Park being her residence, and probably the poem "A Nocturnall on St. Lucy's Day" was also in her honour. Structurally the two poems are close, and could be called companion pieces: one deals with unrequitted love and springtime, the other with winter and death's desolation. In these oblique expressions of Petrarchan love, one can see the awe in which Donne held his patroness. Seven of Donne's verse letters are addressed to Lady Bedford. Lines like:

> Therefore I study you first in your Saints
> Those friends, whom your election glorifies,
> Then in your deeds, accesses, and restraints,
> And what you reade, and what your selfe devize.
> . . . .
> And rest on what the Catholique voice doth teach;
> That you are good: . . ."[5]

are revealing of the regard Donne had for her; language as simple as that can not all be flattery. Lady Bedford exchanged verses with Donne, and Donne wrote some elegies for her kinfolk, as her brother, Lord John Harington; and for Lady Markham and Cecilia Bulstrode. We can imagine Lady Bedford as a vivacious, out-going benefactoress. Lady Bedford was godmother to Donne's second daughter, Lucy, in 1608, and it was to her that Donne applied for help to clear his debts before he accepted Holy Orders. Their friendship was genuine, but it seems there was some coolness on her part about the time of Donne's ordination, as seen in a letter of Donne to Goodyer. However Donne preached before her in 1621. Lady Bedford died in 1627.

[5] Shawcross, *op. cit.*, p. 221.

Donne celebrated other ladies such as Lady Carey and her sister, Mrs. Essex Riche, daughters of Sir Robert Riche, in a verse letter probably written in Amiens while Donne was with Sir Robert Drury (1611-12); and the Countess of Salisbury, Lady Catherine Howard, wife of William Cecil, second Earl of Salisbury. Donne's second "Epithalamion" was written in honour of the Countess' sister, Frances Howard, and her marriage to the Earl of Somerset. Using hyperbole, Donne equates the ladies with virtue, and its ennobling power.

Donne compliments his women friends and acquaintances in poems and letters as well as in prose. Extant copies of the manuscripts prove that these complimentary essays were meant to be circulated, even though addressed to individuals. In his works Donne uses farfetched images, fantasy, metaphysical conceits, and paradoxes. He also follows the courtly love tradition of eulogizing the women he admires. But the depths of serious piety that he sounds in his essays are revealing of his character and his relationship to the women. However mundane his thoughts, they soar towards the spiritual; the young courtier-lover progresses to a divine.

BIBLIOGRAPHY

Clements, A. L., ed. *John Donne's Poetry, A Norton Critical Edition.* New York: W.W. Norton & Co. Inc., 1966.

Coffin, Charles M., ed. *The Complete Poetry and Selected Prose of John Donne.* New York: Modern Library, 1952.

Gardner, Helen, ed. *The Elegies and the Songs and Sonnets of John Donne.* Oxford: Clarendon Press, 1966.

LeComte, Edward. *Grace to a Witty Sinner.* New York: Walker & Co., 1965.

Milgate, W., ed. *The Satires, Epigrams, & Verse Letters of John Donne.* Oxford: Clarendon Press, 1967.

Miner, Earl. *The Metaphysical Mode from Donne to Cowley.* Princeton: Princeton University Press, 1969.

Shawcross, John T., ed. *The Complete Poetry of John Donne.* New York: Anchor Books, 1967.

Warnke, Frank J., ed. *John Donne Poetry and Prose.* New York: Modern Library, 1967.

ROMANTICISM METHODIZED IN POPE

Pope speaking to his friend, Joseph Spence, about his youthful epic, "Alcander," said, "I endeavoured in the poem, to collect all the beauties of the great epic writers into one piece: there was Milton's style in one part, and Cowley's in another: here the style of Spenser imitated, and there of Statius; here Homer and Virgil, and there Ovid and Claudian."[1]

Imitating and emulating the great masters of antiquity, the Renaissance, and his own era, Pope has left a corpus of poetry, much of which can be termed an amalgam of the classical and the romantic mode, and unique in its brilliance.

Pope perfected the heroic couplet, using it for almost all of his poetry. He did experiment with other verse forms as the octosyllabic couplet, the tercet or triplet, and the Spenserian stanza, and had hoped to write an epic on Brutus, the mythical progenitor of the British, in blank verse, but he found his medium in the heroic couplet. He perfected it to "correctness," a much belaboured word of the critics, since first introduced to Pope as a literary discipline by Walsh. Within the framework of the couplet Pope structured and designed and patterned his poems; and using the caesura, shifting pauses, differing vowel tones, and carefully weighed, modulated and facile words, gave the couplet variety and charm. In Pope's hands this classical discipline in verse became the vehicle for some of the greatest romantic poetry of the early eighteenth century, and a precursor of Byron and Keats and Shelley and Wordsworth. In all of Pope's work there is a spontaneity of expression and movement that transcends the restriction of the couplet. The classical clarity and

[1] Reuben A. Brower, *Alexander Pope, the Poetry of Allusion* (London: Oxford University Press, 1968), p. 1.

simplicity of the lines vie with the ebullience of the descriptions in *Windsor Forest,* the emotions in *Eloisa to Abelard,* the antics of the aerial sylphs in *The Rape of the Lock,* the hope-inspiring cadences of *The Messiah,* and the scintillating wit of "An Essay on Criticism."

Johnson, who was an excellent Latin scholar, translated Pope's *Messiah* into Latin poetry, while he was an undergraduate at Pembroke College, Oxford.[2] Johnson, the pedant, admired the *Messiah,* but R. K. Root in 1938, conceding the excellence of its music and craftsmanship, said of the poem, and of *Windsor Forest,* that they have "very little more."[3] Yet the *Messiah* offers a wealth of material. The *Messiah* is an imitation of the Fourth and the most famous of Virgil's *Ecologues,* where Virgil prophesied the birth of a royal child. Written in the grand style the *Messiah* seemingly conveys Pope's deep religious convictions, though critics like R. K. Root would not agree with the statement.[4] Pope was highly ethical and professedly a Roman Catholic, though of Erasmus' leanings, as Pope himself wrote to Swift. To Atterbury he said that he adhered to Catholicism because of his mother. If Pope wrote the *Messiah* thinking of his parents, he also partook of the last sacraments on his death bed. Keeping this emotional climate in mind, the *Messiah: a Sacred Ecologue* becomes romantically charged. The poem first appeared in *The Spectator* (No. 378) in May of 1712 anonymously with Steele's editorial comments. In November of that year *The Spectator* (No. 534) acknowledged Pope as its author. Fashioned on Isaiah's Messianic prophecies and Virgil's *Pollio,* it has the flavour of Milton's "On the Morning of Christ's Nativity." The poem has the romantic and mystical in its fibre as well as the Biblical and the Virgilian pastoral. The following sylvan metaphor embodies these concepts:

> From Jesse's root behold a branch arise,
> Whose sacred flower with fragrance fills the skies:
>
> (*M*. 9-10)

[2] Gilbert Highet, *The Classical Tradition* (New York: Oxford University Press, 1957), p. 295.

[3] Robert Kilburn Root, *The Political Career of Alexander Pope* (Princeton: Princeton University Press, 1938), p. 52.

[4] *Ibid.*, p. 60.

In its mystic expanse the thought is Donnian and metaphysical. The romantic imagery is carried further in reference to Christ's baptism and the descent of God's Spirit as a dove; making the images vibrantly beautiful. Keatsian intensity is seen in lines such as:

> A God, a God! the vocal hills reply,
> The rocks proclaim th' approaching Deity.
> Lo, earth receives him from the bending skies!
>
> (*M*. 31-33)

Romantic and pastoral images aptly paraphrase Biblical passages and prophecies, as the one on peace:

> No more shall nation against nation rise,
> But useless lances into scythes shall bend.
> And the broad falchion in a ploughshare end.
>
> (*M*. 57-62)

or convey the characteristics that make a shepherd good as in Psalm 23:

> As the good shepherd tends his fleecy care,
> Seeks freshest pasture and the purest air,
> Explores the lost, the wandering sheep directs,
>
> (*M*. 49-51)

or pursue the theme of peace further in an iridescent and sensuous picture of nature; a Popian paraphrase of the eleventh chapter of Isaiah:

> The smiling infant in his hand shall take
> The crested basilisk and speckled snake,
> Pleased the green lustre of the scales survey,
>
> (*M*. 81-83)

Pope achieves these highly romantic effects by the use of colour, "apostrophes and grand imperatives [to] set a tone of . . . 'surprise,' . . . unexpected combinations, . . . comic miracles [such as] 'And harmless serpents lick the pilgrim's feet' (M. 80), descriptive epithets, . . . [and] startling contrasts."[5] And in an

[5] Brower, *op. cit.*, pp. 36-37.

amalgam of classical and romantic images "shifts from one tone to another . . . from prophetic calm to prophetic rhapsody in the 'Messiah'."[6] He brings the poem to a close with Miltonic splendour; the Messiah's cosmic effulgence shatters all that is mundane.

As a disciple of Dryden, Pope copies Dryden's Virgilian style in the *Messiah;* and with Biblical overtones and his keen poetic imagination, gives an exuberant romantic poem within a well-wrought classical framework. Anticipating utopian peace and perfection at the advent of the Messiah, Pope also shows himself a romantic rebel:

> The sick and weak the healing plant shall aid,
> From storms a shelter, and from heat a shade.
> All crimes shall cease, and ancient fraud shall fail;
> Returning Justice lift aloft her scale;
>
> (*M.* 15-18)

In a hymn in 1712, with an identical and unmistakable religious fervour, Pope enshrined the triumphant Messiah in a blaze of romantic glory:

> Rise, crowned with light, imperial Salem, rise!
> Exalt thy towering head and lift thine eyes!
> See heaven its sparkling portals wide display,
> And break upon thee in a flood of day.
> . . . .
> Thy realm shall last, thy own Messiah reigns.[7]

Tillotson says the *Messiah* is "Pope's youthful grand public voice."[8] The same voice is carried to *Windsor Forest.*

Windsor Forest written between 1704 and 1710, exemplifies Pope's romantic mode in fetching vignettes. A patriotic poem written in the reign of Queen Anne and revised by Pope at the time of writing the *Messiah, Windsor Forest* expresses the same

[6] Rebecca Price Parkins, *The Poetic Workmanship of Alexander Pope* (New York: Octagon, 1966), p.138.

[7] *The Hymnal of the Protestant Episcopal Church* (Norwood, MA: Plimpton Press, 1943), Hymn 389.

[8] Geoffrey Tillotson, *Pope and Human Nature* (Oxford: Clarendon Press, 1958), p. 265.

optimism as the *Messiah*, except that it hopes for a secular order instead of the religious. Dryden in creating a fresh interest in Virgil, had given the lead, and Pope turned to *The Georgics* for *Windsor Forest*. "From Dryden he learned to imitate without loss of originality,"[9] and like Dryden he used the Horatian "style of public address . . . moulding the speech idiom to the patterns of the couplet."[10] The poem begins with an invocation in the classical style, and then through the use of colour and design, light and shade, mythological allusions, and flights of fancy moves from picture to picture while giving an organically unified poem. The poem celebrates the Peace of Utrecht. Structurally the invocation is followed by a recapitulation of the beauty of Windsor forest. It has a panegyric on Queen Anne and her peace-restoring reign. As compared to the tyrannies of mediaeval Norman kings and their hunting prerogatives, England under Anne is a haven, says Pope. Windsor is "At once the Monarch's and the Muse's seats" (*W.F.* 2). This brings Pope to the joys of hunting and fishing in the Forest. He praises the mythological Diana and addresses the Thames, "great father of the British floods!" (*W.F.* 219). Then follows a wonderful passage which looks forward to *An Essay on Man* (II: 1-2). Like Marlowe's Faustus after man "unlocks the learned store, . . .[he] Bids his free soul expatiate in the skies" (*W.F.* 247, 254). Pope thinks of other poets who frequented Windsor forest and were inspired to paint their own romances. Root points out that structurally *Windsor Forest* depends on Denham's *Cooper's Hill*. Cooper's Hill was on the eastern precincts of Windsor forest, while Pope's home, Binfield, was in the west. Denham's reference to commerce on the Thames and hunting in the forest may have suggested similar themes in *Windsor Forest*. Pope's trees are akin to "Denham's and Virgil and Ovid (Pope's inspiration is always partly literary)."[11] Eventually "the Thames in 'Windsor Forest' bursts the pastoral bounds by being seen as the artery of British Commerce, internationalism, and naval greatness."[12] The most striking feature of *Windsor Forest* is that it has "order in variety" (*W.F.*15), and yet in an oxymoronic image it is "harmoniously confused" (*W.F.* 14). This

[9] Brower, *op. cit.*, p. 1.

[10] *Ibid.*, pp. 3-4.

[11] Geoffrey Tillotson, *On the Poetry of Pope* (Oxford: Clarendon Press, 1950), p. 88.

[12] Geoffrey Tillotson, *Pope and Human Nature* (Oxford: Clarendon Press, 1958), p. 249.

singularity adds to the romanticism of the images, which abound in the poem.

Many of the lines are outstandingly beautiful, such as the lacy shadows of the metaphysical couplet:

> Here waving groves a chequered scene display,
> And part admit, and part exclude the day;
>
> (*W.F.* 17-18)

or the mosaic of his gem-like landscape, with its predominant purples:

> Here in full light the russet plains extend:
> There wrapped in clouds the bluish hills ascend.
> Even the wild heath displays her purple dyes,
>
> (*W.F.* 23-25)

or the lines showing his interest in the hunt and his journalistic observation on the pheasant wounded in flight. Pope displays great tenderness for injured and maimed creatures. His description of the galloping coursers is onomatopoeic as well as extremely clever: as "earth rolls back beneath the flying steed" (*W.F.* 158). For himself the poet wants solitude and communion with nature:

> Bear me, oh bear me to sequestered scenes,
> The bowery mazes, and surrounding greens:
>
> (*W.F.* 261-2).

These Wordsworthian and Keatsian pictures of nature seem to be inspired by "emotions recollected in tranquility," but they are also reminiscent of Alcinous' garden in the *Odyssey*, a work that Pope translated, of Milton's Eden, and Pope's own essay on the "natural" in the formal garden, published six months after *Windsor Forest*. Symbolically the ordered, peaceful scenes of *Windsor Forest* can be equated with the peace brought by Marlborough's victory after the internecine wars abroad and political unrest at home. Pope's love of nature is seen in his description of the happy man:

> Whom Nature charms, and whom the Muse inspires:
>
> (*W.F.* 237)

Because of his exaltation of nature, Pope was termed a deist. He has a "vivid feeling for natural life . . . [and in him] any humanizing of nature is really a partnership with nature. . . . The process of nature-feeling which created the Greek myths, and which Keats understood so well in his own fluid personifications, enjoys an equal perfection here."[13] For Pope Nature and Homer were the same. He turned to Athens as did his followers, Collins, Keats and Shelley.[14]

In this partnership of man and nature, Pope sets the stage for Goldsmith's *The Deserted Village* and Crabbe's *The Village*. Like them and with Byronic bitterness he recalls England under tyrannical rule:

> A dreary desert, and a gloomy waste,
> To savage beasts and savage laws a prey,
> . . . .
> Cities laid waste, they stormed the dens and caves,
>
> (*W.F.* 44-49)

and ironically adds:

> (For wiser brutes were backward to be slaves.)
>
> (*W.F.* 50)

His indignation is that of the incensed romantic at the lot of the rustic destitute:

> In vain kind seasons swelled the teeming grain,
> Soft showers distilled, and suns grew warm in vain;
> The swain with tears his frustrate labour yields,
> And famished dies amidst his ripened fields.
> What wonder then, a beast or subject slain
> Were equal crimes in a despotic reign?
>
> (*W.F.* 53-58)

As a true romantic, he not only decries the destruction of the fields and cities, but that of the Gothic:

[13] G. Wilson Knight, *The Poetry of Pope—Laureate of Peace* (London: Routledge & Kegan Paul, 1955), pp. 18-21.
[14] Tillotson, *On the Poetry of Pope*, p. 3.

The fields are ravished from th' industrious swains,
From men their cities, and from Gods their fanes:
The levelled towns with weeds lie covered o'er;
The hollow winds through naked temples roar;
Round broken columns clasping ivy twined;
O'er heaps of ruins stalked the stately hind;
The fox obscene to gaping tombs retires,
And savage howlings fill the sacred quires.

(*W.F. 65-72*)

Windsor Forest has allegorical and mythological allusions in its couplets. References to Chaos, the Olympians, and the Roman gods and goddesses abound in the poem. The poem also refers to historical and semi-historical figures and events, to geographical locations, to the exciting New World and new discoveries; and relays the felicity of nationalistic harmony in contemporary England. The poem ends with a reaffirmation of faith in a world at peace. Pope the romantic visionary rises above his love for England to a concern for all people, "to a vision of all nations joined by the seas, of imagination enriched by the knowledge of remote peoples and places, of a world without slavery and subject peoples."[15]

Pope's renewed faith in man at peace with himself, is a Blakian affirmation of the New Jerusalem.

"One of Pope's terms of commendation is the then newly invented 'romantic', and he plans poems which were to have been very wild."[16] The intensely romantic *Eloisa to Abelard* does not only display Pope's knowledge of Ovid's *Heroides*, but his interest in the mediaeval. In *Eloisa to Abelard* Pope moves from the sacred ecologue of the *Messiah* and the sylvan pastoral of *Windsor Forest* to the heroic tradition, and uses the dramatic monologue to give a theatrical and psychological interplay of human emotions. The poem is an "Ovidian elegy and epistle."[17] Structurally " 'Eloisa to Abelard' presents a series of scenes and moods all about equal in the number of their lines, one leading properly into another, all of them arranged to fit the psychological progress of Eloisa's mind."[18]

[15] Brower, *op. cit.*, p. 59.
[16] Tillotson, *On the Poetry of Pope*, p. 7.
[17] Brower, *op. cit.*, p. 65.
[18] Tillotson, *On the Poetry of Pope*, p. 47.

Having loved Martha Blount and Mary Wortley Montagu, Pope knew the suffering of love. The poem dates about the same period, 1716 and 1717. and could be said to embody experienced moods. In his pastorals Pope had written of the shepherd's lament for his love, but the intensity of the lyrical sorrow found in *Eloisa to Abelard* is more in line with Keats' *Ode to a Nightingale* or Donne's "Batter my heart, three-personed God." *Eloisa to Abelard* derives "its extra-ordinary dramatic power from the opposition of natural impulse and transcendental authority,"[19] and the blending of sexual and mystical love.

Pope builds the atmosphere of the poem by the use of rhetorical devices and declamation, by metrical balance and poetic conceits, sound effects and word play, and a romantic intensity seldom matched. Byron said of it, " 'If you search for passion, where is it to be found stronger?' "[20]

The setting of the monologue is a nunnery, an old Gothic building, dark, sombre and isolated, with austere monastic cells rejecting all that is sensuous. Like the Norman Abbey of Byron, it suggests a ruin and symbolically the ruined and thwarted personality of the protagonist. Contemplative melancholy reigns there as in *Il Penseroso*. Pope's preamble to the poem suggests the occasion; Eloisa's discovery of an old letter of Abelard to a friend. The poem thus is the upshot of a trend of thoughts and anguish, ostensibly dormant for years. The conflict is between the finality of Eloisa's situation and her welling emotions:

> What means this tumult in a Vestal's veins?
> Why rove my thoughts beyond this last retreat?
>
> (*E. to A.* 4-5)

Pope's use of meaningful adjectives and participles adds to the poignancy of the situation: "deep solitudes," "awful cells," "ever-musing melancholy." "long-forgotten heat," "dear fatal name," "holy silence," "close disguise," "loved Idea"; so does his use of pathetic fallacy: "relentless walls," "ye rugged rocks," "grots and caverns," "black melancholy." The balanced phrases suggest an unrelenting doom:

[19] Knight, *op. cit.*, p. 6.
[20] Tillotson, *On the Poetry of Pope*, p. 44.

No, fly me, fly me, far as Pole from Pole;
(*E. to A.* 289)

Alas, how changed! what sudden horrors rise'
(*E. to A.* 99)

And alliteration adds to the mood:

Relentless walls! whose darksome round contains
Repentant sighs, and voluntary pains:
(*E. to A.* 17-18)

Binding sense to sound the onomatopoetic phrases and lines become instinct with pathos; as the sibilants:

Oh name for ever sad! for ever dear!
Still breathed in sighs, still ushered with a tear.
(*E. to A.* 31-32)

or infused with the sensuous joy of past pleasures:

Those smiling eyes, attempering every ray,
Shone sweetly lambent with celestial day.
(*E. to A.* 63-64)

The use of the anaphora accentuates a point, as in the subtly nostalgic couplet:

Far other dreams my erring soul employ,
Far other raptures, of unholy joy:
(*E. to A.* 223-24)

and the trenchant chiasmus bespeaks finality and the futility of escape:

Yet here for ever, ever must I stay;
(*E. to A.* 171)

These plus other tropes, repetitions, antithesis and epigrams, metaphysical conceits (as "And truths divine came mended from that tongue," *E. to A.* 66) have been used by Pope to create an atmosphere of love, longing, chagrin and romantic rebellion. In its intensity of emotion *Eloisa to Abelard* can be termed "wild"; its rhetoric of passion and disquieting imperatives are overwhelming.

Eloisa to Abelard is not only a dramatic story, but is literature of protest. Flamboyant in its emotional extravagance, it rebels against conventions that debar the freedom of love to the monastic. In a state of great agitation Eloisa chafes at "the convent's solitary gloom!" (*E. to A.* 38) and questions the justice of the lovers' punishment, for she says, "I have not yet forgot myself to stone." (*E. to A.* 24). She cannot commit herself wholly to God for "Still rebel nature holds out half my heart;" (*E. to A.* 26). Abelard to her is the prototype of Divine Love: "Where mixed with God's, his loved Idea lies:" (*E. to A.* 12).

Her love for Abelard is "the best of passions" (*E. to A.* 40), which religion is unable to quench. Abelard, she argues, is more charitable than those who condemned him. She recalls her innocent admiration for him that turned into love, and rebelliously says she would not reverse it:

> Nor wished an Angel whom I loved a Man.
>
> (*E. to A.* 70)

She advocates free love, for like Belinda's sylphs:

> Love, free as air, at sight of human ties,
> Spreads his light wings, and in a moment flies.
>
> (*E. to A.* 75-76)

Like the romantics she asserts her will, and hers is a clarion call for freedom.

In rhetorical questions Eloisa recalls the scene of her final vows and sees the image of Abelard before her instead of the crucifix. The reality of her enforced retirement is more poignant for the ecstacy of their passion. She expresses it in the Miltonic line:

> But now no face divine contentment wears,
>
> (*E. to A.* 147)

The macabre and ironic statement that only death can unite

them, poses the question of monastic celibacy. The palliative powers of her romantic fancy conjure up dream images of a walk through wastes and Gothic ruins, but prove illusory; nostalgia alone remains.

The poem is a penetrating and moving study of the female mind. Like the metaphysicals, Eloisa's spiritual lyricism appears in:

> I waste the Matin lamp in sighs for thee,
> Thy image steals between my God and me,
> Thy voice I seem in every hymn to hear,
> With every bead I drop too soft a tear.
>
> (*E. to A.* 267-270)

Eloisa is the true votary; the devotee who sees nothing but the image of the beloved, hears naught except for his voice. Abelard and God have coalesced.

The poem is of heroic love, has perfect control, is restricted by its metrical couplet, yet overflows with poetic abandonment. It deals with isolation, solitariness, self-confession, and the melancholy of a living death. It has Gothic images and suggestions of the supernatural. Psychologically it shows the conflict between ethical standards and logical human relationships; "one state of mind or feeling is . . . qualified ironically by its opposite."[21] In *Eloisa to Abelard* Pope "naturalized an alien literary tradition and form,"[22] the dramatic monologue, and gave it the potency of a lyric. The poem imitates the Horatian ode, but is a profound statement of romantic love. Pope shows deep understanding of the human psyche, perhaps more so than the romantics, and a fire that excels Donne and Keats; "the main impression of 'Eloisa' is one of almost luxurious pleasure."[23]

The supernatural machinery in *The Rape of the Lock* is another proof of Pope's kinship with the romantics. "No poet has confined himself as strictly as Pope did to a confined metre, yet managed so often to astonish the reader with the unpredictable."[24] *The Rape of the Lock* astonishes as it delights A mock heroic masterpiece, it carries all the machinery of the

[21] Brower, *op. cit.*, p. 83.
[22] *Ibid.*
[23] Tillotson, *On the Poetry of Pope*, p. 71.
[24] *Ibid.*, p. 138.

epic, and enraptures with its images, turns of speech, wit, irony, and kindly good humour; and with its gnomes and fairies. It is a satire on the Augustan society, on its values and manners, yet its charm and appeal are perennial. R. K. Root says, " 'The Rape of the Lock' contains such infinite riches of poetic fancy within the short compass of its five cantos, that one is in danger of forgetting that its playful machinery of Ariel and his sylphs and the descent to the Cave of Spleen put it also into the 'visionary and allegorical kind of poetry' of which 'strict verisimilitude' is not required . . . one of its essential ingredients is sheer romantic fancy. It is this ingredient . . . which raises it so far above the brilliant play of wit into the regions of great poetry."[25]

The first two cantos of the poem appeared anonymously in Lintot's *Miscellany* in 1712; and the completed poem in 1714, and in the collected works in 1717. For his models of the trivial and insignificant treated in the heroic manner, Pope had Chaucer's *Nun's Priest's Tale*; Boileau's *Lutrin* (1683) translated by Ozell in 1708, a poem in the mock-heroic style where the placing of a new lectern led to a battle royal between contending Parisian priests; *Dispensary*, a poem dealing with the quarrel of the apothecaries and doctors; and *Secchia Rapita*, the "raped bucket" of Tassoni (1662); but Pope's supernatural machinery is unique. His sylphs grew out of the Rosicrucian doctrine of spirits and their belief that the four component elements had their own particular spirits as the gnomes, sylphs, salamanders, and nymphs. Pope uses the sylphs and gnomes. His examples of the fairy-world were from literature. Spenser's Archimago in the *Faerie Queene* conjures for his own nefarious designs two small spirits, one of whom summons a dream from the Cave of Morpheus; Marlowe's Faustus invokes supernatural beings; without Ariel and the other figments of Shakespeare's imagination *The Tempest* would have lost its magic power to inspire. These and other mythical creatures of literature and lore were the forebears of Pope's airy denizens. An omnivorous reader, Pope had tried to emulate the great luminaries of literature; and with the inherited tools of Spenser and Shakespeare, Milton and Dryden, his own fertile genius created a new mythology. Like Blake's his mythical creatures were romantically potent, and not half as befuddling. "Where is there a better piece of mythological 'seeing' than in

[25] Root, *op. cit.*, p. 72.

the vision of the sylphs in which the human and the natural interchange with the fluidity of metamorphosis."[26] The diaphanous sylphs and angry gnome are crucial to the drama of Belinda. Joseph Warton derides Pope's imaginative creatures, but by their inclusion Pope gives the poem a cosmic dimension and the idea of an immense natural order, unseen but involved. "By deftly linking his invented deities with popular country beliefs and with the 'Heathen Mythology' of Fate and Jove, Pope makes us feel the presence of forces greater than Belinda and the Baron and their friends. . . . Not only the mock apotheosis and the sylphs, but the whole drama of 'The Rape of the Lock' is a piece of wonderful myth-making."[27] Pope borrows Ariel from Shakespeare, the industrious, concerned sylphs are his own invention, but the supernatural and romantic go beyond them, for the Ombre cards also assume mythological, Homeric personalities. The passion and ardour of the lovers, the belles and beaux have the elemental characteristics of the Rosicrucian spirits; the gnome is the only avenging spirit. Basil Willey points out that Pope has no Satan in his poem, because his was an optimistic philosophy of life in tune with his times, and it had the desire "to explain and to explain favourably . . . an order of things in which evil appears, but only appears to exist."[28] Pope's sylphs are creatures of ethereal beauty:

> Some to the sun their insect wings unfold,
> Waft on the breeze, or sink in clouds of gold;
> Transparent forms, too fine for mortal sight,
> Their fluid bodies half dissolved in light,
> Loose to the wind their airy garments flew,
> Thin glittering textures of the filmy dew,
> Dipped in the richest tincture of the skies,
> Where light disports in ever-mingling dyes,
> While every beam new transient colours flings,
> Colours that change whene'er they wave their wings.
>
> (*R. of the L.* II 59-68)

Pope's imagination is fertile, but it does not run riot. The balanced control of the couplets with their well-placed pauses on the

[26] Brower, *op. cit.*, p. 151.
[27] *Ibid.*, pp. 156-157.
[28] Basil Willey, *The Seventeenth Century Background* (New York: Doubleday, 1955), p. 293.

fourth or fifth syllables makes for precision and exactitude in these romantic images.

Belinda is the heroine of romance and the courtly tradition, and bestows her favours from a distance. She is a priestess at the altar of her dressing table, the altar that transforms her into a goddess inspiring erotic love. Like Cleopatra on the Cydnus she is the cynosure of all eyes on the Thames, but like the bright-eyed Athene she is distant though benevolent:

> Bright as the sun, her eyes the gazers strike,
> And, like the sun, they shine on all alike.
>
> (*R. of the L.* II 13-14)

On the other hand Lord Petre, like Chaucer's Palamon, worships at the Altar of Love "built of twelve vast French Romances" (*R. of the L.* II 37-38). Pope's romantic imagination was playing riot with his fancy, but keeping it methodized within the epic mode and the strict bounds of the couplet. Varying the couplet with the pauses, rhetorical questions, zeugmas, apostrophes, enjambments, trochaic inversions, exquisite and sensuous images, repetitions, contrasts, mythical allusions, alliteration, assonance, and other devices Pope builds this trivial story into an epic burlesque and romance. He satirizes the superficiality of the court of "great Anna," where husbands and lap dogs are of equal value. Pope's censure is mild and playful, yet there are points where his ire rises and he is unduly caustic:

> The sun obliquely shoots his burning ray;
> And hungry Judges soon the sentence sign,
> And wretches hang that jurymen may dine;
>
> (*R. of the L.* III 20-23)

or as in Clarissa's didactic speech, where in one sweep he shows the ephemeral character of physical beauty and mindless frivolity:

> Oh! if to dance all night, and dress all day,
> Charmed the smallpox, or chased old age away;
>
> (*R. of the L.* V 19-20)

The seventeenth and the early eighteenth century, a time when the Ptolemaic theory of the cosmos was giving place to the newer

Copernican, and the telescope had revealed new stars and planets, Pope's preoccupation with the the Moon is interesting. For Pope it is still the changeable, fickle lunar sphere of the romantic, where things that hurt or jar or are futile on earth, find refuge: the hypocritical tears of heirs and the momentary smile of the harlot, death-bed generosities and "heroes wits," "beaux snuff boxes" and "broken vows." And in a firmament which contains such a moon, a new star rises like a comet and trails the severed lock, giving Belinda her romantic immortality.

The Rape of the Lock can be termed literature of social protest, berating the artificiality of meaningless conventions, yet its use of the romantic, the astonishing, the beautiful has placed it on a pedestal in the literary world. Its oft-quoted and much-loved passage describing the sylphs, in its gem-like quality may have inspired the opalescent beauty of aerial creatures in Shelley and Blake; the former's skylark, the latter's spectre of Tharmas, the Zoa. Burns, the romanticist, is so enamoured of the sylphs, that he lifts four verses from the *Rape of the Lock* for Duan Second (Verses 3-6) in his *The Vision*. Keats' "I Stood Tiptoe Upon a Little Hill" has lines with the gossamer lightness of the sylphs:

> Shapes from the invisble world, unearthly singing
> From out the middle air, from flowery nests,
> And from the pillowy silkiness that rests
> Full in the speculation of the stars.
>
> (ls. 186-8)

Umbriel's descent to the Cave of Spleen is reminiscent of subterranean passages in Spenser and Milton; and echoes of Milton, often in parodies, abound in the work. But there is always "a certain awed wonder in Pope,"[29] that makes him a precursor of the romantics.

Emulating Dryden's "prologue-satirical style with the heroic"[30] and combining it with the romantic, Pope gave *The Rape of the Lock*.

A consummate craftsman Pope is precise and succinct in his choice of words and thoughts. Almost each line of his heroic couplet conveys an idea or a picture complete in itself, yet the over-

[29] Cleanth Brooks, *The Well Wrought Urn* (New York: Harcourt Brace, 1947), p. 8.

[30] Brower, *op. cit.*, p. 4.

all structure of his poems is organically whole. The conclusion of each poem is beautifully contrived and the music of his numbers melodious. Passion, a desire for reform, almost a deistic love of nature, mythological symbolism, an interest in the Gothic and the exotic are all present in Pope. "The Wordsworthian gospel of nature was implicit, though in a much subtler form, in the verse of the Augustan Deists. Nor was the meaning of 'nature' as typical human experience altered between Pope and Wordsworth. . . . For there were not only different degrees, but very different kinds of romanticism."[31]

In Pope romanticism is methodized.

[31] Douglas Bush, *Mythology and the Romantic Tradition in English Poetry* (New York: Norton, 1963), p. 42.

BIBLIOGRAPHY

Adler, Jacob H. *The Reach of Art A Study in the Prosody of Pope*. Gainesville: University of Florida Press, 1964.

Bloom, Harold, ed. *Romanticism and Consciousness Essays in Criticism*. New York: Norton, 1970.

Brooks, Cleanth. *The Well Wrought Urn*. New York: Harcourt Brace, 1947.

Brower, Reuben A. *Alexander Pope, The Poetry of Allusion*. London: Oxford University Press, 1968.

Bush, Douglas. *Mythology and the Romantic Tradition*. New York: Norton, 1963.

Clark, Donald B. *Alexander Pope*. New York: Twayne, 1967.

Dobrée, Bonamy. *Alexander Pope*. London: Oxford University Press, 1966.

Fletcher, Angus. *Allegory: The Theory of a Symbolic Mode*. Ithaca: Cornell University Press, 1964.

Grierson, H. J. C. *Cross Currents in English Literature of the Seventeenth Century*. Baltimore: Penguin, 1966.

Highet, Gilbert. *The Classical Tradition: Greek and Roman Influences on Western Literature*. New York: Oxford University Press, 1957.

Keats, John. The Poetical Works. London & Glasgow: Collins' Clear-Type Press. (Undated).

Knight, C. Wilson. *The Poetry of Pope, Laureate of Peace*. London: Routledge & Kegan Paul, 1955.

Parkin, Rebecca Price. *The Poetical Workmanship of Alexander Pope*. New York: Octagon, 1966.

Platzner, Robert. L., and Hume, Robert D. "Gothic versus Romantic." *PMLA*, 86, No. 2 (March 1971), 266.

Renwich, W. L. *English Literature 1789-1815*. Oxford: Clarendon Press, 1963.

Root, Robert Kilburn. *The Poetical Career of Alexander Pope*. Princeton: Princeton University Press, 1938.

Stephen, Leslie. *English Literature and Society in the Eighteenth Century*. London: Methuen, 1966.

The Hymnal of the Protestant Episcopal Church. Norwood, MA: Plimpton Press, 1943.

Tillotson, Geoffrey. *On the Poetry of Pope*. Oxford: Clarendon Press, 1950.

———. *Pope and Human Nature*. Oxford: Clarendon Press, 1958.

Willey, Basil. *The Seventeenth Century Background*. New York: Doubleday, 1955.

Wimsatt, William K. Jr., ed. *Alexander Pope Selected Poetry and Prose*. New York: Holt, Rinehart and Winston, 1951.

EXPERIMENTATION OF THE ROMANTIC MODE, 1725-1800

The years 1725-1800 saw the burgeoning of new forces in England. Industrialisation and economic growth, fresh trade routes, colonial expansion, consciousness of mass culture, of social justice and growing internationalism, involvement with the psyche, exploration of the mediaeval and the Gothic, and national pride saw the shift of emphasis in literature from the neo-classic of the Restoration to "romantic tendencies" that were a precursor of the Romantic Movement.

James Thomson was an early exponent of the new mode. Son of a clergyman, reared in the countryside of Southdean and Jedburgh in Teviotdale, in 1715, at 15 he entered Edinburgh University, hoping to take Holy Orders. His early association with the farmer-poet, Robert Riccaltoun (whose poem *A Winter's Day* may have had a bearing on Thomson's *Winter*), the spirit of independence since the Scottish Union of 1707, and his own leaning towards literature, some of his poems being already published in the Edinburgh press, made Thomson adventure to London in 1725. He never returned to Scotland, but his nature poems figure the Scottish heath and highland. In his approach to neo-classicism Thomson is ambivalent, though he eschews their logico-rhetorical mode. But in relation to the romantic trend he is an important transitional force. Partially a neo-classicist and partially a romanticist, his poems, especially *The Seasons*, exerted a tremendous influence on 18th century Europe. Goethe praised it.

The Seasons seems to be an amplification of Thomson's *Of a Country Life*, published in the *Edinburgh Miscellany* in 1720. Describing the sounds and sights of the country in the poem, he stressed the progress of the seasons, devoting four lines each to Spring and Summer, two to Autumn and sixteen to Winter, a constant love. His *Hymn on the Power of God* foreshadows the hymn at the end of *The Seasons* in 1730, and exhorts man to praise "the God of Nature." From his youth Thomson was a Nature Poet, and remained so except that his maturer works have philosophical reflections in line with the thought that nature and philosophy are one.

The Seasons is a long poem of uneven merit. Divided into Spring, Summer, Autumn and Winter, it formulates the working of Creative Nature and moves in a framework of the progressive year. The movement is continually from the material to the spiritual. The poem has rhythms and echoes of Milton, and in some areas the sublimity of Milton but not sustained on an even keel. His pictures of Nature have a sensitive charm, that of a landscapist, and his light images a mystical quality. In the preface to the poem, modelled on Norris Bemerton's *To the Reader* in his 1687 *Collection of Miscellanies*, Thomson refers to Nature as "all that enlarges and transports the soul," and to its "wild" and "romantic" quality. Thomson's approach to external Nature is that of Wordsworth, almost that of a Deist or a Pantheist, with a Stoic's acceptance of it. In Nature he envisages a Golden Age. *The Seasons* is a compendium of knowledge, of contemplative reflections on humanitarianism and domestic bliss, of sentimental optimism looking backwards to a Golden Past and forward to a Golden Age. It brings in pastoral episodes, contemporary travels and discoveries, mentions Newton, his prism and the telescope, historical events as the plague at Marseilles, prison reforms. Along with Miltonic cadences it uses colloquialism. In it Thomson shows a sense of wonder and delight, but not the fervour of the romanticists. Thomson revised his poem several times, and made it more historical and philosophical with each revision.

His poem *Liberty* (1735-36) is also a harbinger of the Romantic Movement. Written as one of the opposition when Walpole was in power and giving the history of civilisation, its burden is that civilisation can only flourish when there is freedom. Thomson honours the new science in *To the Memory of Sir Isaac Newton* whom he greatly admired, and there he proves himself more a neo-classicist.

The Castle of Indolence, written in the Spenserian stanza, tries to capture the aura of the neo-classical by using archaic words and phrases, but has a fresh and simple directness of expression. It is lightly satiric and the numbers are sensuously musical. Indolence, the enchanter, is genial, but Thomson moralizes by bringing in the King of Arts and Industry, who is a product of savagery forced on poverty. The poem has a delightful spontaneity as it portrays idleness in a playful mood. Had Pope, a friend of Thomson's, lived he would have appreciated the mood of this 1748 poem, though laughed at ideas such as the Wordsworthian return to the innocent state of childhood. Pope had died in 1744; Thomson died in 1748. Thomson was gentle and genial with a great love for men and animals. He opposed slavery and was a pacifist and endorsed organised charity and brotherhood. Thomson was a romanticist, had their ardour as well as their prolixity. He lacked complete control—a problem of the romanticists, and at times his images were absurd (as the deer weeping in autumn). His didacticism often spoilt the charm of his poems, yet he stands as a precursor of the romantic movement. His highly personal and subjective approach to Nature and man is in line with the romantic tendencies.

T. S. Eliot said of the 18th century that poetry no longer was courtly and seemed to be written by country parsons. George Crabbe was one of the latter. His education had not been formal, though he had been apprenticed to a surgeon and later took orders, but life had prepared him for the work of a poet. Born the son of a minor revenue officer in 1754 at Aldeburgh, Suffolk, a poor rugged seaside town, he wrote of his birthplace in *The Village* and *The Borough*. Edmund Burke befriended him, enabled him to move in literary circles, and had him placed in a church. His poem, *The Library*, was published in 1781, *The Village* in 1783 and *The Newspaper* in 1785. Then for 22 years he gave himself to pastoral duties and his home. A volume of his poems was published in 1807; *The Parish Register* was in it. Crabbe's poems were popular in his own day, for his was a realistic approach to poetry. As a critic he could not reconcile himself to a poet being relegated to the spheres of fancy and the imagination alone when he lived in a world of stark reality. Because of their realism his poems are powerful. There were two periods of his poetic output starting with the anonymous *Inebriety* in 1775 and *The Candidate* in 1780 when he was in his twenties, and ending with *The Tales* (1812) and *Tales of the Hall* (1819). The works of the latter period show no appreciable difference in development in the spirit, thought or manner of the poems. Crabbe is an anomaly. Called the "Poet of the Poor," he shows no particular emotional involvement. The American and French revolutions occurred when

Crabbe was 22 and 35 respectively, "an angry young age," but Crabbe's works do not reveal his reactions. He disapproved of problems nearer home, as infidelity. He was a poet of the commonplace, an Augustan writing in an age fast becoming Romantic. He says a great deal in protest of the existing conditions and uses a photographic technique to do so. In an age exploding with the beauty of romantic poetry, he tells of his concerns in drab and colourless language. His iambic pentameter couplets are reminiscent of Pope, without Pope's scintillating brilliance. He is a romantic rebel, but pedestrian. He wants the idyllic state for his rustic, but presents the life of the rustic poor in unidealized and sombre colours like a news reporter and unlike a pastoral poet. His contemporary popularity was due to his poems being newsworthy. A shrewd observer, he writes in an easy frigid style with little music to his lines. He has keen sympathy for the oppressed, and some of his lines do show intense passion like the romanticists. His character studies are careful observations and indicate a wide view of society. As a concerned parish priest he knew his people, their homes, their problems and their joys, yet writes of them with the objectivity of a novelist.

Crabbe had visited Scott in 1822 in Edinburgh, and Scott refers to him in *Waverly* as the "English Juvenal" and again in *The Heart of Midlothian* as "the British Juvenal." Like Scott Crabbe was a story writer, though in verse and with a dry satiric humour. His stories were more statements and lacked the complexity of developed plots. His direct vision portrayed the poor, the deserted, the betrayed, the condemned, the hurt, with sympathy; the prosperous, the arbitrary, the proud in sardonic comedy.

He projects the coarseness of the situation and the poor of Aldeburgh in *The Village*. The poem was admired, for Crabbe uncovered "ungeneralised truths and revealed elemental humanity." His early hardships made him sensitive, but not analytic of others. In *The Village* he has sociological overtones that are frightening as ". . .cast by Fortune on a frowning coast." The statement has the darkness of mediaeval predestination and the sombre cadences of the *Book of Job*. There is bitterness in his editorial comment as he bewails that no Goldsmith is there to champion the cause of the rustic, the farmer and fisherman, the smuggler, the ailing, the fatigued, the overburdened, the starved and emaciated, the cold, the aged and the lonely; or expose the beadle, the greedy doctor, the time server. Using an architectonic technique, such as that of Thomas Hardy, Crabbe makes the poem a social worker's paradise. It ends with an ironic note on the graveyard.

The Parish Register is written in three parts and carries the theme further, but in a happier mood. Crabbe in recounting the memories evoked by the entries remembers his own romantic experiences as a priest. As compared to the wide sweep of *The Village* it has minute characterisation. Its stories were appealing to Scott and Charles James Fox, and an opera, *Peter Grimes*, came from it. Dickens included a poem of Crabbe's in his *Hard Times*. Crabbe, a late Augustan, is a romantic rebel.

The last among the early romantics is William Cowper. He retired early into the country, fearing the loss of his intellect. Cowper's is a complex and complicated personality. At times he is morbid and doleful, suffering intensely on account of his Calvinistic religion and its hidebound ideas of predestination, at other times joyful as John Gilpin. Shy and oversensitive, he died as a hypochondriac in an "insane asylum" in 1800, at the age of 69. A lawyer's apprentice in London, he had a happy attachment to his cousins, Harriet, Lady Hesketh, with whom he carried a long correspondence, and Theodora. His recovery from a mental illness became the occasion of his involvement with the Methodists and spending the rest of his life in the countryside of Olney. Mrs. Unwin, his kindly housekeeper, who looked after him, he enshrined in *To Mary* and the sonnet *Mrs. Unwin*. Cowper's religious experience inspired the beautiful *Olney Hymns*, which, contrary to his despair, reaffirm hope, but his despondency shows in *The Task* and more so in *The Castaway*.

The Task is a new art form, the forerunner of Wordsworth's *The Prelude* and Tennyson's *In Memoriam*, the long autobiographical poem. Cowper was a poet of the English countryside, of the park and garden, the small denizens of the garden—the birds and hare and pet animals. They helped him fight his melancholia. He said of his poetry that all of it was from his observation of Nature and his own experiences, and that the galloping burlesque, *John Gilpin*, was written in one of his most pensive and sad moods.

In *The Task* he imitates the cadences of Milton, and structures the poem on blank verse, but he lacks Milton's imagery. *The Task* is a romantic confessional poem and a mental exercise to keep the mind in form. Cowper uses a series of romantic tensions, and develops the artistic element of the poem more than the subject matter. Its poetic diction is simple but musical and comes nearest to Wordsworth. Like Thomson Cowper revels in the glory of Nature, for reunion with Nature emancipates him; he is free in the country. The poem is reminiscent of Bunyan in its simplicity, and like Wordsworth's *Tintern Abbey* has a sense of dedication and renewal as it anticipates a millennium of the Golden Age. In his solitude Nature is a solace for Cowper. In the poem he recalls Dr. Cotton, the physician who helped to restore his sanity thus acknowledging the skill of a learned man of medicine. In spite of it Cowper shows a strong romantic pose when he expresses disdain of learning. Cowper also expresses antipathy towards science. Newton, the great god of science, was extolled by Thomson in the early part of the century, but men like Goldsmith and Cowper were suspicious of him, and Blake considered Newton a villain, for Newton advocated the enforcement of order and discipline like the God of the Old Testament, a concept totally alien to the romantic mode. Cowper calls Newton "a childlike sage," he admires him, but is sceptical of science. *The Task* is a highly religious and moral poem, the work of a fundamentalist, also a pantheist as he sees God "in all." The central theme is the permanence of God's grace, and its acceptance by the soul. The medium is Nature, for it is through nature that the message comes to man, Nature the Wordsworthian teacher. There is sincerity in the poem as Cowper affirms his contentment with God's gifts to him. The poem is the work of a romanticist who like Wordsworth seeks tranquillity in Nature, and basks in "emotions recollected in tranquillity." Cowper decries the corruption in London, a city where there is much that he loves, but it is also "spotted with all crimes." Wordsworth knew and loved London, even though he preferred the country. His descriptions of London in *The Prelude*, if isolated, could almost make him an urban poet.

The Castaway has romantic despondency. The sea that Cowper battles is overwhelming for it clouds his intellect:

> . . .Waged with death a lasting strife,
> Supported by despair of life.

Cowper's preoccupation with a fundamental belief, his fear of damnation, coupled with his sensitive soul and poetic nature were responsible for his suffering and romantic agony.

The culmination of "romantic tendencies" of the 18th century are seen in the poetry of Robert Burns and William Blake. Burns is a true romanticist in himself. He was a peasant, found "at the plough," he lived in the country away from a corrupt city, saw in Nature a mentor and a disciplinarian, loved and used the native literature and folklore, coined his own words and pronunciations, and was a poet. An Ayrshire lad, Burns's national pride exceeded that of MacPherson and Scott. He was keen to revive a language that was almost lost, and write of actual people and situations that he loved. His *The Holy Fair* is realistic in recalling the yearly observance of the sacrament. It gives the early morning scene, portrays a freshness in his resolution of independence, and is a combination of religious feelings and bawdiness, also a sly commentary on Calvinism. He starts the poem in a mediaeval and allegorical vein and exposes hypocrisy. The description of the crowds at the fair and nine different individuals who are there is delightfully dramatic. The poem is satiric yet highly romantic. It too has the Wordsworthian anti-intellectualism: drink, he says, gives him more "than either school or college." Apparently as a folk ballad it had an influence on Wordsworth.

The Twa Dogs is a poem of social protest. It is satiric and highly perceptive, and in a dialogue structure portrays the absurdity of class distinction and poverty. Luath, the Scot pie-dog gives the hard lot of the peasant but adds, "They're maistly wonderfu' contented." This is the burden of the song, the joy of life in the highlands after the gruelling labour, the relaxing around the hearth for fun and fellowship. Poverty and hardship do not affright the peasant as he is accustomed to them! It's a political comment and shows Burns a romantic rebel. *Address to the Deil* is entrancing. It has the peasant's belief in the supernatural, still current in the highlands, and reviews the Devil's role in history. Inspired by Milton's Satan, it admires the spunk of the arch rebel as well as warns him that he will meet his match in Archangel Michael. Being romantic rebels themselves, Milton's Satan was of great interest to both Burns and Blake. Burns's short life (1759-1796) covered a period in history when the western world was in ferment. Two revolutions, the American and the French, had come and gone, initiating the Romantic epoch, and establishing ideals that were primarily secular. The stress was on instinctive pleasures rather than divine grace. The human imagination for the romantics had infinite range and the gifts of nature were there to be utilized to transcend limitations. This was the milieu in which Burns and Blake lived and worked.

The full impact of the times is seen in the works of Blake; in his chagrin at over-industrialisation and iniquities ensuing from it, in the desire for intellectual freedom that breaks all tyranny of restricting conventions and traditions, and in an ardent belief in Christ's all-pervading love freeing man from the shackles of Jehovah of the Old Testament. "Liberty" was Blake's watchword. Burns and Blake both suffered poverty; they were the "impoverished and neglected geniuses." Their very lives were responsible for the democratization of literature. They took for their subjects not only the external world, the supernatural, the Gothic, folk legends and fables, but sensations, feelings and ideas; and gave themes and thoughts that set the romanticists, Wordsworth, Coleridge, Byron, Keats and Shelley, aflame, giving them new dimensions of consciousness and self-awareness. The emphasis was on actual human experience for self-realisation.

In the plethora of material that proves the importance of the 18th century to the development of the Romantic Movement, the works of Burns and Blake become the very heart blood of the movement. In them the "romantic tendencies" had a full flowering. The 18th century gave literature the great romantics of 1789-1815.

BIBLIOGRAPHY

Blake, William. *Complete Writings*. Ed. Geoffrey Keynes, London: Oxford University Press, 1969.

Bloom, Harold, ed. *Romanticism and Consciousness*. New York: W.W. Norton, 1970.

Bredvold, Louis I. *et. al.*, eds. *Eighteenth Century Poetry and Prose*. New York: Ronald Press Co., 1956.

Burns, Robert. *Poems and Songs*. Ed. James Kinsley, London:Dutton, 1970.

Cowper, William. *Poems*. Ed. Hugh I'anson Fausset, London: Dutton, 1966.

Dobrée, Bonamy. *English Literature in the Early Eighteenth Century*. London: Oxford University Press, 1959.

Kroeber, Karl. *Backgrounds to British Romantic Literature*. San Francisco: Chandler, 1968.

Renwick, W. L. *English Literature 1789-1815*. Oxford: Clarendon Press, 1963.

Thomson, James. *Poetical Works*. Ed. J. Logie Robertson. London: Oxford University Press, 1965.

THOMAS WARTON, THE YOUNGER: A POET OF HIS TIMES

An entry of 1778 in the *Early Diary* of Frances Burney, Madame D'Arblay, reads, "Dr. Warton of Winchester, a very pleasing man. His brother, Mr. Tom Warton, the greatest clod I ever saw, and so vulgar a figure with his clunch wig that I took him for a shoemaker at first."[1]

Thomas Warton may not have appealed to the rather superficial though the prominent, fastidious and courtly Fanny Burney, for even as a poet laureate in 1785, Warton was careless of his appearance, but as a critic of literature in the eighteenth century he stood 'second alone to Dr. Johnson. A poet, a literary historian, a critic, an Oxford don, Thomas Warton belonged to the romantic precursors in literature; the *literati* who were turning away from the Augustan neo-classicism and its rigid propriety.

Descendants of Sir Michael Warton, a loyal friend of Charles I. Thomas Warton, his father Thomas Warton, Senior; and older brother, Joseph, were "a select and influential group of scholar-poets,"[2] whose works, though not of consistent merit, rank with those of their contemporaries, Thomson, Young, Blair, Collins, Gray, and Dyer.

Thomas Warton, born on January 9th, 1728, in Basingstoke, remained under the tutelage of his father, an ex-professor of poetry at Oxford and a friend of Pope's, until, at the age of sixteen, he entered Trinity College, Oxford. At Oxford he won several honours; he was elected Fellow of Trinity, Professor of

[1] Eric Partridge, ed., *The Three Wartons* (London: The Scholartis Press, 1927), p. 15.

[2] Wylie Sypher, ed., *Enlightened England* (New York: W.W. Norton, 1962), p. 635.

Poetry from 1757 to 1767, Fellow of the London Society of Antiquarians in 1771, and in 1782 a member of the Literary Club. Two years later he was appointed Camden Professor of History at Oxford, and five years before his death, in 1785, became Poet Laureate.

In a century beset with religious, political, economic, industrial, and colonial-expansionist cross-currents, Thomas Warton's life at Oxford seems comparatively peaceful and uneventful, but his tremendous output, and the change in his literary media from poetry to criticism and research for his *opus magnum,* his literary history, his observations on the *Faerie Queene,* and the editing of Milton, are indications of the flux and transient nature of the age as well as of his own versatility.

Early in his career Warton saw Oxford, not only as a seat of learning, but a place for petty politics and bickering and lax living for some, and in the satiric neo-classic vein of Pope he lampooned the situation:

> Our pupil's hopes, tho' twice defeated,
> Are with a scholarship completed:
> A scholarship but half maintains
> And college rules are heavy chains:
> In garret dark he smokes and puns,
> A prey to discipline and duns,
> And now, intent on new designs,
> Sighs for a fellowship—and fines.
>
> . . . .
>
> When calm around the common room
> I puff'd my daily pipe's perfume!
> Rode for a stomach, and inspected,
> At annual bottlings, corks selected:
> And din'd untax'd, untroubled, under
> The portrait of our pious Founder![3]

His satirical works include "Journal of a Senior or Genuine Idler," and "Companion to the Guide, and Guide to the Companion." The mock Miltonic burlesque "The Oxford Newsman's Verse," the lines describing the beauties of Oxford in "The

[3]Clarissa Rinaker, *Thomas Warton*—Critical Study (Urbana: University of Illinois Press, 1916), p. 16.

Triumph of Isis," and the Horatian "A Panegyric on Oxford Ale," can be classed with the early eighteenth century poetry of journalistic statement. Warton's "Progress of Discontent" is Swiftian.

If Warton enjoyed satirical verse, he was also enamoured of the poetry of Spenser and Milton and Chaucer. To break away from the Augustans he reached for Longinus' idea of the sublime, the grand style, and became imitative of the great masters. His "The Pleasures of Melancholy," published anonymously in 1747, is fashioned on Milton's "Il Penseroso," and "is full of personifications of abstractions and Miltonic epithets and diction."[4] The poem is written in blank verse, and its melancholic strain is reminiscent of the graveyard poets, Young, Blair, and Gray. Clarissa Rinaker, Warton's 20th century biographer, affirms that Gray's elegy was inspired by "The Pleasures of Melancholy."[5] Like Thomson, Warton has some Wordsworthian descriptions of Nature in the poem:

> Let others love the summer evening's smiles,
> As listening to some distant waterfall
> They mark the blushes of the streaky west:
> I choose the pale December's foggy glooms;[6]

Yet in his descriptions, Warton has a classical restraint, different from the exuberance of the romanticist. He does not exult in Nature with the abandonment of a Shelley of the heady, cloying sweetness of Keats, for in this period of transition the neo-classic influence of restraint, of balance and order is still evident.

If Warton was an imitator, he was also an innovator. An antiquarian and a lover of the Gothic, he is original in his ". . .introduction of the Gothic and medieval subjects. . . [and in starting a new movement, classified by] repudiation of pseudo-classical models, Spenserian and Miltonic revivals, the return to Nature, the cult of solitude, the melancholy of the 'graveyard school,' the interest in the supernatural, and the Gothic revival."[7]

"The Grave of King Arthur," though written in iambic tetrameter couplets, is an example of this innovation:

[4] *Ibid.*, p. 25.
[5] *Ibid.*, p. 27.
[6] Partridge, *op. cit.*, p. 103.
[7] Rinaker, *op. cit.*, p. 24.

And bade her spirits bear him far,
In Merlin's agate-axled car,
To her green isle's enamell'd steep,
Far in the navel of the deep.
O'er his wounds she sprinkled dew
From flowers that in Arabia grew.[8]

The love of the Gothic appears in "The Pleasures of Melancholy":

Beneath yon ruin'd abbey's moss-grown piles
Oft let me sit, at twilight hour of eve,
Where through some western window the pale moon
Pours her long-levell'd rule of streaming light;[9]

The subtle pictorial quality of Warton's descriptions approximates the art of Sir Joshua Reynolds, whom he extols in "Verses on Sir Joshua Reynolds' Painted Windows at New College, Oxford."

Warton was constantly experimenting with different literary forms and genre. He wrote pastorals and sonnets, some of the latter in imitation of Milton, arousing a fresh interest in sonnets. His sonnets vary from the reflective and personal "Winslade in Hampshire" to the purely academic "Written at Stonehenge."

Among Warton's associates and friends were men such as Thomas Coxeter, a collector of dramas; Francis Wise, an archaeologist attached to the Bodleian; Bishop Percy, a researcher of ballads; Dr. Johnson, for whom he secured an honorary M.A. at Oxford; and above all his brother, Joseph. Their inspiration and encouragement were incentives for Warton to proceed with his literary criticism and history. Two hundred years before Edward LeComte's *Yet Once More*, Warton wrote ". . .Milton copies from himself. . . . There are likewise other strokes, both of expression and sentiment, which Milton has transformed, from the smaller poems, into his Great Work."[10] Warton's love for Milton came from his father. He quotes from Milton's prose, his early and late poetry, the prolusions and Latin poems; analyzes

[8] Partridge, *op. cit.*, p. 173.

[9] *Ibid.*, p. 102.

[10] Thomas Warton, *Observations on the Fairy Queen of Spenser*, 2nd ed. (London: Pall-Mall, 1762), p. 22.

Milton's works, and recognises in Milton ". . .the ideas of a mind deeply tinctured with romance reading."[11] In addition echoes of Milton abound in his works, and he edited Milton's minor poems.

Warton's criticism of Spenser is important, for in it he adopted a new critical method. He put an end to the existing rules and rigidity of neo-classical criticism when he said, "It is absurd to think of judging either Ariosto or Spenser by precepts which they did not attend to."[12] Warton liberated criticism further by bringing new ideas from the romance languages, and exploding theories such as Johnson's "fancy beyond reason [is] insanity."[13] The new criticism considered the author's purpose, his work in its historical context, and the relation of the mediaeval to contemporary literature. Warton's study of Spenser took him to Malory's *Morte d'Arthur* and Chaucer, the allegory and the moralities, the masque and dumb shows; for him mediaeval studies were as important as Homer and Plato and Aristotle.

Though Warton continued to write poems as occasional pieces, and biographies such as those of Sir Thomas Pope, founder of Trinity, and Ralph Bathurst, a president; and letters ripe for the publishers, the major part of his last years was occupied with *The History of English Poetry*. He had mentioned his literary history to Bishop Percy as early as 1765. With his friends' help, and his own diligent search and research, the three volumes of his work, comprising 1761 pages, appeared in 1774, 1778, and 1781. The work was acclaimed by his circle of friends and by journals such as *The Gentleman's Magazine* and *The Monthly Review*, but he met with adverse criticism from Walpole; and from the antiquarian, Ritson, who was vituperative in accusing Warton of plagiarism. A hundred years later Hazlitt tried to rectify some of the discrepancies in the work. The history is invaluable for its insights, topicality, Warton's methods of research, and for reference to works now obsolete. Considering Warton's limited resources and the erratic availability of material, (a third edition of *Venus and Adonis* was discovered by Warton amidst "bacon, red-herring, and old iron. . ."[14] in a small Salisbury shop!) the work was monumental.

[11] *Ibid.*, p. 33.
[12] Rinaker, *op. cit.*, p. 38.
[13] *Ibid.*, p. 39.
[14] *Ibid.*, p. 81.

Thomas Warton was a man of his age. An Anglican divine, he appears a Deist in his Nature poems; in criticism he breaks away from the rigidity of rules; and along with his contemporaries paves the way for romanticism, though still governed by Augustan discipline. He sounds the trend of his age when he says:

> Thro' Pope's soft song tho' all the Graces breathe,
> And happiest art adorn his Attic page;
> Yet does my mind with sweeter transport glow,
> . . . at the root of mossy trunk reclined,
> In magic Spenser's wildly-warbled song.[15]

[15] Partridge, *op. cit.*, p. 106.

BIBLIOGRAPHY

Baine, Rodney M., ed. *The Augustan Reprint Society. Thomas Warton. A History of English Poetry: and Unpublished Continuation.* Lo Angeles: University of California, 1953.

Bartell, Roland, ed. *Johnson's London.* Boston: Heath & Co., 1956.

Bredvold, Louis I., et al. *Eighteenth Century Poetry and Prose*, 2nd ed. New York: Ronald Press, 1956.

The Encyclopaedia Brittanica. Eleventh Edition. Volume XXVIII. Cambridge, England: the University Press, 1911.

Ford, Boris, ed. *From Dryden to Johnson.* Baltimore: Penguin, 1968.

Partridge, Eric, ed. *The Three Wartons.* London: The Scholartis Press, 1927.

Rinaker, Clarissa. *Thomas Warton, A Biographical and Critical Study.* Urbana: University of Illinois, 1916.

Sypher, Wylie, ed. *Enlightened England, An Anthology of English Literature from Dryden to Blake.* New York: W. W. Norton, 1962.

Warton, Thomas. *Observations on the Fairy Queen of Spenser.* 2nd ed. London: Pall-Mall, 1762. (Reproduced by Duopage Process in the U.S. of America. Original in Ohio State University Library, Columbus, Ohio).

THE EMANATIONS OF THE FOUR ZOAS IN BLAKE'S "CYCLIC VISION OF LIFE"[1]

In the milling, changing, never-static vision of *The Four Zoas* Blake encompasses man's spiritual and emotional history. In a series of dramatic vignettes he carries the mind back and forth from the pristine and prelapsarian stage of life to its many faceted and complex patterns, contemporary to any period. His vision progresses within the "Circle of Destiny,"[2] and each character, in spite of its amorphous form, stands out distinct and powerful, emerging, fading, and reappearing in an eternal cycle. Not least among the four mighty Zoas, Luvah, Tharmas, Urizen and Urthona, are their emanations. Each emanation is distinctive, and an integral part of the whole. The emanations being equated with the female principle are vital to the psychological epic.

The epic begins with elliptical sentences referring to the Aged Mother, Vala or Eno, whose song it is to be. The first few lines show the elements in flux and set the stage for a mighty, almost terrifying drama, where forces larger than man are at play. Yet the four Zoas are the component part of Eternal Man, punitive though psychologically gigantic. Vala is Nature before the fall of the Eternal Man, Albion. In Night Seven of "The Four Zoas" Enitharmon refers to Vala as "the lilly of the desart"[3] of whom Albion became enamoured and from whom their son, Urizen, was born. Later Albion discovered Vala to be an androgyne, dividing herself into Luvah and Vala, love and the female principle. Horrified Albion tried to return to the prelapsarian state, but eternity was barred to him. He flourished for a while, but conspiring Luvah and Urizen brought about his fall and disintegration. Thus

[1] Angus Fletcher, *Allegory the Theory of a Symbolic Mode* (Ithaca: Cornell University Press, 1970), p. 176.

[2] William Blake, "Vala or the Four Zoas," *Blake Complete Writings*, ed. Geoffrey Keynes (London: Oxford University Press, 1969), p.267, 1. 101.

[3] *Ibid.*, p.326, 1. 238.

Vala and Luvah remain the complementary elements in the poem; she the emanation, he a Zoa.

> The Fallen Man takes his repose, Urizen sleeps in the porch,
> Luvah and Vala wake and fly up from the Human Heart
> Into the Brain from thence; upon the pillow Vala slumber'd,
> And Luvah seiz'd the Horses of Light & rose into the Chariot of Day.[4]

Vala, though asleep, is with Luvah at this crucial and psychological moment of the drama. Love is in ascendance over Urizen (reason divorced from imagination) having seized the horses of Light, like Phaeton. This pivotal point gives new ramifications to the theme for Vala is left in her primordial garden: "Weeping for Luvah lost in bloody beams of your false morning."[5] Vala, the cruel *Nature*, who had abandoned Fallen Man, now suffers with Luvah in an orb of blood, "alone, forsaken, in fierce jealousy," though still attracted to him. Devoid of love Nature becomes a chaotic and blind mass:

> Vala remain'd in desarts of dark solitude, nor Sun nor Moon
> By night nor day to comfort her; she labour'd in thick smoke.[6]

But as the vision is cyclic, the hermaphroditic principle is reunited. Meanwhile the Zoa, Urizen, builds his mundane shell. Urizen eschews compassion and the tenderness of love, being hard calculating mechanical reason devoid of all pleasure. He binds Love in chains and forces it into his furnaces. The changeable Vala at this juncture displays the most sadistic part of her wanton self. She callously feeds the furnaces of Urizen, helping to torture and consume Luvah, her complementary self, and leaves herself a heartless entity: "In joy she heard his howlings and forgot he was her Luvah."[7] She forgets that Luvah was her spiritual

[4] *Ibid.*, p. 271, ll. 261-264.
[5] *Ibid.*, p. 272, l. 287.
[6] *Ibid.*, p. 475, 11. 417-418.
[7] *Ibid.*, p. 282, l. 78.

mentor and had helped in her metamorphosis from an earthworm to a serpent, then a dragon and finally a child. This sadism does not help, for separated from Love she becomes a Wanderer, her ardour fades, she is destroyed; and self-consumed she turns to ashes. Her ashes, mingled with mortar, help to erect Urizen's hall of science; Nature separated from compassion can be ruthlessly exploited by Reason. Like the phoenix, she cyclically rises from her ashes and labours, shadow-like, in Urizen's brick kilns. Her resurrection has made her one with the oppressed of England who worked in the "dark Satanic mills." Luvah to her is now part of the infernal machines, a non-entity. Her preoccupation with the grinding labour is so acute that when Luvah, in compassion and pity, appears to her Christ-like, like Mary Magdalene she does not know him. Ahania, Urizen's emanation, in a vision of Beulah, sees Vala withdrawn as far as the east is from the west, from Luvah, presaging their actual division; life for Vala was all confusion. Bloom calls Vala diabolic, "a prime Villainous of the work,"[8] for first she seduced the Eternal Man:

> Where is sweet Vala. . . the lovely form
> That drew the body of Man from heaven into this dark Abyss?[9]

and then had tortured Luvah, proving Boehme's theory of good and evil, that all manifestation involves opposition. Yet as personified hatred Vala herself suffered; she became a shadowy female "wither'd by winds."[10] Her mission became to assuage the uncontrolled furies of Orc, a form of Luvah; Orc was energy and zeal without the alleviating factor of compassion. Instead of mollifying Orc, her caresses move him to further fury. Another facet of her character is revealed, the cause of Orc's fury; she is "Urizen's harlot solidus. And the Harlot of Los & the deluded harlot of the Kings of the Earth."[11] Orc's jealousy made the "*femme fatale*" the vortex of the raging battle around her. Orc rent her, and self-consumed mingled with her "dolorous members" which were scattered over the Abyss; in their disintegration

[8] Harold Bloom, *Blake's Apocalypse* (Ithaca: Cornell University Press, 1963), p. 193.
[9] Blake, *op. cit.*, p. 306, l. 46.
[10] *Ibid.*, p. 311, l. 227.
[11] *Ibid.*, p. 336, l. 138.

too the cyclic visions unite and Vala "joys in all the conflict."[12] She revels in the conflict; like a banshee she goes howling, wading through fens, delighting in the horrors of the war. At her worst, almost demented with the heady wine of war, she melts at a word from Tharmas, and discloses her immense suffering. She acknowledges her "secret faults" and pours out her sorrows, for her children are in Urizen's war, Luvah has been metamorphosed into Orc and accuses her of Sin, and she herself is condemned to eternal flames of torment. In spite of her degeneration from pristine Nature and her being the cause of the loss of "heaven and bliss" Vala still has a spark of nobility in her. She exclaims in Biblical overtones that she will not leave Luvah, her beloved, to remain in chains. The daughters of Beulah commend this resolve in her. Luvah will be resurrected.

Vala uses her erstwhile nefarious life to accomplish her work. As Urizen's harlot she enmeshes him in his own net of reason. She had absorbed "The enormous Sciences of Urizen,"[13] and was determined to free Luvah and to "deliver all the sons of God."[14] Being the counterpart of Luvah, Vala was to play a vital role in the act of salvation. As a "shapeless and indefinite cloud"[15] she overcomes Urizen, who is already a victim of his own sorrow and lust, and so opens the way to liberty. Yet nature being cyclic her diabolic character shows itself in her secret league with Satan; Blake identifies her with Rahab, the highly institutionalised Church of England:

> A False Feminine Counterpart, of Lovely Delusive Beauty
> Dividing & Uniting at will in the Cruelties of Holiness,
> . . . .
> When view'd remote she is One, when view'd near she divides
> To multitude, . . .[16]

Perverted, but she is the church triumphant in her scarlet robes

[12] *Ibid.*, p. 338, l. 213.
[13] *Ibid.*, p. 344, l. 144.
[14] *Ibid.*, p. 345, l. 156.
[15] *Ibid.*, p. 345, l. 175.
[16] *Ibid.*, p. 348, ll. 278-283.

and gems. It was the lament of Enion and Ahania that made Vala realise the enormity of her faults:

> He saw the Harlot of the Kings of Earth and saw her Cup
> Of fornication, food of Orc & Satan, press'd from the fruit of Mystery.
> But when she saw the form of Ahania weeping on the Void,
> And heard Enion's voice sound from the caverns of the Grave,
> No more spirit remain'd in her.[17]

She emerges repentant and shriven (though still weeping over her burning robes and jewels!) to begin a regenerate state of life. In Night IX of the epic, Vala and Luvah become the resurgence of the consummated Orc. Having passed the state of innocence and then experience, they are reunited.

They re-enter the golden age of Beulah. In lovely, lyrical lines, Blake gives a duet (almost a stichomythia) of the two, Love and Nature. Love supersedes Nature, and life is again at its idyllic best, for Vala is now "the sinless soul."[18] Luvah enshrines her in pearl and ivory. Selfless she can attain heaven, for "To be shut up in selfhood was Blake's idea of hell."[19] Once she reaches the state of celestial purity, another mystery of her life is disclosed; Tharmas and Enion emerge as her children. In the pure atmosphere of Beulah, Tharmas and Enion revert to the state of childhood and innocence; the eternal return to nature. Blake's cyclic vision brings them to the prelapsarian state, where in Miltonic form and diction: "He took her hand reluctant; she follow'd in infant doubts";[20] Vala's mission is completed, paradise is regained. At the Bacchanalia, the orgiastic feast of the Zoas' sons and daughters, Vala appears. But matron-like she goes back with the others to work at the Golden Loom. Yet her industry and reincarnation as the unspoilt female principle, do not help to save her. The rejuvenated Eternal Man, incensed at the orgy casts

[17] *Ibid.*, p. 356, ll. 602-606.
[18] *Ibid.*, p. 369, l. 458.
[19] Max Plowman, *An Introduction to the Study of Blake* (London: Frank Cass & Co., 1967), p. 72.
[20] *Ibid.*, p. 371, 1. 552.

Vala and Luvah and their progeny into the world of shadows and chaos to rework their salvation in the Circle of Destiny. The function of the male and female, psychological and physical love is unending.

Blake's ominous cyclic forces, his cosmic whirlpools, the plenitude and exuberance of his imagery surfeit, but the design is clear. For him Godwin's rational persuasion does not mean right action; it is love and instinctual understanding and liberty of thought and action that can bring about oneness with the Creative Principle, and so salvation for a chaotic world.

Enion encountered as the small daughter of Vala is the emanation of Tharmas. It is with her quarrel that the epic opens. Bloom calls her "the earth-mother,"[21] Erdman says she stands for "anyone,"[22] and like Vala she is the female principle. But unlike Vala, her affection for her male counterpart is unwavering. She is constant even at the time she asserts her will in jealous tantrums and loses him. Tharmas is a Parent Power; his quarrel with Enion is domestic. Jealousy is at the root of it for he has shielded the beautiful Enitharmon, his daughter, and Enion can not forgive him. In a heart-stirring Blakean passage he sues for her understanding:

> Why wilt thou Examine every little fibre of my soul,
> Spreading them out before the sun like stalks of flax to dry?
>
> . . . .
>
> O Enion, thou art thyself a root grown in hell,[23]

"Tharmas realises that he is being destroyed because he is confronted by a separate Female Will . . .[and so] he is compelled to sink into chaos."[24]

Enion's will is adamantine; she is assertive of her rights, and would have agreed with Mary Wollstonecraft's *Vindication of the Rights of Woman* (1792). Enion's stand is just as courageous as Mary's, except that she suffers "romantic agony." She loses Tharmas. Nine days and nights she weaves her woes and an animated

[21] Bloom, *op. cit.*, p. 196.

[22] David V. Erdman, *Blake: Prophet Against Empire* (Princeton: Princeton University Press, 1969), p. 253.

[23] Blake, *op. cit.*, p. 265, 11. 47-57.

[24] Bloom, *op. cit.*, p. 197.

continent grows out of her loom, terrifying and transfixing her. She yearns for Tharmas and all she encounters is his hollow, soulless spectre. Her anguish is portrayed by some of the most beautiful lamentations, reminiscent of the *Psalms* and the *Song of Songs*. At the nadir of her despair the Spectre of Tharmas unfolds itself, a form of gold with diaphanous wings and gems glistening in his crystal body. Once he finds her, he dominates her mind. She knows that in destroying Tharmas by her feigned indifference and petulence, she has destroyed the souls of her children, among them that of the murdered Enitharmon. Her own jealousy communicates itself to the Spectre of Tharmas, and he announces:

> . . . In my jealous wings
> I evermore will hold thee, when thou goest out or comest in.[25]

In mid-air their love is consummated. Blake's description of this union has an ethereal and opalescent charm seldom matched in imaginative literature. Enion's ecstasy is ephemeral; she returns to her rock still burdened with guilt. The union produces two powerful mythic figures, Los and Enitharmon. Los is postlapsarian creative imagination, his counterpart, Urthona, having been the inspired creative imagination before the Fall. Enion conceived Urthona and Enitharmon, but Urthona impatient of his imprisonment, like Athena and Sin, had sprung from Enion's brain. His spirit returned to implant Los in his place in Enion's womb. Enion nourished her offspring with her strength, and Los and Enitharmon emerged as a god and goddess, scornful, arrogant and beautiful. As she gave of herself, the mother drooped and wilted. Weak, aged, and hoary-headed, she became "a shadowy survival of her true self,"[26] and at their naptial feast, while Los and Enitharmon sat discontented, she sang another poignant lament, in which she questioned Providence. In her song Blake asks the eternal questions: why do the innocent suffer and why is justice so oblique. Using bird and beast imagery, Blake gives the song greater pathos and poignancy. Eternal Death and chaos follow this outburst. To avoid death at the hands of Urizen, Urthona flees to Enion, but is swallowed up in the caverns of Tharmas to

[25] Blake, *op. cit.*, p. 269, l. 177.
[26] Bloom, *op. cit.*, p. 200.

become a monster. Enion sinks further "into the deathful infinite,"[27] and sings another great lyric of oppression, in which Blake voices the whole humanitarian movement. "The terrible poignancy of her song is in its absolute universality of reference . . . our joys and our virtues are founded upon the suffering of others."[28] Meanwhile Urizen's world has crashed and Tharmas has revived. His bellicose thunder filled with hatred frightens Enion still further and, though blind and bent with age, she plunges into the cold primeval waters. From the deep, still lovelorn, she sues for his love and understanding. Tharmas cries after her wraith asking her to return, and he acknowledges his share in the abject state of his emanation:

> For now no more remain'd of Enion in the dismal air,
> Only a voice eternal wailing in the elements.[29]

Tharmas bewails her loss and is nostalgic for her; Ahania joins her in her own plight; and Vala accuses her and the other emanations of converting Luvah to Orc. Enion does not appear after this until almost the end of the epic, but there are references to her throughout. In spite of her approaching end, to Ahania, in the caverns of the Grave, she gives an optimistic reflection on life. Through the experience of suffering she had learnt to look beyond herself. The veil is rent, she says, and the Lamb of God will redeem the scattered remains of mankind and rejuvenate the Eternal Man, who is collective life, for "all things that live are holy."[30]

It is in Beulah that Enion ultimately joins Tharmas. They return to Vala innocent and child-like, but they are just shadows in Vala's world. Enion still sombre and morose, remains aloof from Tharmas; the female Will is a strong element, not easily diverted. A strange phenomenon occurs at the feast of the reincarnated Eternal Man. Enion rises like a beam of light and in the midst of eerie happenings, announces that she is ready to leave her death shell and reunite with Tharmas. All nature revives, and Tharmas, jubilant, fills the heavens with the triumphant sound of trumpets, and they are welcomed to the feast. Their mutual rejection is

[27] Blake, *op. cit.*, p. 290, l. 383.
[28] Bloom, *op. cit.*, p. 219.
[29] Blake, *op. cit.*, p. 297, ll. 205, 206.
[30] *Ibid.*, p. 195, l. 10.

gone. In the cyclic vision death and disintegration are no barriers to life in Beulah.

Ahania, an outcast along with Enion, first appears in the epic at the moment of Urizen's cold, calculated triumph. Urizen had thrown Luvah into his furnaces, and conquered love; he had inspired stern regimentation, planning, mathematical precision of square and rhomb and cube, commerce and industry, and unrelenting education. And man, spurred by Urizen, had been caught in his own nets of exquisite workmanship and enthralled by the beauty of soul-limiting music. As the "Architect divine" Urizen was the inspirer of a quadrangular pile. The edifice had twelve halls, and like the Byzanti churches, three central domes which surrounded Urizen's Golden Hall. It was in this palace of Gold, built with sweat and blood (its mortar mixed by female slaves contained the ashes of Vala) that Ahania is encountered. She appears as Urizen's "Shadowy Feminine Semblance . . . repos'd on a white Couch."[31] She is bright and beautiful; at Urizen's smile she is "Like a bright Cloud in harvest."[32] But when Urizen becomes inhuman, calculating and hard, Ahania, the joyful spirit of reason, weeps over the misuse of reason. She trembles at Urizen's ruthless aggrandisement, and she courts death. Her daughters, the votaries of right reason, keep Ahania alive by sacrifices offered at her Golden Altar. When left to herself, with the light from the West illuminating her, she manages to live. She is Urizen's nobler self, the joy and pleasure of science. Urizen's connotations are sinister, but with the other Zoas he was essential to the Eternal Man. He only needed the complementary humanity of Ahania. Paradoxically for her survival live sacrifices had to be offered on slave-constructed altars of brass; apparently even wisdom and right reason survive on the blood of martyrs.

In Urizen's absence, Ahania languishes. On his return she welcomes him, yet her humanitarian wisdom can no longer comingle with his mechanistic intellect:

> Two wills they had, two intellects, and not as times of old.[33]

[31] *Ibid.*, p. 284. l. 181.
[32] *Ibid.*, p. 284. l. 183
[33] *Ibid.*, p. 285. l. 206.

Enitharmon gleaned this division in their soul. A tantalizing entity herself, she decides to divorce their souls, and does it when the moment arrives. By his "strong Power" Urizen had built his "Mundane Shell"; he had calculatingly seen all his "wondrous works" materialize out of nothing and emerge like Satan's exhaled Pandemonium; he had thousands subordinate under him. He was at the zenith of his prowess, the peak of his triumph, and his world toppled like that of Ibsen's "Master Builder," for he had no love or joy. Los and Enitharmon "Conduct the Voice of Enion to Ahania's midnight pillow,"[34] and Ahania realizes the futility of cold reason in its application to experience:

> What is the price of Experience? do men try to buy it for a song?
> Or wisdom for a dance in the street? No, it is bought with the price
> Of all that a man hath. . .[35]

Enion's midnight lament championed the cause of the oppressed and the poor; unveiled the irrationality of war and oppressive prisons and their serious aftermaths; exposed the hardships of slave labour, and sounded a sympathetic chord in Ahania. Blake's design exposed more than the gory phase of the French Revolution, it described the urgency of change that was of moment to every thinker.

> Ahania heard the Lamentation, & a swift Vibration
> Spread through her Golden frame. She rose up e'er the dawn of day
> When Urizen slept on his couch: drawn through unbounded space.
> On to the margin of Non Entity the bright Female came,
> There she beheld the *Spectrous* form of Enion in the Void
> And never from that moment could she rest upon her pillow.[36]

[34] *Ibid.*, p. 287, l. 290.
[35] *Ibid.*, p. 290, ll. 397-399.
[36] *Ibid.*, p. 291, ll. 419 ff.

Troubled, Ahania comes to Urizen seeking alleviation for her seared soul and intellect. In her address to him she seemed to be convincing herself of his greatness and supremacy, knowing fully well that he was fallible. He disillusions her further. All his power, he says, is for the service of another, a Prophetic boy, whose darkness he has to illumine with his own light of reason. Ahania weeps and meditates over it for seven days. She blames Urizen for having given the steeds of light to Luvah thus changing the entire course of events. In her words of wisdom she decries all the regimentation that Urizen has perpetuated, and so curbed justice and liberty. Nostalgically, in Miltonic terms, she exclaims:

> . . .O how unlike those sweet fields of bliss
> Where liberty was justice, & external science was mercy.[37]

Urizen cannot accept this tirade from "thou little diminutive portion!"[38] He compares her wisdom with Vala's love of power, and with scathing words casts her out. She falls like lightning, and her sons abandon Urizen. Her fall has repercussions throughout nature and cracks the Mundane Shell of Urizen. Joy leaves science and Urizen petrifies.

Ahania falls into the Caverns of the Grave, far into Non Entity. Wandering in the realms of the aged Enion, she is always apprehensive of a greater fall. Like Athena she is a bright-eyed goddess of wisdom, but unlike her she suffers like a mortal. Enitharmon encounters her weeping in her dreary caverns; Tharmas tries to escape her wailing voice. She is oblivious to things around her; her concern is Urizen. Ahania sings her song of the pestilences, a morbid song of extreme dejection and filled with weird imagery. Enion, more optimistic, tries to console her, and Los weeps for her.

Urizen, admonished by the Eternal Man (now resurrected) for deforming his magnificent form and for engendering war by his sciences, weeps. His quest was futile, for everything he searched was already there. He newly realizes that inspiration, art, humanitarianism, and even revolution are facets of science.

[37] *Ibid.*, p. 292, 11. 39-40.
[38] *Ibid.*, p. 295, l. 117.

This knowledge liberates him, and like Milton's Satan, he soars magnificent into the heavens, a pyramid of fire, recreated and rejuvenated. This release liberates Ahania; in great exultation she joins him, only to expire at his feet. The daughters of Urizen watch over her, and in his threnody the Eternal Man prophesies her resurgence, when she and all her sex "shall learn obedience!' Urizen converted, sows a new generation, a basic concept of the epic. Ahania is resurrected in "majesty divine." Urizen dances for joy, and their jubilant sons and daughters fill the air with songs. The intellect with its beauty and joy is restored.

Enitharmon is "the courtly love Queen of Heaven,"[40] the "willful queen of joyless abortion,"[40] "that sympathy which a brutal condition of life provides as the poet's inspiration, and the female principle . .. [in her] all the sins of inharmonious sexuality begin . . . cruel coyness, false modesty, hypocritical restraint."[41] She and Los are the "fierce children of Experience."[42] Enitharmon, Eve-like, combines in herself all these traits, and in some ways is a greater creation than her pristine Miltonic prototype. She is an outstanding example of Blake's "Contraries." "Blake conceived that the life of the human spirit proceeded out of a union of what he called Contraries. Without Contraries is no progression. Attraction and Repulsion, Reason and Energy, Love and Hate, are necessary to Human existence.' "[43] Enitharmon exemplifies the statement. Born of the soulless spectre of Tharmas and the sensitive Enion, she displays all the vagaries of a daughter of Eve, and especially in relationship to her counterpart, Los erstwhile Urthona, and for a period two entities. She hovers between the two, a cause of great chagrin to Los. Though nurtured in Eno's beautifully ornamented Beulah, she is the cause of strife. Sits discontented through an epithalamium and a nuptial feast, and flies from the bosom of Urthona to seek protection of Tharmas. She is murdered and embalmed by Enion, but resurrects. She yearns for Los yet scorns him. Protean, she tan-

[39] Bloom, *op. cit.*, p. 218.
[40] Erdman, *op. cit.*, p. 254.
[41] Mark Schorer, *William Blake, The Politics of Vision* (New York: Vintage Books, 1959), p. 235.
[42] Bloom, *op. cit.*, p. 217.
[43] D.J. Slos and J.P.R. Wallis, *William Blake* (Oxford: The University Press, 1964), p. 22.

talizes Los by taking the form of other emanations, then blames him for making overtures to her as Ahania. He finds her a corpse in his arms and dies; she returns and sings him back to life. In Enitharmon Blake shows his ambivalence towards women. She is the centre of contention between Tharmas, Los, and the spectre of Urthona, and eventually is bound in chains and molten iron by the combined efforts of Los and the spectre.

It is the birth of her son, red Orc, that changes Enitharmon's personality. Los builds Golgonooza for her, and in a way imprisons her in columns of gold and silver and brass. In his jealous rage he nails the fourteen-summers-old Orc to an iron mountain (1785 saw the building of the first iron bridge in England) where the fierce young spirit grows roots and cannot be extracted. It sobers Enitharmon. Blake's Enitharmon grows in stature. From an erratic young woman, she becomes the stable, concerned mother, and then the counterpart of Eve as the helpmeet and inspirer of Los, and finally, having united Urthona and Los, watches over the sepulchre of Christ. She reaches sainthood when she helps to build Jerusalem, the symbol of liberty, and rears a new generation. She, too, reassembles with her Zoa in the revived Eternal Man.

Blake has used the Zoas and their emanations and spectres to personify the life forces that are beyond the comprehension of man, yet direct his life.

"He learned enough of the doctrines of Emanuel Swedenborg to be convinced that man is divisible into separate entities called body, mind, and spirit, or material form, spectre, emanation. . . ; that creation consisted in successive emanations of God, so that each material creature, being separated from God, is a fallen creature and requires a process of regeneration by which it returns into the divine unity after internecine strife and passage through successive states of happiness and sorrow."[44]

In line with the radicalism of the French Revolution, Blake's epic stresses freedom from laws and institutions to reach this ultimate unity of love and brotherhood.

The epic is an archetypal human tragedy, resolving itself aesthetically in unity. The emanations of the Zoas play an important role in regeneration and in the processes that spell liberty.

[44] W. L. Renwick, *English Literature 1789-1815* (Oxford: Clarendon Press, 1963), p. 115.

BIBLIOGRAPHY

Bloom, Harold. *Blake's Apocalypse*. Ithaca: Cornell University Press, 1963.

———, ed.*Romanticism and Consciousness Essays in Criticism*. New York: W.W. Norton, 1970.

———. *Shelley's Mythmaking*. Ithaca: Cornell University Press, 1969.

Erdman, David V. *Blake: Prophet Against Empire*. Princeton: Princeton University Press, 1969.

Fletcher, Angus. *Allegory, the Theory of a Symbolic Mode*. Ithaca: Cornell University Press, 1970.

Frye, Northrop. *Fearful Symmetry*. Princeton: Princeton University Press, 1947.

Houtchens, C.W. and L.H., eds. *The English Romantic Poets and Essayists*. 2nd rev. ed. New York: 1966.

Keynes, Geoffrey, ed. *Blake Complete Writings*. Oxford: Oxford University Press, 1969.

Kroeber Karl. *Backgrounds to British Romantic Literature*. San Francisco: Chandler Publishing Co., 1968.

Plowman, Max. *An Introduction to the Study of Blake*. London: Frank Cass & Co., 1967.

Renwick, W.L. *English Literature 1789-1815*. Eds. F.P. Wilson and Bonamy Dobrée. Oxford: Clarendon Press, 1963.

Saurat, Denis. *Blake and Milton*. New York: Russell and Russell, 1965.

Schorer, Mark. *William Blake, the Politics of Vision*. New York: Vintage Books, 1959.

Sloss, D.J. and Wallis, J.P.R. *The Prophetic Writings of William Blake*. Oxford: Clarendon Press, 1964.

SOME BIOGRAPHICAL INSIGHTS IN KEATS' LETTERS TO FANNY KEATS

On January 23, 1818, Keats wrote to his brothers, George and Tom, that Richard Abbey resented his visits to their 14-and-a-half-year-old sister, Fanny, at the Abbeys' home in Walthamstow.[1] Fanny had been with the Abbeys since the death of the Keats' grandmother, Mrs. Jennings, in December of 1814, and was kept virtually a prisoner.[2] John Keats as the eldest in the family, eight years Fanny's senior, the one who had sat by their mother's bedside and seen tuberculosis take its toll, who was soon to nurse Tom through a similar ailment, shows a constant concern for his young sister, for "Fanny was growing up thin and listless, more and more resembling Tom. . . ."[3] Richard Abbey was an austere and unsuitable guardian. He tried to isolate Fanny from Keats, but when he forbade "even letters, Keats protested angrily . . . [and won] the concession of a letter every fortnight."[4] For Fanny her brother's letters were precious. The 44 letters she preserved so jealously are a compound of playfulness, tenderness, and solicitude. They are also a treasure trove for the student of Keats.

The letter dated September 10, 1817, is in a jocular mood but has underlying anxiety: "Let us now begin a regular question and answer . . . as a pleasant method of my coming at your favourite little wants and enjoyments, . . ."[5] Keats' catechism is not just to gauge Fanny's creature needs, but to discover her in-

[1] Frederick Page, ed., *Letters of John Keats* (London: Oxford University Press, 1954, reprinted1968), p. 67.

[2] Joanna Richardson, *The Everlasting Spell* (London: Trinity Press, 1963), p. 25.

[3] Aileen Ward, *John Keats, The Making of a Poet* (New York: Viking Press, 1963, reprinted 1967), p.258.

[4] *Ibid.*, p. 247.

[5] Page, *op. cit.*, p. 21.

tellectual moiety. He enquires about her preference in books, mentioning books as diverse as the *History of King Pepin*, Bunyan's *Pilgrim's Progress*, *Cinderella* and Moor's *Almanack*. (Incidentally *Pilgrim's Progress* is mentioned by Severn as one of the books which he read to Keats during his last illness.[6]) At Fanny's age Keats had enjoyed the fellowship of Charles Cowden Clarke, an intellectual, a teacher and a friend, who recognizing Keats' great potential had stimulated his mind with works such as Gilbert Burnet's folio *History of His Own Times*, William Robertson s *History of America*, Andrew Tooke's *Pantheon*, John Lempriere's *Classical Dictionary*, Joseph Spence's *Polymetis*. Among the books Keats won as prizes at the Clarkes' private school in Enfield was John Bonnycastle's *Introduction to Astronomy*. He was exposed to Leigh Hunt's political radicalism and liberalism in *The Examiner*, to which the Clarkes subscribed.[7] Having had mentors such as the Clarkes, Keats was anxious about his sister's education specially in the stultifying, unsympathetic atmosphere of the Abbeys' home, where the child was not even allowed the comfort of her dog.[8] In his letter Keats instructed his sister to read diligently each week and to discuss with him what she had read, for his comments. Had this been done in writing what a wealth of material could have come to posterity.

In the same letter Keats writes at length about his visit to Oxford and his stay at Magdalen Hall with Benjamin Bailey (who in after years recalled Keats as a glorious Apollo). Keats visited Bailey in the autumn of 1817, after a stimulating summer with the Reynolds, the Dilkes and James Rice. Charles Wentworth Dilke was a man of letters and an admirer of William Blake; his wife, Maria Dilke, took a kindly interest in young Fanny. The Dilkes and Benjamin Bailey were mutual associates of the Reynolds, and it was at the Reynolds' that Keats met Bailey, and was invited by Bailey to Oxford ere the University reopened. Keats enjoyed the autumn serenity of Oxford, and wrote of its cloisters and groves, its spired and turreted buildings, and its quadrangles, and called it "the finest City in the world."[9]

[6] Walter Jackson Bate, *John Keats* (Cambridge, MA: Harvard University Press, 1964), p. 692.

[7] Douglas Bush, *John Keats—His Life and Writings* (New York: Collier Books, 1966), p. 20.

[8] Bate, *op. cit.*, p. 29.

[9] Ward, *op. cit.*, p. 126.

Keats found Oxford conducive to his poetic genius and writing. In poetic prose he tells Fanny that he is composing a bucolic poem, where a goddess of the Moon falls in love with a handsome young shepherd; and hopes Fanny is familiar with mythological stories so essential to aesthetic insights; he is eager to share classical myths with her in case she does not have access to them. Keats may have felt that Miss Tuckey's boarding school was not giving Fanny a liberal education. "Endymion" was born in Oxford.

Keats' visit to Bailey was of tremendous value, for he read and assimilated the books on Bailey's shelves at a rate commensurate with his own phenomenal growth, maturity, and perfection. Bailey and he discussed "Plato and Aristotle, medieval commentary and seventeenth-century poetry, Milton's theology and Coleridge's metaphysics, . . ."[10] It was there that he read Plato's the *Phaedo*, and it was at Oxford that Keats resolved to make Milton his special study. Shakespeare was part of his thinking; with Charles Cowden Clarke, Keats had made Spenser his own;[11] with Bailey he learnt to love Milton.

Keats' education of Fanny continues in the letter when he mentions George and Tom's trip to the continent and gives her a delightful catalogue of sounds and sites they heard and saw, though nothing, he says, excelled their own green and pleasant land. He mentions the great heritage of Europe that they saw: "Cathedrals, Manuscripts, Fountains, Pictures, Tragedy, Comedy," and in sheer joviality adds to the list "Washerwomen, Lamplighters, Turnpikemen, Fish kettles, Dancing Masters, kettle drums, Sentry Boxes, Rocking Horses. . . ."[12]

It seems that Keats was overworking himself for he complains to Fanny of mental fatigue, but is confident that he will complete the third book of "Endymion." He asks Fanny's opinion on Jane and Ann Taylor's *Essays in Rhyme*, which he had sent her, because she had enjoyed an earlier work of theirs, *Original Poems for Infant Minds.*[13] Keats' teaching process of Fanny continues in his letters, but he also emerges as a friend, for instance in his reflections on French and Italian; he confides that Italian is a

[10] *Ibid.*, pp. 127-128.
[11] *Ibid.*, p. 28.
[12] Page, *op. cit.*, p. 23.
[13] *Ibid.*, *op. cit.*, p. 19.

richer language, though he was conversant with Voltaire and Ronsard.[14] Keats gives Fanny his theory of writing. He says, "Write all you think about, never mind what—only let me have a good deal of your writing—You need not do it all at once—be two or three or four day[s] about it, and let it be a diary of your little Life."[15] Had Keats known his immortality when he exhorted his young sister, "You will preserve all my letters . . ."[15] or was he just helping her to improve her prose style and writing habits?

The letter of August 18, 1818, is written to Fanny ten days after his return from the walking tour of Scotland with Charles Brown. He apologizes for being tardy in writing and complains of a sore throat, the sore throat which was the first symptom of the consumption that took his life. Among the places he and Brown visited, he writes to Fanny of Inverness, the bucolic Island of Mull where he got his "sore throat," Cromarty from where he had his first sea voyage back to London, Perth, his mail depot, the Island of Icolmkill, where he picked pebbles for his sister, and the Mountain of Cairn Gorm,—Cairn Gorm had all the charisma of Keats' supernatural and Gothic fairy stories, but he was not able to visit it.

Brown, Keats' knapsack-carrying companion and nine years his senior, belonged to the Dilke circle. He was a writer and of Scottish ancestry and proved one of Keats' choice and close friends. It was he who persuaded Keats to accompany him on the walking tour of northern England and Scotland. They began their tour at Lancaster, one of the first cities to be industrialized. Aileen Ward feels that Keats' tirade against the Florentine merchants in "Isabella" may have been occasioned by the poverty he saw at Lancaster.[16] The Island of Mull that Keats mentions to Fanny was mountainous and his thirty-mile walk through it in bad weather hardly exhilarating. It was while taking shelter in a shepherd's hut that Keats caught the cold which hounded him the rest of his short life. Brown and Keats threaded their way through the rugged and gorgeous north, in foul and fair weather. The trip was strenuous and by the time they arrived in Inverness, Keats was too exhausted and his throat badly ulcerated to

[14] Ward, *op. cit.*, p. 8.
[15] Page, *op. cit.*, p. 24.
[16] Ward, *op. cit.*, p. 189.

proceed further,[17] yet they walked to Cromarty, a two-days' walking distance from Inverness, and Keats took the nine-day packet back to London. In the month and a half of the tour, Keats had seen the country of Wordsworth and of Burns, he had gone through the experience of bidding his brother George and the peerless Georgiana farewell at Liverpool, and had drunk deep of the beauty of crag and hill and lake and river, seen historic Iona, and lived with the prototypes of Meg Merrilies and the Cumberland Beggars. "The visual result was to show in the grandeur of the landscape of *Hyperion*."[18] While on the tour, inspired though he was with all the beauty around him, Keats had a great deal of fun writing doggerel and puns and quips to entertain his companion and himself and his friends in London. He literally claps to the music of the country dancers, when he tells Tom, "No, they kickit and jumpit with mettle extraordinary, and whiskit, and friskit, and toed it and go'd it, and twirl'd it, and whirl'd it, and stamp't it, and sweated it, tattooing the floor like mad; . . . beating up a batter pudding."[19] And expressed a desire to learn the Highland fling ere he returned. He wrote a poem about Meg Merrilies for Fanny, and quoted it in his letter of July 3rd to Tom. Living surrounded by the majesty of Nature, Keats reaffirmed his belief in himself as one who would give incomparable poetry to the world, "I shall learn poetry here and shall henceforth write more than ever."[20] In his letter to Fanny he promises her all the details of the tour, and expresses anxiety for George and their sister-in-law, not knowing the Settlement they would be heading for on their arrival in Philadelphia. He mentions "Endymion" as the title of his new book, and says Fanny will soon have a copy of it. He commiserates with her about her canary, and humours and encourages her, especially about her well-written letter.

Chagrined at Abbey's treatment of Fanny, on October 26, 1818, he writes to her to be prudent in what she reveals to the Abbeys. He says he does not advocate duplicity, but he does not wish his little sister to suffer because of imprudence in chance remarks. Keats was himself most forthright, for that was part of the Romantic credo. Even when courting Fanny Brawne he could

[17] Richardson, *op. cit.*, p. 27.
[18] Bush, *op. cit.*, p. 83.
[19] Page, *op. cit.*, p. 133.
[20] *Ibid.*, p. 126.

not bring himself to prevaricate or be false. From Winchester, after having been away from her at the Isle of Wight, he wrote, "I see you through a Mist: as I dare say you do me by this time. Believe in the first Letters I wrote you: I assure you I felt as I wrote—I could not write so soon. . . . Remember I have had no idle leisure to brood over you—'tis well perhaps I have not."[21] But he cautions his sister prudence. As her champion, Keats was unafraid of Abbey, but legally unable to rescue the child. In the letter of December 30, 1818, he shows deep concern for Fanny's schooling. Apparently Richard Abbey had decided that Fanny's formal education had reached the zenith allowable to a girl. Keats is incensed, "I shall not neglect any chance of an endeavour to let you return to School—"[22] (a school whose name he hardly got correctly! Perhaps the informality of "Misses Tuckey" was responsible for his mental block). However ardent and enthusiast he was for women's liberation, he was unable to persuade Abbey regarding Fanny's schooling, and so advised her to continue her education independently, and assured her of his constant support. There is a morbidity in the letter not occasioned by the circumstance alone, but seemingly by a preoccupation with impending doom. On Mrs. Abbey he satirically comments, "You can't stop an old woman's crying more than you can a Child's—The old woman is the greatest nuisance because she is too old for the rod."[23] He exhorts Fanny to continue with her reading and amuse herself with music and gardening, and tries to enliven her with jokes and puns and pleasantries.

On March 13, 1819, Keats's letter to Fanny dances with *joie de vivre*, though he is still anxious for news of George. Keats has been to a birthday party, done windowshopping in Leicester Square looking at the famous Tassie seals, and almost buying one for Fanny. With great abandon he promises her anything but livestock, and the latter brings to his mind a catalogue of creatures as entrancing as the ones Noah must have rounded; birds and mice and fish—"the whole tribe of Bushes and Brooks."[24] The magic of the images brings Keats' poetic fancy into play. He sees an enormous globe of gold fish in a picture-frame window overlooking Lake Geneva, and wreathed with myrtle and

[21] *Ibid.*, p. 298.
[22] *Ibid.*, p. 109.
[23] *Ibid.*, p. 218.
[24] *Ibid.*, p. 221.

japonica; and sees himself in a brown study behind it. The "Song About Myself," written for Fanny, is reminiscent of his joy in wild creatures of bush and stream.[25] In 1816 he wrote:

> Linger awhile upon some bending planks
> That lean against a streamlet's rushy banks
> . . . .
> Where swarms of minnows show their little heads
> . . . .
> Sometimes goldfinches one by one will drop
> From low-hung branches: little space they stop;
> But sip, and twitter . . .[26]

Keats' letter to Fanny on March 31, 1819 may have been especially meaningful to her. He signs himself "Your affectionate Parson John—,"[27] and painstakingly explains the sacrament and ritual of the Confirmation. He wants her to examine the book he has sent her on Confirmation and discusses the rite pointwise giving references from the Old and New Testament to substantiate his points. The question is whether this is a testament of Keats' own belief. He himself had been confirmed soon after his mother's death[28] at a period trying and puzzling for him. While an interne at Guy's Hospital, like many of his compeers, Keats had become a sceptic and rather blasphemous, often writing limericks on theological concepts.[29] For Keats, religion was aesthetics; truth was beauty; truth was a complex abstraction with many facets but enduring. To George and Georgiana he wrote in December 1818, "I may be speaking sacrilegiously—. . . I never can feel certain of any truth but from a clear perception of its Beauty."[30] His correspondence with his theologian friend, Bailey, shows that to Keats religion was an unsubstantial mystery of life as was poetry; and neither was "proveable."[31] Yet after the death of his 18-year-old brother, he said, "I have scarce a doubt of im-

[25] Ward, *op. cit.*, p. 13.
[26] Horace E. Scudder, ed., *The Complete Poetical Works of John Keats* (Cambridge, MA: Houghton Mifflin, 1899), p. 15.
[27] Page, *op. cit.*, p. 120.
[28] Ward, *op. cit.*, p. 18.
[29] *Ibid.*, p. 53.
[30] Page, *op. cit.*, p. 207.
[31] Ward, *op. cit.*, p. 170.

mortality of some nature or other. . . ."[32] About Christ he said, "That he was so great a man that though he transmitted no writing of his own to posterity, we have his Mind and his sayings and his greatness handed to us by others . . . . [and] see his splendour. . . . I am straining at particles of light in the midst of a great darkness—without knowing the bearing of any one assertion of any one opinion. . . . I strive to know myself."[33] Keats' religion was that of a philosopher in search of ultimate truth. He owned theological books such as the works of Bishop Beveridge and Saint Ambrose along with a folio Prayer Book and books on Church history.[34] In spite of his letter to Fanny, Keats did not subscribe avowedly to the 39 articles of faith of the established Church, neither was he enamoured of the clergy whose popularity depended, as he tells Fanny, on the "cock'd hat and . . . lady meal, violet smooth, dainty scented, lily white, feather soft, wigsby-dressing, coat-collar-spoiling whisker-reaching, pig-tail loving, swans down-puffing, parson-sweetening powder. . . ."[35]

Among the gifts Keats showered on his little sister were flowering plants. In the Spring of 1819 he wrote to her that he had ordered some bulbs for her, and added that the heaths were in bloom. He hoped that "the Princess of flowers," her double violets were thriving, for "in a shower of rain [they were] almost as fine as barley sugar drops . . . to a school boy's tongue [and to the delight of a little girl]. I suppose this fine weather the lambs tails give a frisk or two extraordinary—"[36] Summer was approaching, but by this time the aftermath of the Scotch tour and his enervation were keeping Keats quietly at home.

From Wentworth Place, on April 17, 1819, Keats wrote to Fanny that he was anxious to see her, but it was a long distance to walk, and he could not afford a stage coach fare "to *chez vous* [as though dramatically] going into the Boxes by way of the pit."[37] Keats' penury was no subject for a joke, for in his state of health he needed the money. Abbey was withholding his annuity, and Keats found dealing with Abbey perplexing.[38] Had Abbey been

[32] Page, *op. cit.*, p. 191.
[33] *Ibid.*, pp. 123-124.
[34] Ward, *op. cit.*, p. 262.
[35] Page, *op. cit.*, p. 230.
[36] *Ibid.*, p. 227.
[37] *Ibid.*, p. 229.
[38] *Ibid.*, p. 364.

more generous in parting with what was their own, Keats may have suffered less and lived longer. It was not until Fanny came of age, and with a great deal of pressure by Dilke and Fanny Brawne, that Abbey was induced to hand over her inheritance.

Keats always felt exhilarated with fine weather. To him nothing mattered more than clear skies and health and as he says to Fanny all other sensuous things: books, the countryside, "a contented Mind, and Diligent habit of reading and thinking, and an amulet against ennui."[39] Echoing lines from the "Ode to a Nightingale":

> O for a draught of vintage! that hath been
> Cool'd a long age in the deep-delved earth,
> Tasting of Flora and the country green,[40]

he adds "and, please, heaven, a little claret-wine cool out of a cellar a mile deep . . . [and] a strawberry bed to say your prayers to Flora. . . ."[39] He wistfully lists the need of "two or three spiteful folkes to spar with; two or three odd fishes to laugh at and two or three numskuls to argue with. . . ."[41] Had he in mind the Dilkes and Reynolds, Bailey and Brown, Hunt and Haydon, Rice and Taylor, and the other friends? "But for that incurable philistine, Mr. Abbey, everyone within the charmed Keats circle gave him immediate, devoted friendship."[42] Writing of his friends in her first letter to Fanny Keats, Fanny Brawne says, "I am certain he has some spell that attaches them to him, or else he has fortunately met with a set of friends that I did not believe could be found in the world."[43] Brown gave Keats a home and financial security on the death of Tom, and through his *mémoire* left the world a wealth of material on Keats; the Dilkes and Reynolds's took Keats into their social circle—his entrée to the coterie of writers and artists; Bailey provided him with deep spiritual friendship and a few first glimpses into the world of literature; Hunt with his radicalism proved a mentor to him of current thoughts and ideologies. Hayden's work Keats admired, but

[39] *Ibid.*, p. 230.
[40] Scudder, *op. cit.*, p. 144.
[41] Page, *op. cit.*, p. 230.
[42] Richardson, *op. cit.*, p. 11.
[43] Fred Edgcumbe, ed., *Letters of Fanny Brawne to Fanny Keats* (London: Oxford University Press, 1937), p. 4.

sparred with him on his religious leanings. He admired Haydon's *Christ's Entry Into Jerusalem.* In Haydon's studio Keats saw the face of Christ become more and more like Haydon's as Haydon touched and retouched the painting, while Wordsworth and Lamb and Hazlitt and Newton paid homage to him, and from one corner of the picture Voltaire sneered at him. Keats saw himself as a spectator in the painting. In November of 1816, overwhelmed by the company of Haydon the previous evening, Keats composed and dedicated his soaring sonnet, "Great Spirits now on Earth are sojourning" to Haydon and sent it to him with the note, "My dear Sir— Last evening wrought me up, and I cannot forbear sending you the following— Yours unfeignedly John Keats.—"[44] His brilliance and charm and impulses such as this endeared him to men and women alike. Yet measuring himself with the magnetism of his brother George, he said of himself, "I do think better of Womankind than to suppose they care whether Mister John Keats five feet high likes them or not."[45]

Unlike his compeers Shelley and Byron, Keats did not express his political views often, but in an era seething with political upheavals and his own great sensitivity to life, it was inevitable that he should show its effects in his works. In his early youth Bishop Burnet's *History of My Own Time* and *The Examiner* made him cognizant of the vagaries of politics. During the years after the cessation of the Napoleonic wars (1812-15), and the unpopularity of the Prince Regent in England, voiced so emphatically by Leigh Hunt in *The Examiner* and Hunt's polemical writings and subsequent arrest, Keats was an apprentice at Hammonds. Keats' radical views and indignation are seen in four of the poems of this period.[46] In "On Peace" he asks for ordered freedom in England and Europe. In the poem addressed to Leigh Hunt on his release, Keats glories in liberty. In "Infatuate Britons" he protests the right of a king to rule by the accident of birth and not competence. As an interne at Guy's, Keats' views had become more and more anti-establishment; anti-State and Church. His friends, Clarke, Haslam and Wylie, had influenced him. Cooper, who like Wordsworth, had experienced the French

[44] Page, *op. cit.*, p. 2.
[45] *Ibid.*, p. 154.
[46] Ward, *op. cit.*, pp. 34-37.

Revolution[47] and was a renowned surgeon at Guy's, and Keats' fellow students, as Spurgeon and Matthew, were idealistically and romantically revolutionary. Keats expressed his radicalism in poetry. On the acquittal of the radical journalist, William Hone, he wrote a parody, "Nebuchadnezzar's Dream." His political criticism in the "Dream" echoes lines from "Endymion."[48] Keats also celebrated the triumphant return to London of the radical orator, Henry Hunt. Hunt's triumph was built on the Manchester Massacre, and his reception by the London crowds betokened a fresh zeal for freedom, as Keats wrote to George.[49] Keats expressed his dissatisfaction with current politics and related matters to George and Georgiana in October 1818:

> . . .as for Politics they are in my opinion only sleepy because they will soon be too wide awake. . . . There is, of a truth, nothing manly or stirling in any part of the Government. . . . there are many Men like Hunt who from a principle of taste would like to see things go on better . . . but there are none prepared to suffer in obscurity for their Country. . . . We have no Milton, no Algernon Sidney—Governors in these days lose the title of Man in exchange of that of Diplomat and Minister. . . . All the departments of Government have strayed from Simplicity which is the greatest of strength. . . . A man now entitled Chancellor has the same honour paid to him whether he be a Hog or a Lord Bacon. No sensation is created by Greatness but the number of Orders a Man has at his Button holes. Notwithstanding the part which the Liberals take in the Cause of Napoleon, I cannot but think he has done more harm to the life of Liberty than anyone else could have done: not that the divine right Gentlemen have done or intend to do any good—no they have taken a Lesson of him. . . . [and prophetically adds] The worst thing he has done is, that he has taught them to organise their monstrous armies.'[50]

Keats predicts that Russia might overthrow China as it will Tur-

[47] *Ibid.*, p. 52.
[48] *Ibid.*, p. 149.
[49] *Ibid.*, p. 319.
[50] Page, *op. cit.*, p. 180.

key, and that Northern Russia will be in league with France against the rest of Europe. He voices Godwin's and his disciple Dilke's "idea that America will be the country to take up the human intellect where England leaves off,"[51] and yet he says America though great will lack the sublimity of men like Milton and Sidney. In August 1819 Keats says to Fanny with a frivolous carelessness, "I can pass a summer very quietly without caring much about Fat Louis, fat Regent or the Duke of Wellington."[52] Politics indeed were mundane for one who had eternity in his grasp.

In June 1819 Keats wrote to Fanny that he was proceeding to the Isle of Wight where he hoped to work at his compositions. He said he was tired of the town, and was accompanying an ailing friend, Rice, to the Isle. Having been unsuccessful in getting any of their funds from Abbey, he reiterated his annoyance with the Abbeys and their hypocrisy; that was an ever-rankling thorn for him. He also gave Fanny the news of the birth of a niece in America. He did not mention his straitened circumstances overtly, but told her that he was reconsidering working for an apothecary or trying the press again, and hoped that he would be reimbursed by those who had borrowed money of him. In spite of all his jollity and ironic innuendoes, Keats continually gives the feeling of being enmeshed. And his personality is so strong that he invests the letters with a real presence.

Keats offers to send Fanny a profile of him done by Brown, as he could not afford the head Severn did of him. He was always humoring his little sister. From Shanklin, Isle of Wight, he wrote describing his coachmates to her, especially the French travellers and their excessive courtesy to the ladies. He paints for her the view of the cliffs and the sea across the housetops, but makes it plain that he is bored. Shanklin is pretty and romantic for retirees, he says; a place where he could make his fortune like the troubadours of old with their lute and a song, but adds he is reluctant to experiment with it himself. He does not mention Fanny Brawne to Fanny at this stage or that his restlessness and boredom were part of his separation from Miss Brawne.

On August 28, 1819, Keats wrote to Fanny from Winchester, where he was glad to be near a library, a prime reason for his

[51] *Ibid.*, p. 181.
[52] *Ibid.*, p. 307.

leaving Shanklin. He found Winchester with its 300-year-old history and its Cathedral and environs enthralling. He described the sites, the Collegiate School, a Nunnery, the Foundation of St. Croix, but deplored the desertion of the great city by the well-to-do. Keats tells Fanny of the tragedy he was writing, hoping very much that Kean would play the leading role in it. Kean was about to leave for America, and that was causing Keats some anxiety. Kean was an exceptional artist and actor, and Keats had seen him on the stage. In December 1817, on first seeing Edmund Kean, Keats had written to his brothers of his role as Richard III, also that in compliance with the request of Reynolds, Keats had written a critique of the play.[53] Like Keats "Kean was very short, but by sheer intensity managed to convey an effect of heroism on a grand scale."[54] Brown and Keats collaborated in writing *Otho, the Great*, and were eager to have Kean in it, for as Keats says to Fanny, "There is not another actor of Tragedy in all London or Europe. The Covent Garden Company is execrable. Young is the best among them and he is a ranting coxcombical tasteless Actor—A Disgust A Nausea—and yet the very best after Kean—What a set of barren asses and actors!"[55] Shelley too had little sympathy for actors, especially those of the Restoration dramas. In spite of the four-letter words he uses, Keats does give the current and topical opinions of the critics.

As for his writings, he tells Fanny in the letter of October 26 or 30, 1819, that it is only when he works consistently that he covers a great deal of material. In May 1817 he had written to Haydon that he studied and wrote about eight hours each day. He also shares with Fanny the fact that he had become a vegetarian, and so supposedly nobler in the great chain of being; also the rather depressing familial news that George had some reverses in his enterprises. George had not been successful as a merchant in Kentucky, a cause of distress to his ever-concerned older brother. But as usual in the kindly, conversational manner of his letters to Fanny, he cheers her with the mention of some pretty shells he has for her. In December 1819 he tells her that he has been busy composing poems to be published in the spring, and that his play has been accepted at Drury Lane for the following season. He appears more optimistic about his suc-

[53] Scudder, *op. cit.*, p. 276.
[54] Ward, *op. cit.*, p. 150.

cess in the world of literature and his dream coming to fruition. Like Milton, Keats wanted immortality, a prerogative only of the elect of letters. Keats ends the letter to Fanny with a frivolous appraisal of his brother George's handwriting on an envelope not addressed to them, thus beyond their reach. Like a detective by gauging each letter of the script, he comes to the conclusion, perhaps to the great amusement of his little sister, that all is well with George in America.

In February 1820, Keats tells Fanny of the pneumonia he had contracted and all the kindness he had met from his friends. He makes some merry comments on the death of George III, and then entertains her with a list of sights he enjoys from his sick couch; each sight pregnant with images for poems: "Old women with bobbins and red cloaks and unpresuming bonnets I see creeping about the heath. Gipseys after hare skins and silver spoons. Then goes by a fellow with a wooden clock under his arm that strikes a hundred and more. Then comes the old french emigrant (who has been very well to do in france) whith his hands joined behind on his hips, and his face full of political schemes."[56] In the letter he mentions Mrs. Brawne, the mother of Fanny Brawne, for the first time to Fanny, though he must have known the family since his return from the Scottish tour.[57] In December of 1818 he had mentioned Mrs. Brawne and "her daughter senior . . . .[whom he thought] beautiful and elegant, graceful, silly, fashionable and strange . . ."[58] to George and Georgiana. By the summer of 1819 Keats was desperately in love with Fanny Brawne, and wrote some of the most impassioned love letters to her; his "Minx" and his "Heloise." Perhaps he considered his sister Fanny too young to understand his relationship with Miss Brawne, hence his silence on the subject.

Ill as he was, he tells Fanny in April 1820 to be brave, for anxiety and despondency are enemies of health. Lack of recognition, illness, penury, and the intensity of his love for Fanny Brawne were all contributing factors to the tension and frustration in those last months of Keats' meteoric life. In May 1820 he says to Fanny, "You will forgive me when I confess that I endeavour to think of you as little as possible. . . . the reason being that I

55 Page, *op. cit.*, p. 307.
56 *Ibid.*, p. 384.
57 Ward, *op. cit.*, p. 215.
58 Page, *op. cit.*, p. 195.

am affraid to ruminate on anything which has the shade of difficulty or melancholy in it, as that sort of cojitation is pernicious to health . . ."[59] yet, as always, he is solicitous of her welfare. In June he had hoped to visit Fanny, with a copy of his newly published poems, when a serious haemorrhage prevented him. July saw him more pensive and despondent, preparing himself for a winter in Italy; but a mischievous note creeps in his letter when he seems to delight in the misfortune of Hodgkinson who had partnered Abbey in adding to their fiscal misery. He goes on to tell his sister that if he recovers at all it will be a slow process, also that he has directed his publishers to send her a copy of his poems. He does add a cheerful note in saying that he is happy in Hunt's company and in the books he reads, but decries the city calls and "ballad singers, and street music"[60] (unfortunately lost in a large measure to the twentieth century). He still hopes for a "trump card" to brighten the fortunes of the family.

Keats' next letter to Fanny is addressed from the home of Mrs. Brawne; perhaps the happiest period of his short life when Fanny Brawne was his constant companion. Keats had passed through a period of doubt regarding Fanny Brawne's love for him. Her vivacity and Brown's proximity to her were the cause of intense jealousy for Keats. He wrote to Fanny Brawne, "I would show some one in Love as I am, with a person living in such Liberty as you do. . . . Hamlet's heart was full of such Misery as mine is when he said to Ophelia 'Go to a Nunnery, go, go!' . . . I should like to die. I am sickened at the brute world which you are smiling with."[61] It was very heaven for him to be under the same roof as Fanny Brawne and be assured of her undivided love. In the same letter to his sister, Keats mentions Shelley's invitation to him from Pisa. Shelley was incensed at the reception afforded Keats' poems by the press, especially the *Quarterly Review*, and critics as Lockhart; and was convinced that Keats' illness was partly due to it. Shelley's was an invitation of the great "Ariel" to "Adonäis." While exhorting his sister to remain cheerful and healthy, Keats makes a rather snobbish and un-egalitarian remark that health is the prerogative of scavengers and cinder-sifters alone; an ironic early eighteenth-century truism.

In the last letter written to Fanny before he sails for Italy in

[59] *Ibid.*, p. 211.
[60] *Ibid.*, p. 416.
[61] *Ibid.*, p. 420.

September 1820, Keats refers to Fanny Brawne, "I have accepted the assistance of a friend [Fanny Brawne], who I have desired to write to you when I am gone. . . ."[62] Fanny Brawne took this behest seriously and befriended Fanny until she came of age, and married Valentine Llanos.

Apparently Fanny Keats received no other letter from her brother, but Keats had her constantly in mind. According to Severn, in line with Keats' wishes her unopened letters and those of Fanny Brawne were interred with Keats. Writing to Brown from Rome Keats had said, ". . . the difference of my sensations with respect to Miss Brawne and my sister are amazing. The one seems to absorb the other to a degree incredible."[63] Keats's last letter to Brown, dated November 30, 1820, has the sensuous poignancy of his lyrics, "I have an habitual feeling of my real life having past, and that I am leading a posthumous existence," thinking of his little sister before signing his name—perhaps for the last time, he says, ". . . [she] walks about my imagination like a ghost—she is so like Tom." And ends, "I can scarcely bid you good-bye even in a letter. I always made an awkward bow."[64]

[62] *Ibid.*, p. 428.
[63] *Ibid.*, p. 431.
[64] *Ibid.*, p. 437.

BIBLIOGRAPHY

Adami, Marie. *Fanny Keats*. London: John Murrav. 1937.

Bate, Walter Jackson. *John Keats*. Cambridge, MA: Harvard University Press, 1964.

Bush, Douglas. *John Keats—His Life and Writings*. New York: Collier, 1966.

Edgcumbe, Fred, ed. *Letters of Fanny Brawne to Fanny Keats*. London: Oxford University Press, 1937.

Frye, Northrop. *A Study of English Romanticism*. New York: Random House, 1968.

Jones, John. *John Keats's Dream of Truth*. London: Chatto and Windus, 1969.

Murray, John Middleton. *Keats*. U.S.A.: Minerva Press, 1955, reprinted 1968.

Page, Frederick. *Letters of John Keats*. London: Oxford University Press, 1954, reprinted 1968.

Richardson, Joanna. *The Everlasting Spell—A Study of Keats and His Friends*. London: Trinity Press, 1963.

Scudder, Horace E., ed. *The Complete Poetical Works of Keats*. Cambridge,: Houghton Mifflin, 1899.

Talmon, J. L. *Romanticism and Revolt*. Norwich, Great Britain: Jarrod and Sons, 1967.

Trilling, Lionel, ed. *The Selected Letters of John Keats*. New York: Farrar, Straus and Young, 1951.

Ward, Aileen. *John Keats—The Making of a Poet*. New York: Viking, 1967.

Weller, Earle Vonard, compiler. *Autobiography of John Keats*. Stanford, CA: Stanford University Press, 1933.

A TALK ON WAUGH'S *DECLINE AND FALL*

Evelyn Waugh's *Decline and Fall* is most entertaining. The plot and many of the characters are incredible, and he gives a string of farcical situations, through which the naïve Paul Pennyfeather, like Candide, comes out unscathed, though initiated. Ironically, the 25-year-old Waugh has struck at the very base of British society. For centuries the aristocracy and the gentry and traditional institutions were the norm of stability in the island. Suddenly the post-World War I years saw the emergence of an unprincipled and amoral society, for which the old Christian values or rather the values of decency had little meaning. Integrity, devotion, loyalty, and with them chivalry, seemed to have peeled off like a veneer, leaving animal lusts for aggrandizement, sexual appetites and the devil-may-care-for-the-other-fellow attitude bare. For an essentially upright and pious young man, like Waugh, this was a situation that called for, if not Juvenalian, Horatian satire. And he does it beautifully. His expressions, his choice of words and phrases, show his comic genius for satire though at times his tone is moralistic and banal. His agglomeration of anti-social attitudes and situations is farfetched, as are most of his characters; and he formulates no solutions. He just exposes the malaise of society. His humour lacks the usual British subtlety, but is delightful. A great deal he writes from personal experience, and some of the incidents parallel his life. The areas that I have picked seemed to me the most pertinent to the insanity that Waugh derides.

When Waugh ridicules Oxford, he strikes at the very heart of British prestige. The orgy of the Bollinger Society is understandable, but their sadistic rapacity is disturbing: it not only denudes but expels the unsuspecting Paul. The irony is that the "Boller" consists of the scions and the cream of society; the traditional backbone of British life; Waugh's sarcasm is also visible in showing the callousness of the Dean and Master of Scone.

The expulsion proves a rustication for Paul. In spite of the treatment meted out to him, Paul is drawn back to the University. As he is inconsequential, he returns unrecognized—his only disguise being a moustache and a commoner's gown! For practical purposes he retains his name, and thinks of himself as a cousin many times removed of the expelled man. In *A Little Learning* Waugh devotes a long chapter to his three years at Oxford. Like Pennyfeather, he was a serious student at Hertford College, a member of the Oxford Union, and interested in the League of Nations. Waugh went back to Oxford soon after graduation, and to identify himself with the Oxonian undergraduates wore the modish polo-neck sweater and the Oxford bags. Did Waugh see himself in Paul?

On his expulsion, and after being defrauded of his inheritance by an unscrupulous guardian (for the legal profession was also suffering from the general malaise), Paul finds that the only profession open to an unqualified and expelled Oxford man is teaching. He is hired by Fagan on a salary well below par, for a situation like his had to be exploited!

Waugh had been an outstanding student at Hertford, but had not done too well in his final examinations, passing with a 3rd division. On account of it he felt debarred from all professions but teaching. As a teacher he went to a remote Welsh town, and later moved to a boys' school for misfits near London. These two institutions were his models for Llanabba Castle.

Waugh satirizes the public schools to the nth degree. At the Castle the older boys wear dinner jackets, but the younger ones are in Eton suits. Grimes, the Second-Master and an inveterate rogue, is a Harrow man. Dr. Fagan stoops to practices far befitting the Head of a public school. The school schedule is unorganized; a Sports Day is sprung on the teachers, just because some influential parents are visiting the area. Paul, to his great surprise, finds that he is expected to teach subjects of which he has no knowledge, and has to be deferential to boys of leading families. Discipline is non-existent and students have little respect for the masters. The Dickensian Fagan has some semblance to a Headmaster, but the two Second Masters are caricatures. Grimes limps on a wooden leg lost after a drunken bout, and glories in his cups and his homosexual propensities. Prendergast is guilt-ridden for he is a defrocked priest. His only crime is a questioning mind, which the established Church could not bide.

His heresy was an innocent, "Why did God create the world?"

In *A Little Learning* we meet the prototypes of these characters. The headmaster of the Flintshire School, Mr. Vanhomrigh, before employing Waugh, made sure that Waugh had an evening jacket! Mrs. Vanhomrigh is not unlike Miss Dingy Fagan. The second-master at Flintshire suggested Grimes to Waugh. Waugh says of Llanabba Castle, "When later I came to write a novel which introduced a private school in North Wales, I lavishly embellished it. . . ." He did, by giving it a satirical twist. Unlike the 18th century preparatory school, which Waugh attended at Heath Mount, and the mediaeval Anglo-Catholic public school at Lancing, he made Llanabba grotesque—the folly of a *nouveau riche* industrialist, who thought of it as his "impregnable medieval castle"—a monstrosity towered and turretted. The Lancashire Mill owner had used cheap labour to build it—seemingly as an act of mercy to keep his underpaid employees from starving. Here Waugh attacks the industrialists, their accumulated wealth, their mimicry of the aristocrats, and failure even in philanthropy; for at the centre of it all is self-interest.

In his autobiography Waugh's students are healthy and clean and fine, but Pennyfeather's students are little monsters, ruthless and sadistic. Pennyfeather is sized up by them on the very first day. To be liked he has to resort to white lies and Fagan's studied poses and a firm deafness to gossip. Waugh ridicules the traditions of the public schools in Grimes' stories. Grimes was oftener in trouble than out, but he invariably escaped, thanks to his being a public school man, and public school men never let each other down. They transmute death sentences and courts martial! And let the scapegoat remove himself to Ireland—the forgotten land—too distant a place to pose a problem!

Part of the discipline of the private schools was a travesty of religion. Instead of using the set epistle and gospel of the liturgy, Fagan opens the Bible at random, and reads a meaningless passage at the assembly. His disciplinary action on the cigar found in the boiler room is typical of a private school. The culprits are given until lunch time to confess; but here, when prevarication is, the order of the day, this code of honour is farcical.

Fagan's daughter, Flossy, has a beautiful broad accent. In speech she and the cockney butler, Philbrick, complement each other. Philbrick is quizzical and complex. He has a novelist's imagination, and sees himself the hero of each episode he fabricates.

He confesses to having been an associate of the notorious crook, Toby Cruttwell. (Alec Waugh points out Evelyn's intense dislike of the name Cruttwell, as the antipathy between him and Dean Cruttwell of Hertford was proverbial.) In these characters Waugh is satirizing not only the con men, the crooks, but the commoner.

It is at Llanabba that we meet the callous Countess of Circumference. Waugh recounts in his autobiography that she was suggested by the mother of a friend, whom he calls "Hamish Lennox." She has all the arrogance of the aristocrat. She shocks others by her utterances, wears manly tweed, rides roughshod over all without any qualms. It is for her that Fagan has all the fanfare on Sports Day. Fagan gets intoxicated by the excitement of the event, forgets all discretion; usually parsimonious, becomes insanely extravagant, but the countess is not moved. She is only moved when crossed. Her little Lord Tangent is shot in the foot, but that hardly bothers her. Eventually he dies.

It is Peter Beste-Chetwynde's mother, Margot, who takes Pennyfeather's breath away. She enters the arena "like the first breath of spring in the Champs Elysées." She sports a handsome Negro and uses him like a bauble, except he is too serious to remain a plaything.

"King's Thursday," her country seat is symbolic of her, Though a Tudor construction of the 16th century, it had nothing to commend it architecturally, and from the 20th century point of view had no conveniences or labour-saving devices. Once Margot decides to rebuild it, there is a hue and cry, especially from the antiquarian clergymen; and their only consolation is that it may be re-erected in Cincinnati! Waugh's satire here is double-edged. He is making fun of the conservatives and of Margot's insensitive extravagance. All she asks of Otto Friedrich Silenus, the architect, is, "Something Clean and Square;" with its glass and chrome symbolic of modernity and affluence; a thing of "a different species" like herself. Silenus, the impecunious philosopher-architect, a disciple of Corbusier, knows Margot. When he speaks of her in Corfu, he sees her hanging on dangerously to the fast-moving wheel of life; thrilled with its dynamic motion, uncaring for the rest of the world. Silenus too is on the wheel of life, but his poverty has made him a sycophant, and shoved him to the static centre. Pennyfeather remains untouched, as he is flung off the wheel, and watches its revolutions from a seat in the amphitheatre. Paul is on the wheel only during the short contact with Margot; a woman "fresh and exquisite as a 17th c. lyric." She alone roused Paul from his static state; the height of his activity was the trip to Marseilles. It is at King's Thursday that Paul meets the Dickensian characters: the Minister of Transportation, appropriately called Sir Henry Maltravers; Lord Parakeet, Pamela Popham, Miles Malpractice. They are the new, noisy and bored pseudo-aristocrats who have taken over from the Pastmasters.

Candide-like Paul's associates keep cropping up and recropping in the novel. Fagan writes to him of his erstwhile butler, as Sir Solomon Philbrick, a candidate for Llanabba. Philbrick is Protean. He greets Paul in the Blackstone Gaol, himself a useful and affable inmate. In Oxford Paul sees him smothered in furs on the backseat of a Rolls Royce, looking intellectual enough to be dubbed, "Arnold Bennett." Grimes is in and out of the picture; the last time escaping like Magwich in a fog. He is so optimistically affable that Paul associates him with Bacchus, the dying and the reviving god. Crime in post-war society is hydra-headed and illusive.

Arthur Potts remains single-minded, and makes international criminals his special business. He is the do-gooder in the League of Nations, and his efforts legally kill Paul. Prendy returns to the Church, but as a Modern Churchman. His problems remain the same. He can no more control the prisoners than the boys, and loses his life. Augustus Fagan reappears with an M.D. and owning a little run-down but large nursing home, with Dingy as his presiding nurse. Their "Decline and Fall" takes them to a more sophisticated life of crime. Fagan's last appearance is also immortal; Paul gets his book, *Mother Wales*, dedicated as a wedding present to Fagan's wife—which wife?

The 20th century English prisons had not improved much since the time of *Caleb Williams*. Waugh gives a catalogue of punishments and hardships inflicted on the prisoners. The only difference is that the Col. MacAdders have turned into Sir Wilfred Lucas-Dockeries. The MacAdders' adage was, "If you make prison bad enough, people will keep out of it," and "Give hell to the man immediately below you and it will be passed on." The Dockeries, the radicals, gloried in applying the wrong psychology and physio-therapy; giving sharp tools to a maniac, because like Joseph of old, he was a godly carpenter. His visions made him decapitate Prendy; and the men sang "O God, our help in ages past."

The charming Margot, guilt-ridden enough to ease life in prison for Paul with dainties and copies of recent publications, among them the latest Virginia Woolf, lets others suffer vicariously for her. But unlike Paul, she is not unscathed. On seeing her in prison, "Paul is greatly pained at how little he is pained"; but Margot at last sees herself as Silenus saw her. Silenus had given her another ten years, perhaps she gives herself less. Already ostracised by the blueblooded Lady Circumference and Lady Vanbrugh and Fanny Simpleforth, she realises that only one who had risen from the ranks, and through sheer perseverance, like Maltravers, could become a Metroland. Yet her mood and nefarious ways are not quite over; Trumpington remains her new diversion.

Trumpington like Bedivere watches Paul sail to Corfu. Waugh in *A Little Learning* mentions his own preoccupation with Bedivere. For him Bedivere was the symbol of disillusionment and nostalgia. Trumpington muses on Paul's "Decline and Fall," himself unwittingly its initiator. In Oxford Paul is about to take Holy Orders when the "Boller" meets again; this time in Peter Pastmaster's room. A wiser Paul advises Peter to be more abstemious, and the young Earl replies, "Oh, damn, what else is there to do?" Recalling Gibbon's work, *Decline and Fall* is a serious piece of writing. Waugh's characters suggest the Morality Plays. How denunciatory was Waugh of a society that seemed materialistic, hypocritical, degenerate, and completely amoral?

ENGLISH IN INDIA

A question asked in general of a stranger anywhere in the vicinity of an Indian village is, "*Sahib, time kya hai?* (Sir, what is the time?)" The sentence is more of a greeting than a query requiring an answer, but the word *time*, pronounced "taime," is unmistakable. This is just one instance of the infiltration of English into the sixteen main regional languages of India and several hundred dialects. A person asking the question may be oblivious of *time* being an alien word, and in all probability has lost the synonym for the word in his own language or dialect. Statistics show that over 3,000 English words are now in use in Telegu alone,[1] Telegu being one of the sixteen main languages.

In 250 years of India's association with the British, English in its own peculiar form and with its own aura has come to stay. Constitutionally the language has been adopted as the second official language of the country; functionally it serves as the main language of communication within the borders of the country and outside.

In spite of English words having become an intrinsic part of Indian speech, a command of English is limited to a comparatively small percentage of India's 500 million people. The reason for it is that literacy is still low. Approximately sixty percent of India's people are illiterate. Of the forty percent literate, about fifteen percent are women. Since India's independence in 1947 the number of primary and secondary schools have tripled, and almost every village can boast of a primary school; but the curricula in these schools and the calibre of teachers are far from satisfactory. In spite of English being declared the second *lingua*

[1] Braj B. Kachru, "English in India: A Pan-Indian and International Link," *English Around the World*, ed. John I. B. McCulloch, No. 4 (New York: Publication of the English-Speaking Union of the United States, May 1971), p. 4.

franca of the country, it is not taught universally. A great deal of it is due to a top-heavy bureaucracy, who can not agree about the status of English in primary schools. There are two distinct opinions: one of a fanatical worship of the regional language and the fostering of its natural development in the child; the other is of imposing the two languages of the country, Hindi and English, on the child at an early age. The latter advocates tri-lingual education for every child attending school. Education now for the six to eleven-year-olds is compulsory. As for teaching English, each State Department of Education has its own regulations, and so there is no uniformity. This poses problems for the country as a whole.

India is still a part of the British Commonwealth, but the withdrawal of the English from India in 1947 has made English suffer a "sea change." English, except in a few church-related and private schools, is no longer the English taught at Eton and Harrow; and few Oxford and Cambridge dons continue to remain as teachers. This withdrawal has affected not only the structure of the written word but the enunciation and pronunciation of the language. Among the English-speaking populace of India, English is spoken not with an "Indian" but a regional accent. Anyone having the least familiarity with the intonation of a regional native language, can single out a person speaking English as belonging to that particular area. It can be said, there is Bengali English, Tamil English, Punjabi English, Gujrati and Marathi English, Hindi English, Malayalam English, and so on. English has not only taken the vowel and consonantal variations of these regional speeches, but also their dialectical idiom and cultural pattern. The usage and turns of speech in English follow the patterns of the respective native language. At times it requires ingenuity to decipher sentences spoken in English if one is not conversant with the language of that particular region. The difference is due to the rhythm of speech, stresses on different syllables, and the use of gutturals or velars unwarranted in English English. Then there are "hybrid words" as *her memsahibship, tickety, fashionwali, Englishdan, motorwala, cycledidukan, garamcoffee*; which mystify. These words have either "a native stem and a foreign ending"[2] or, vice versa, a foreign stem and a native suffix. Other

[2] Otto Jespersen, *Growth and Structure of the English Language* (New York: Free Press, 1968), p. 98.

shortcomings that are usually pointed out in Indian English are the use of ornate bookish language, clichés, obsolete words, and Shakespearian, Miltonic and Victorian phraseology. When a colloquial term or slang is used, it hardly rings true. At times the ludicrousness of the situation comes nearest to Dickens *(Pickwick* II, 13) where "Bob Sawyer asked 'I say, old boy, where do you hang out?' Mr. Pickwick replied that he was at present *suspended* at the George and Vulture";[3] and in the paraphrase of " 'A rolling stone gathers no moss' . . . [as] cryptogamous concretion never grows on mineral fragments that decline repose."[3]

Justly or unjustly the myth of Indians speaking and writing bad or *baboo* English has been perpetuated since Ellis Underwood gave his findings on Indian English in 1885. His verdict was that Indian English has "a fondness for 'tall' writing, a delight in 'six-foot' words and . . . grand expressions, magniloquence of style . . . coupled with colloquialism, . . . the use of 'fine imagery often derived from ancient classical sources,' the practice of 'interlarding or . . . embellishing . . . periods with misplaced or misguided idioms or phrases, forced allusions, tags, quotations and such bits of Latin or French as those picked up second hand' and mistaking 'garishness for splendor, tinsel for ornament.' "[4]

Examining the works of nineteenth-century Indian writers of English, such as Raja Ram Mohan Roy, Bankim Chandra, Toru Dutt, the statement quoted here seems somewhat exaggerated and prejudiced. Almost eighty years after Underwood, in 1964, V. K. Gokak gave his appraisal of Indian English. In Indian English he saw "the evolution of a distinct standard—a standard the body of which is correct English usage, but whose soul is Indian in color, thought and imagery. . . ."[4] Gokak is closer to a just evaluation of the speech and writing of the speakers and writers of English in India today. They have evolved an Indian idiom of English "which is expressive of the unique quality of the Indian mind while conforming to the 'correctness' of English usage."[4] The works of Indo-Anglian writers, such as Minoo Masani, Mulk Raj Anand, Kamla Markandaya, Kushwant Singh, Raja Rao, Jawaharlal Nehru, Mahatma Gandhi, Sirvapallai Radhakrishnan, the Milton scholar B. C. Rajan, Sarojini Naidu, Rabindranath

[3] *Ibid.*, p. 137.

[4] C. Paul Verghese, "Indian English," *India News* (Washington, DC: Embassy of India, Sept. 4, 1970), p. 3.

Tagore, Santha Rama Rau, and others, exemplify the mode and styles of Indians writing in English. Yet the excellence of their work is no encomium for English in India today.

For an Indian, who has not been exposed to English English since childhood, and whose mother tongue is a derivative of Sanskrit with its special "positions of articulation . . . as the 'cerebral position' . . . where the tip of the tongue articulates against the hard palate. . . , its consonantal system . . . , its infixed nasals and polysyllabic words,"[5] enunciation of English words is difficult to master. Mastery of it "entails phonetic modification"[5] of his own speech pattern.

The vowel lengths in Indian languages differ from those in English. Words such as *seed, hard, tool* sound like *sid, had, tul.* A *head-master* becomes a *hudmastur,* a *rose* is a *rauj. Lost* sounds as *laust, trend* as *tarend, thought* as *thaut, level* as *laywal, matter* as *maytar, realizing* as *rilizing, got* as *gat, return* as *ritarun, satisfaction* as *sayteezfakshun, develop* as *dawalup.*

The Indian idiom can be seen in sentences such as, "There is a chance in a million that her intellectual level may be the same as mine." "When it happens it happens." "I can't come to know people I am not a friend of." These are literal translations, as it can be noticed, from native languages. (The words and sentences quoted here were tape-recorded in March 1973 at an informal gathering of Indian students in New York.) The consonant "v" poses difficulties in all the Indian languages. It is used interchangeably with "b" and with "w," "b" for "v" is common in Bengal, and "w" in the Punjab and Uttar Pradesh. The sound "zhu" as in *azure* is absent from most of the languages, and "j" becomes its substitute. There are phonetic difficulties for a learner.

Due to different regional intonations, pronunciations and enunciation, inter-provincially spoken English in India is difficult to follow. Educationists today are convinced that English should be spoken as English wherever it is taught, not only among the opulent families who can afford expensive English education and English tutors for their children. They feel that as in pre-independence days, English should be free of provincial accent and the strong accentual bias of the mother tongues; yet they

[5] Edward Sapir, *Language*, 1st ed., 1921 (New York: Harcourt, Brace, & World, 1949), pp. 52, 72, 196, 197.

concede the influence of the latter can never quite be eradicated.

For all interstate political and business purposes, English is the *link* language. It is in use in schools and colleges, universities, offices and law courts. As Hindi, the main official language, was found more problematic, in December 1967, by an amendment of the Indian Parliament, English was proclaimed as the language of communication between the Union Government and the States that had not adopted Hindi as their official language. This edict also charged that for clarity, all Hindi communications should be translated into English where the former was not understood. In some quarters there was a strong feeling that to keep the Indian sub-continent united, English had to be maintained as the *link* language. India also realizes that English is essential for international communication, and it would be folly to lose this great heritage. India is quite conscious that for its economic and scientific and technological advancement it depends on English. In spite of it, the standard of English has deteriorated considerably since Independence. Teachers are no longer amused at the "howlers" in the written returns of their students; they are appalled. The students' comprehension of the language is poor, but their expression is poorer still. Someone tersely remarked that in India there are "as many kinds of English as there are students." The examiners today grade their students only on the substance of the answer, not on language skill—a fatal dichotomy. English is only functional.

For a teacher of English in India, the response of the students to the language, let alone literature, is disheartening. The majority of the students find the simplest structures of English difficult. Educators are concerned at the situation. They know that even in the scientific fields a knowledge of the accepted, international terminology is not enough; that the terms have to be studied in the context of the thesis. Translations and adaptations generally lose the essence of the work. Thus a solution is that English should be an essential part of the school curriculum, and each child be required to study it.

As the most receptive period for languages in a child is age 4 to 10, and the secondary stage, 11 to 14, the child should be exposed to the language from the kindergarten. Although psychologists have "claimed that it is only in the mother-tongue that a child goes through the socialising process that helps him to master language. He acquires his second language intellectually, not via the emotions. . . . ,"[6] experience has proved that bilingualism ("the practice of making alternate use of two languages,"[6]) or trilingualism in a small child, make the second and third language as naturally his as the mother tongue. Thought and converse in them come spontaneously and effortlessly. The syntax and grammar acquired in those early years become the means of his later mastery of the language and its literature. V. K. Gokak has pointed out that the structural method of teaching English in India today is the most effective. He says, "Achieve the result by modern methods of teaching . . . like the structure method of teaching English."[6]

"Many State Departments of Education have adopted a structural syllabus now. The 'grammar and translation' method is not openly advocated by any department or institution. It lingers here and there in the actual teaching work of teachers who are not convinced of the utility of the structural approach. . . . The use of textbooks prepared on structural principles is bound to be beneficial. Both the vocabulary and sentence-patterns are controlled and graded in these books and this makes it somewhat easy for the student to learn the language."[6]

The books aim at giving the child in the first six years of his schooling, a working knowledge of over 250 basic structure forms and a vocabulary of at least 2500 words. Besides the textbooks, India needs teachers who have the skills to use these modern methods. The most competent can be drawn from the English medium schools, for the English medium schools have tried to maintain and uphold the standards on which they were founded; some over 150 years ago. These schools still use the phonetic method of oral instruction; their classes are small enough to allow for the tutorial method; their stress is on composition. Declamations, debates, and recitals of literary passages are often part of their school year. But there is a dearth of such schools, and the students who graduate from them have plans other than teaching in primary schools of the mofussils of India.

Along with the simplified English texts, the educationists advocate for the teachers "a second knowledge of General Linguistics . . . to analyse precisely a prescribed literary text . . . to

[6] V. K. Gokak, *English in India: Its Present and Future* (Bombay: Asia Publishing House, 1964), pp. 22, 23, 31, and 68.

formulate . . . the relation between language and literature . . . in contemporary English. [To be effective the teachers have to] study their own local variety of English . . . and phonetics of English."[7] The problems of the non-English speaking child are linguistic. Correct English phonology can make the language live for him. It is the teacher's mission to help him understand the language and to communicate intelligibly in it.

The Central Institute of English, at Hyderabad, and the English Language Teaching Institute at Allahabad have been doing research in the subject for almost fifteen years. Their goal is to improve the teaching of English in India. The other States are trying to implement their programmes of English teaching and English teacher education by establishing similar institutes in their own regions. The British Council in Delhi, Calcutta, Bombay and Madras, has been giving short refresher courses for teachers of English and supplementing the work of the training colleges and universities. In conjunction with the British Council the Government of Madras has had special campaigns for reorientation of primary school teachers of English; and the seminars offered were popular.

Along with the research at Hyderabad and Allahabad in English for the masses, the University Grants Commission in India is inviting visiting professors of English from the U.K. and the U.S.A. It is holding seminars for its teachers and giving grants to some for study abroad. Overseas, the University of Leeds offers special courses in Indo-English literature and invites Indian professors to conduct seminars. The Ford Foundation is helping to stimulate interest in American Literature, and is bringing American scholars to India. The U.S. Education Foundation is deputing young U.S. graduates to help as tutors of English in some of the Indian colleges.

India's association with English started in the 16th century with the ambassadors of Queen Elizabeth I at the court of the Moghul Emperor, Akbar. Elizabeth's charter to the merchants of the City of London, allowing trade with India, was another link in the association. Before this, the bards of England, like Chaucer, had mentioned the wealth and beauty of India in their song. Early in the 19th century due to the mounting interest of

[7] *Ibid.*, p. 48.

scholars in the Indian languages and the classics, and of the Christian humanitarians in the Indian people, the English Parliament, by a special Act, established English medium schools in the country. The Sanskrit-Latin studies, first explored in the 16th century, were incorporated in 1786 in the Bengal Asiatic Society. Sir William Jones, "the father of comparative linguistics,"[8] was the founder of the Society. Since those early beginnings English has been a formative influence in India. The setback in proficiency came with Independence and the inordinate zeal for everything indigenous; a natural and expected aftermath of independence. It made a whole generation grow up knowing little or no English. The awareness of it has jolted the educationists and the officials. There is a concerted effort to re-establish English as the second *lingua franca* of the country, and once again produce eminent Indians like Gandhi and Nehru and Radhakrishnan, who were as at home in English as in their mother tongue.

[8] Thomas Pyles, *The Origins & Development of the English Language*, 1st. ed., 1964 (New York: Harcourt Brace Jovanovich, 1971), p.86.

BIBLIOGRAPHY

Black, Max. *The Labyrinth of Language*. New York: Mentor, 1969.

Bolinger, Dwight. *Aspects of Language*. New York: Harcourt, Brace & World, 1968.

Gokak, V. K. *English in India: Its Present and Future*. Bombay: Asia Publishing House, 1964.

Iyengar, K. R. Srinivasa. *The Indian Contribution to English Literature*. Bombay: Karnatak Publishing House, 1945.

———. *Indo-Anglian Literature*. Bombay: The International Book House, 1943.

Jespersen, Otto. *Growth and Structure of the English Language*. New York: Free Press, 1968.

Kachru, Braj B. "English in India: A Pan-Indian and International Link." *English Around the World*, ed. John I. B. McCulloch. No. 4. New York: Publication of the English-Speaking Union of the United States, May 1971.

Langacker, Ronald W. *Fundamentals of Linguistic Analysis*. New York: Harcourt, Brace, Jovanovich, 1972.

Pyles, Thomas. *The Origins & Development of the English Language*, 1st. ed., 1964. New York: Harcourt, Brace, Jovanovich, 1971.

Sapir, Edward. *Language*, 1st ed., 1921. New York: Harcourt, Brace & World, 1949.

Verghese, C. Paul. "Indian English." *India News*. Vol. IX, No. 24. Washington, D.C.: Embassy of India, September 4, 1970.

PART II

THE LITURGICAL ELEMENT IN THREE RELIGIOUS PLAYS:

Everyman

Samson Agonistes

Murder in the Cathedral.

CONTENTS

PREFACE

In this thesis the liturgical element in three religious plays, *Everyman*, *Samson Agonistes*, and *Murder in the Cathedral*, are explored in the light of the doxology, the rules and practices of the Anglican services of worship. The plays have often been called *liturgical dramas;* and it has been interesting to note parallels and to equate the theme, the diction, and the ideas in them with the liturgy of the *Book of Common Prayer*. Historically both the liturgy and the religious drama were outgrowths of the patristic Church, and were written to elevate man's spirit Godward; towards the heroic and the high. The plays under discussion are tragedies. They embody philosophical issues built on human experience and suffering, and in the catharsis they effect, bring out theological truths that are of perennial interest. In an age sceptical of religious truths, it is significant that literary minds have been sensitive to ethical concepts and values, and have left imprints of their belief on some of the world's greatest literature.

Chapter I

LITURGY AND DRAMA

Most critics agree that the English drama had its inception in the liturgical worship of the Church, especially in the highly dramatic ritual of the Eucharistic Mass. With the Mass, the ceremonial worship, the first portrayal of the Easter *Quem Quaeritis Trope*, the Church gave the histrionic art. The church already had sculpture and murals, the vitreous windows and chants, to make the Scripture more real to the lay worshipper. Mediaeval learning had become the prerogative of the Church and was confined to the cloisters; it was through the audio-visual approach that religious teaching could best be conveyed to the masses, and what could be better than the medium of art to bring home scriptural truths to the laity? The appeal thus was not only to the emotions of the people but also to their aesthetic sensibility and gave rise to the highest form of adoration and worship, a form in which the love of beauty and the comprehension of the infinite become one.

In studying religious plays, whether scriptural or ethical, the parallels and similarities between the dramatic presentation of the themes, and the liturgical acts of worship of the Church, seem striking and evident, and offer a field of investigation to the student concerned with promoting worship with the aid of the dramatic art. The three great religious tragedies, *Everyman, Samson Agonistes*, and *Murder in the Cathedral*, though written centuries apart, in periods ranging from the mediaeval to the age of the *new philosophy* and the sophisticated, modern times; and by men, two of whom, we know, of profound learning and deep, though different religious convictions, breathe an air of sanctity which conveys religious truths as great as any ecclesiastical homily. The plays, both in their spirit and their manner, are liturgical, and in themselves, acts of worship. Evelyn Underhill aptly points out:

> Worship, in all its grades and kinds, is the response of the creature to the Eternal . . . [it] may be overt or direct, unconscious or conscious . . . [but] is an acknowledgement of Transcendence.[1]

If worship is the transcendence of the human soul over earth-bound shackles and passions, then the three tragedies are indeed acts of worship, for in each one of the three we see the response of the creature to his Creator and the transcendence of the creature's soul over all that is mundane. The author of *Everyman*, Milton, and T.S. Eliot have all joined in worshipping God through their art. These plays, good in themselves as theatrical pieces, have the quality of the Gothic cathedral about them. The amplitude, the depth, the soaring beauty of their lines can be equated with the structural magnificence of the cathedral, and the catharsis they effect, with the sanctifying grace of the benediction.

Oscar Cargill, in *Drama and Liturgy*, observes that Charles Magnin was the first to state the connection between liturgy and drama:

> Charles Magnin, lecturing at the *Faculté des Lettres de Paris*, in 1834, first declared that the Latin liturgy was the source of the mysteries; and Marius Sepet, in 1867, in the most important book published up to that time on the drama, *Les Prophètes du Christ*, advanced a novel and fascinating hypothesis which made it possible to believe that every scene of the plays was a growth from, or a duplication of material already existing in the liturgy of the church.[2]

Cargill does not agree with this point of view of Magnin and Sepet. For him liturgy was closer to poetry than to drama:

1. Evelyn Underhill, *Worship* (New York and London: Harper and Brothers, 1937), p. 3

2. Oscar Cargill, *Drama and Liturgy* (New York: Columbia University Press, 1930), pp. 2-3.

> The only existing historical account of the development of the tropes appears to confirm my contention that they were created for lyrical expression.[3]

But it is an undeniable fact that the tropes and chants of the Church were links in the chain that gave us the English drama. The early mystery and morality plays both in theme and concept were religious:

> dramatic representations . . . popular in their aim, liturgical in their origin, taking as their subjects events which belonged strictly either to sacred history or to accepted legends, [enacted] to bring the events of the Gospels to the 'unlettered people'.[4]
>
> During the ninth and tenth centuries the germs of modern drama appeared in the elaborate ritual of the Easter service in the greater cathedrals and monasteries of Europe. The dramatic liturgies thus evolved consisted originally of a few lines of question and answer chanted responsively by priests, and taken almost literally from the Vulgate Latin lesson for the day.[5]

The liturgy of the Church was the parent stem of all religious plays; and conversely the plays often were the motifs of religious art in the cathedrals and churches.

> It is worth noting . . . that the Plays had a very powerful influence on the other arts, and that many of the arrangements of the scenes which we see in stained glass, in painting, in illuminations, in sculpture such as the English alabasters, have quite clearly been derived from the performances of these scenes in the Mystery Plays.[6]

Before proceeding further on our quest to equate the liturgical elements in *Everyman*, *Samson Agonistes*, and *Murder in the*

3. *Ibid.*, p. 14.
4. Alfred W. Pollard, ed., *English Miracle Plays, Moralities and Interludes* (Oxford: At the Clarendon Press, 1954), p. xii.
5. C.F. Tucker Brooke, *The Tudor Drama* (Boston: Houghton Mifflin, 1911), p. 2.
6. E. Martin Browne, ed., *Religious Drama 2* (New York: Meridian Books, 1958), p. 14.

Cathedral with the liturgy of the *Book of Common Prayer*, we will examine the word *liturgy*. The word is derived from the Greek term, *leitourgeo*. Liddell and Scott give an interesting history of the word. According to the writings of Demosthenes at Athens, the implication of the verb was *to serve expensive public offices at one's own cost* or *to serve these offices for another*; in general, *to perform public duties, to serve people or state*. Later, in the time of Dionysius of Halicarnassus, the verb was used in the sense of *performing religious service, to minister*. The noun forms of the word, *leitourgema* and *leitourgia* carried the meaning *the performance of a liturgy* and *a burdensome public office or duty which the richer citizens discharged at their own expense, properly by rotation but also voluntarily or by appointment*. These duties included sacred embassies, athletic games, payment of and provision for choruses at dramatic performances, and other such offices. Special exigencies of the State called for special *liturgies* as at the time of war. Though the system was chiefly Athenian, liturgies were mentioned in connection with other places of the Greek world such as Siphnus and Mytilene. Aristotle mentions it in his *Politics* and calls liturgy *the public service of the gods (Politics* 7.10.11). The significance of the word *liturgy* for the Greek, therefore, was service for others whether pleasurable or irksome, paid or voluntary; it meant an active participation in ordering the good of the people.[7]

In the Christian tradition, liturgy came to mean the service or ministry of priests as mentioned in II Corinthians 9:12; Philippians 2:30; St. Luke 1:23; and Numbers 8:25. The liturgy was thus the ministration of dedicated men to man's spiritual needs, a ministration which is considered one of the greatest public offices in Christian belief. In the wake of the liturgical force followed the religious plays. Conceived in the rites and ceremonies and dramatic observances of the Offices, the drama emerged as:

> the presentation of Jewish and Christian sacred history in much detail and in one epic sweep toward the fulfillment in Jesus of God's purpose for the redemption of man.[8]

7. Henry George Liddell and Robert Scott, *A Greek-English Lexicon* (New York: American Book Company, 1897), p. 882.
8. Willard Farnham, *The Medieval Heritage of Elizabethan Tragedy* (New York: Barnes and Noble, 1956), p. 137.

The early mystery and morality plays were the Church's didactic effort to bring man nearer to God and to prepare his soul for the much iterated everlasting bliss. Into this effort went the liturgical forms and words and rhythms, which made religious drama a continuous whole with the other liturgical practices of the Church.

On examining the liturgy of the *Book of Common Prayer*, we find that it is a compilation of the thought and work of many minds:

> [It] is not the production of a single author or a single age. It has been formed by operations slow, irregular and intermittent. Its stately fabric, with a general unity of design apparent throughout bears the impress of the thoughts of various epochs. It embodies elements of various kinds, some of which carry us back to the devotions of God's ancient people, Israel, while others took shape in the early dawn of Christianity. The East and the West have conjoined to make it what it is. . . It has been enriched . . . by the genius and the piety of saints and doctors of the Church. . . . The Church of the Fathers has bequeathed to it some of its most precious treasures. Nor are there wanting many traces of the influence of the age of the mediaeval theologians and liturgists.[9]

The religious practices of the *Torah*, the experiences of the early Church, the meditations of the Divines, the Saints, and the Church Fathers, the contemplation of devotees, and the studies of the theologians have left their mark on the liturgies of the *Book of Common Prayer*, and among its forebears, it can count the mediaeval and pre-Reformation hour and service books, the Breviary, the Missal, the Manual, the Pontifical, and the Processional. Fashioned on the Prayer Books of Edward VI (1549 and 1552), Elizabeth I (1559), and James I (1604), it was accepted soon after the Restoration in 1662 as the standard Book of Common Prayer of the State Church in England. Some of the prayers and practices of the liturgies can be traced back to Pope Gregory and the first Anglo-Saxon converts to Christianity. Names, such

9. John Dowden, *The Workmanship of the Prayer Book* (London: Churchman's Library, 1899), p. 1.

as St. Francis, St. Chrysostom, St. Gregory of Nazianzum, St. Athanasius, figure widely in the songs of praise and supplications, the creeds and thanksgiving, the rubrics and rituals. Reformers like Martin Luther, Edward Reynolds, Martin Bucer, Philip Melanchthon have also left their impress on the *Book of Common Prayer*, and to theologians like Bishop Cranmer, Robert Sanderson, and the Roman Catholic Cardinal, Cardinal Quignon, the book owes many of its doctrinal precepts. Primarily the *Book of Common Prayer* is based on the Bible, and in words as beautiful, reiterates ethical truths. The Book, therefore, is a monument of Christian thought and prayer and devotional life. From its liturgical patterns have stemmed many forms of religious art, one of the chief among them being the religious drama.

Although liturgical plays have been of interest to scattered groups all down the ages, the revival of widespread interest in them is comparatively recent. In the mediaeval and the pre-Reformation period every citizen in towns like York and Chester and Coventry had a part to play either as a patron, a participant or a spectator in the cycle of mystery plays, which were enacted annually, and formed part of the Corpus Christi or other festal processions. Later, the fragmentation of life tended to break all unity of interest, for in the wake of this active interest and participation came a disinterested tolerance of religious attitudes and practices. As the cycle of interests has to take man back to the acceptance of reality, religious values have again tended to come to the fore in the last two decades. It was after World War II that Britain revived its interest in the morality and mystery and miracle plays. York has again become a place of pilgrimage like Oberammergau. Historically the last performances of the mediaeval cycle in York is noted in the year 1572, and, now, after almost four centuries the performances have again become a recurring feature. In 1951 a compressed variety of the cycle was given, and there have been other performances since.[10] The growing interest of the people is due not only to a historical pride in their traditions or to attract the tourist trade; their interest is due to a genuine regard for their Christian heritage and its guiding values. It is part of the Liturgical Movement:

> essentially a *return* to the *standards of teaching and wor-*

10. Browne, *Religious Drama 2*, p. 305.

> *ship* to *be found in Scripture and the early Fathers* of the *Church.* Its keynotes are *both evangelical* and *catholic* in the truest sense.
>
> What gives stability and strength to the Liturgical Movement is its foundation of scientific scholarship. . . . The twentieth century has brought its wealth of historical findings into correlation with comparable advances in biblical and patristic studies.[11]

Modern scholarship has revealed many documents, which, till the end of the last century were obscure, such as "the *Didache* with its archaic prayers and rubrics of the second century . . . and the Prayer Book of Bishop Sarapion,"[12] and into the research has gone the study of the source material of the liturgical tradition and its main lines of development.

While dealing with liturgy, we come across facets of worship that are closely linked with man's spiritual urge to live a better and more complete life, a life in line with the highest ethical principles laid down by thinkers through the ages. In the liturgy we note distinct paths to the core of worship; these may be classified as laud or praise of the Highest, thanksgiving, confession and contrition, obedience to the will of God, sacrifice, and the acceptance of God's mercies and blessings, the last being the logical outcome of the soul's triumph over the lower self. Herein lies the theme of salvation which gives purpose to the plays under discussion and leads to the drama of worship.

> Worship, then, at every level, always means God and the priority of God. . . We in our worshipping action are compelled to move within the devotional sphere, with all its symbolic furniture, its archaic survivals, its pitfalls, its risks of sentimentalism, herd-suggestion, and disguised self-regard.[13]

Like the liturgies of the Church, the religious plays are concrete expressions of this spirit of worship and embody much of

11. Massey Hamilton Shepard, *The Liturgical Movement and the Prayer Book* (Evanston, IL: Seabury-Western Theological Seminary, 1946), p. 10.
12. *Ibid.*, p. 12.
13. Underhill, *Worship*, p. 6.

the paraphernalia of life. Man as *embodied spirit* can use only those materials which are at his command to express himself. The mediaeval artist portrayed many vignettes of life on one canvas, thus giving body to scattered thoughts. Similarly the dramatist picks up variegated threads of life and weaves them into a unified act of worship.

> The painted cave of those prehistoric worshippers of an unknown God, . . . the pagan temple, the Christian Cathedral, all are expressions of the same fundamental human need to incorporate, make visible, the spirit of worship; to lavish skill, labour, and wealth on [it].[14]

This skill and labour is finite, because of man's limitations. Words, music, colours, rhythmic patterns, histrionic gestures and movements, imagery, symbols, sacrificial acts, sacramental offerings and human experience are a few limited means that the liturgist or the religious playwright can use as his response to the Ultimate Soul. The outward form of worship takes the shape of

> agreed symbols and established formulas and rites. A religious ritual is an agreed pattern of ceremonial movements, sounds, verbal formulas, creating a framework within which corporate religious action can take place. . . . Its greatest creation—e.g., the Eucharistic liturgy—are sacred dramas, in which the mystery of salvation is re-enacted and re-experienced by the worshipping group.[15]

This relationship of God and man can hardly be expressed outwardly; it is as elusive and nebulous as death. Religious rites try to codify this relationship, and make the appeal of the rituals compelling for the individual as for the group. Liturgy such as that of the *Book of Common Prayer* is so fashioned that it progressively uplifts the soul of the votary from despondency to hope, and provides spiritual sustenance for the seeker after truth. Religious plays perform the same function, for they help man to transcend his earthly failures and desires, and achieve spiritual

14. *Ibid.*, p. 14.
15. *Ibid.*, pp. 22, 32.

sublimity. Though the liturgy and liturgical plays have much in common, it is hardly feasible to equate everything in the *Book of Common Prayer* with the plays under discussion in this paper, but while examining the plays, we come across elements that are reminiscent of the liturgy of the Church; the prayers and supplications, the thanksgiving and adoration, the acquiescence to the Will of God and the acceptance of the inevitable self-sacrifice. These are part of the liturgy as well as the drama of life.

In the conduct of any formal worship, the two essential elements are the voiced conscience, personified by the priest; and the suppliant for grace, the receptive devotee, who for the moment annihilates his individuality and lays himself open to the guidance of a superior power, be it God or his own psyche. The communion between the two elements has to be close and intimate, for the one urges and the other aspires to the highest. In *Everyman*, *Samson Agonistes*, and *Murder in the Cathedral*, the playwrights have used these two aspects of formal liturgical worship most felicitously.

F.H. Brabant says:

> All liturgical acts—whether they use words (ritual in the narrower sense), or actions (ceremonial proper)—have a double function; one directed Godwards, expressing in outward form the thoughts and feelings of the worshippers, the other directed manwards, teaching the worshippers how they ought to think and feel by setting before them the Church's standard of worship.[16]

Here are the two axes, the vertical pointing Godwards, and the horizontal, where earthbound man accepts God's grace through the Church's ministrations; the priest being the agent. In *Everyman*, the priest or verbal conscience, is first provided by Death and then Good Deeds and Knowledge. The Chorus of the Danites and Manoah, by turn, perform the same function in *Samson Agonistes;* while the women of Canterbury in *Murder in the Cathedral*, and paradoxically to an extent, the tempters, echo the thoughts of Becket, who is his own High Priest as well as the protagonist in the play. The three devotees are Everyman, Sam-

16. F. H. Brabant, "Worship in General," *Liturgy and Worship*, edited by W.K. Lowther Clark and Charles Harris (London: S.P.C.K., 1933), p. 12.

son and Thomas a Becket; they are the suers after grace and yet are the prototype of Christ. In words with which Lowther Clark describes Christ's incarnation, we can sum up the playwrights' purpose for our three protagonists:

> The purpose of the Incarnation[is] to live the life of perfect obedience under conditions . . . which hitherto have led men to withhold obedience. . . . And that homage is rendered under the most difficult conditions of all —humiliation, disgrace, and intense suffering—so that the cross is the typical and culminating act of obedience and sacrifice that saves the world. (*Cf.* Phil. ii.8)[17]

In Everyman, Samson and Thomas a Becket, we see the struggling soul; each in its individualty representing the soul of humanity. The struggle is to free itself of the earth, while still attracted by its glamour, the glamour which takes the shape of vice, pride and even martyrdom for the wrong reason. Each is victorious at the crucial moment. Like the death on the cross, each tragedy is a triumph, for man conquers his own unfitness and is deified.

In examining the liturgical elements in *Everyman, Samson Agonistes*, and *Murder in the Cathedral*, we shall follow the Eucharistic Mass, the service of *Matins*, and excerpts from the other offices of the Anglican *Book of Common Prayer*, keeping in mind that the first religious plays in the English language were the outcropping of the liturgy of the Church.

17. Clark and Harris, *Liturgy and Worship*, p. 7.

Chapter II

THE LITURGICAL ELEMENT

Introit

The *Introit*, or the approach of the priest to the altar, is first mentioned in mediaeval literature as having originated in the time of Gregory the Great. It was one of the most spectacular performances of the Church:

> When all the preparations for the Mass were finished and the candles were lit, the *Schola Cantorum*, the Paraphonistae and the boys placed themselves in two rows before the altar, according to their rank, and the chief of the singers, the *Prior Scholae*, intoned the antiphon to the Introit (that is, he gave the air for the psalms or the trope). At this moment the Pontiff, with his retinue, proceeded from the Sacristy into the Church. On arriving at the altar, and after adoring the Holy Host, he gave a sign to the *Prior Scholae* that he was to start the *Gloria* (at the end of the psalm). Bowing to the Pontiff, he obeyed his command. At the end of the *Sicut erat*, the Pontiff went from the altar to his seat, and the whole concluded with the antiphon.[1]

The *Introit* in itself was a dramatic ritual. Its psychological impact was that it gave a corporate sense of interest and unity to the congregation, and helped to align the mind with the service that followed. The approach to the altar was symbolic of the approach to the throne of the King, and required the elaborate

1. Cargill, *Drama and Liturgy*, p. 22.

ceremony described above. In some churches, the *Introit* is still an essential ritual preceding the actual service, and acts as the harbinger of awe and solemnity for the entire proceedings. Its chants can be supplications for guidance and directive; they can also help to inspire and inflame the heart of the worshipper. The voice raised in praise or thanksgiving "greatly aids devotion. It is not only the outlet, but, to a great extent, the exciting cause of devotion."[2] The invocation becomes man's response to God and man's preparation for the final surrender.

With a feeling of awe, such as inspired by seraphic voices intoning the psalms of the *Introit* or the tones of a vibrant organ filling the vaults of the cathedral, one approaches liturgical plays. *Everyman*, a morality, with its four extant English editions, written about the fifteenth century, is a homily, which makes men aware of God's prevening grace and His great act of salvation. Everyman is

> an essential representation of the common run of humanity, which has become more sinful than it used to be, as God declares in his opening words, and is to be chastised by some extraordinary visitation of death such as a plague. [It is] morality adhering to the earliest fashion of abstracting all mankind in one character.[3]

The tragedy, because of its universal character, has a general appeal, death, the leveller, comes to all and salvation is available if desired. The cycle, beginning with the conflict of virtue and vice, is followed by spiritual rebirth, physical death, and rejuvenation, and forms the theme of the play.

With *Samson Agonistes*, a mystery and a morality, we enter a realm of perfection. However virulently Johnson might censure the play as lacking a middle, it is a masterpiece, equalled, if at all, by few. This tragic drama of Milton was a long-deliberated play. As early as 1641, Milton had mentioned Samson as a possible Biblical theme for a play, but it was not till after the Restoration that the tragedy was written. The play is a model of ancient Greek tragedy, although in his introductory note, Milton explicitly states that he has not followed the stanzaic pattern of the

2. Samuel Fuller, *Characteristic Excellences of the Liturgy* (Boston: 1845), p.3.
3. Farnham, *The Medieval Heritage of Elizabethan Tragedy*, p. 203.

Greek tragedies, and that it is modelled on ancient Greek as well as contemporary Italian patterns. It was meant as a closet drama, not to be acted on the Restoration Stage; "Division into Act and Scene referring chiefly to the Stage (to which this work never was intended) is here omitted."[4] Milton could not associate anything of a religious nature with levity. In "An Apology for Smectymnuus," he scathingly says:

> In the colleges so many of the young divines, and those in next aptitude to divinity, have been seen so oft upon the stage, writhing and unboning their clergy limbs to all the antics and dishonest gestures of Trinculos.[5]

To him a Biblical theme like Samson had to be solemn, soaring, and didactic, yet he does indulge in flights of humour, for Milton was far from devoid of humour in the modern sense of the word. *Samson Agonistes* is liturgical. It breathes a sanctity which makes it rank with the best religious literature of the world, and performs the great service of enriching the mind aesthetically and ethically.

Murder in the Cathedral, written for the Canterbury Festival in 1935, and first performed in the Chapter House of Canterbury Cathedral in that year, is also a tragedy based on the Greek models:

> The model is the earlier plays of Aeschylus, as Professor Murray says, "There is one great situation in which the poet steeps our minds, with at most one or two sudden flashes of action passing over it."[6]

Its theme, the martyrdom of Becket, overawes the entire play. Characters other than the protagonist are puppets that revolve around the monolithic figure of the Archbishop. The play has an aura of impending doom; it is only Becket's acquiescence to the Will of God and release from his spiritual pride, which re-

4. John Milton, "Of That Sort of Dramatic Poem Which is Call'd Tragedy," *John Milton, Paradise Regained, The Minor Poems and Samson Agonistes*, edited by Merritt J. Hughes (New York: The Odessey Press, 1937), p.540.

5. John Milton, "An Apology for Smectymnuus," *John Milton Prose Selections*, edited by Merritt J. Hughes (New York: The Odessey Press, 1947), p. 153.

6. Helen Gardner, *The Art of T.S. Eliot* (London and Hartford: E.P. Dutton, 1950), p. 135.

deem the sombre character of the play, and make it rank with the other two liturgical dramas.

The three playwrights have approached their subject with deep religious convictions. They believe in the fallibility of man and do not treat him as a demi-god, however strong he is as the universal man or the elect of the nation or the religious head of a realm. He has still to be sustained by a power greater than himself and a moral force that is transcendent. The human quality of these plays makes the drama of salvation poignantly real and aligns the plays with the liturgical practices of the Church. They too lead the votary to the altar as does the priest in presenting himself before it.

The Invocation

"O send out Thy light and Thy truth, that they may lead me, and bring me unto Thy holy hill, and to Thy dwelling,"[7] cries the psalmist, like one who is blind. The priest iterates the sentence, for himself and his spiritually blind flock, invoking the Holy Spirit at the beginning of the Order for Daily Morning Prayer, for God's presence is essential to worship. Every act of worship, whether formal or only a sigh for the infinite, presupposes a Deity and communion with Him. The suppliant approaches the Deity with awe and with the feeling that, "The Lord is in his holy temple, let all the earth keep silence."[8] In the invocation can be seen "the soul's deep and awestruck apprehension of the numinous."[9] The Eternal Presence may be real for the worshipper, but the mystery around the Presence is just as real and always mystifying. In the offices of the Prayer Book, these invocations are codified into oft-repeated words, yet they have the devotional fervour and spontaneity with which they were first uttered by poets and worshippers. Nor is the dramatic element absent in these liturgical invocations; the cry for assistance is as soulful as that of Everyman in the play:

Our Lord Jesus help me![10]

7. Psalm 43:3, *The Holy Bible,* King James' Version.
8. Habakkuk 2:20, *The Holy Bible,* p. 690.
9. Underhill, *Worship,* p. 112.
10. E. Martin Browne, ed., "Everyman," *Religious Drama* 2, p. 286.

A direct, simple statement, it has all the poignancy of distress, yet its very utterance shows that Everyman is progressing towards salvation. He has entered the lists of those who are militantly determined to be redeemed by invoking God's help:

> O gracious God in the high seat celestial
> Have mercy on me in this most need![11]

Not until Everyman becomes conscious of his jeopardy does he invoke God's help.

The invocation does not come too early in the play; it is when Everyman is dramatically ready to become the humble votary and the suppliant that he calls on God, and like the worshipper, brings his own failures and distress to the altar. The time-old struggle between good and evil continues in Everyman's soul. This is a struggle that accompanies man to the end and evokes deep emotion in him. Bunyan says:

> The Christian . . . deeply sensible of the divine mercy in providing in the blood of Christ a ransom for his guilt, by which he can escape eternal death, involuntarily breaks forth in words, either of penitence or gratitude —his voice spontaneously expresses the emotions of his soul.[12]

Such are the the short, pithy, liturgical cries of Everyman as he sues for grace and invokes God's help.

The very words with which *Samson Agonistes* opens are an invocation for guidance. It is true the words are addressed to the boy who leads Samson forward, but a meaningful depth is sounded in the liturgical plea:

> A little onward lend Thy guiding hand
> To these dark steps, a little further on.[13]

The words convey the protagonist's frame of mind as well as his

11. *Ibid.*, p. 272.
12. Fuller, *Characteristic Excellences of the Liturgy*, p. 2.
13. John Milton, *Samson Agonistes*, edited by H.M. Percival (London: Macmillan and Co., 1916), p. 7, Lines 1-2.

physical state. His wish is to be led into "The breath of Heav'n fresh-blowing, pure and sweet."[14]

Samson, unconsciously, is invoking Nature's benediction to assuage his mental and physical unrest, and to re-create his rudely wrecked integrity and self-respect. In the monologue, he recalls his election and careful upbringing as a Nazarite, his unfortunate enslavement to a woman and then the Philistines; but he is humble, and accepts the will and wisdom of Providence, saying:

> I must not quarrel with the will
> Of highest dispensation, which herein
> Haply had ends above my reach to know.[15]

The words are almost sinister in their portent; they help Samson to build the mental attitude which progressively prepares him for the last act of worship, the final sacrifice and acquiescence to God's will. The invocation is liturgical. It asks for a renewal of the right spirit within Samson, the suppliant, at a time of his worst affliction. Like the psalmist and the priest, the plea is for *light* and *truth*.

The Invocation in *Murder in the Cathedral* takes quite another form. It is voiced in the subtle choric chant, and mirrors the mood of the Archbishop. It is a cry for help to stop the Archbishop from committing the sin of pride in wilful suicide, and to save himself from the *utter, uttermost death of the spirit:*

> I have consented, Lord Archbishop, have consented
> Am torn away, subdued, violated,
> United to the spiritual flesh of nature
> Mastered by the animal powers of spirit,
> Dominated by the lust of self-demolition,
> By the final utter, uttermost death of spirit
> By the final ecstasy of waste and shame,
> O Lord Archbishop, O Thomas Archbishop, forgive us, forgive
> Us, pray for us that we may pray for you, out of our shame.[16]

14. *Ibid.*, p. 7, Line 10.
15. *Ibid.*, p. 8, Line 60.
16. T.S. Eliot, "Murder in tehe Cathedral," *The Complete Poems and Plays, 1909-1950* (New York: Harcourt, Bruce & Co., 1952), p. 208.

It is the *lust for self-demolition* that Thomas must fight, the desire for martyrdom, and he requires assistance to master it. The invocation is to God's strength in him, and the dependence is on prayer, his own and that of the chorus.

The liturgical invocation therefore takes different forms in the plays and the Prayer Book. The Greek and the Mozarabic liturgies, which are two of the sources of the Prayer Book, stressed the Invocation to the Holy Spirit as essential in the Eucharistic Mass, but the rite was modified in the *Book of Common Prayer*. The invocation can be considered a call for God's presence or His help, and a means whereby the devotee can concentrate on worship. In the Eucharist, it becomes a plea for the cleansing action of the Holy Spirit. The invocation has several functions; it can express awe and wonder, gratitude or rededication of the individual, a need for the spirit of worship, and thankfulness for God's blessing. In the plays mentioned above, the invocation is a simple plea for God's help; a plea for a mental attitude preparatory to acceptance of a hazardous quest for the sublime and the necessary annihilation of self-pride. In the invocation lies the germ of the heroic action; the potential that will lead to the catharasis, and exonerate man of all dross and sin.

The Exhortations

The invocatory statements are addressed to a Power beyond man; in them the vertical axis of worship comes into play. In the exhortations that follow, the attention is turned to the horizontal axis, to earthbound man and his failings.

J.H. Snawley, in his essay, "The Holy Communion Service," calls the Exhortations

> . . .a series of formularies dealing with the more immediate preparation of the communicants . . . intended to supply the lack of oral instruction.[17]

He adds that the

> . . .exhortation is a call to self-examination and repentance, and to the right disposition befitting the worthy reception of the Sacrament.[18]

17. J.H. Snawley, "The Holy Communion," *Liturgy and Worship*, ed. Clark and Harris, p. 326.
18. *Ibid.*, p. 326.

The priest urges the worshipper to prepare himself for God's grace in words such as "acknowledge and confess your manifold sins . . . with an humble, lowly, penitent, and contrite heart";[19] "make your humble confession to Almighty God, meekly kneeling upon your knee";[20] "be in perfect charity with all men";[21] "search and examine your own conscience, and that not lightly, and after the manner of dissemblers with God; but so that ye may come holy and clean";[22] "examine your lives and conversations. . .; whereinsoever ye shall perceive yourselves to have offended, either by will, word, or deed, there to bewail your own sinfulness and to confess yourselves to Almighty God, with full purpose of amendment of life."[23] The votary is told to come with "a quiet conscience" and not to have "feigned excuses . . . before God."[24]

The fragmentary exhortations quoted from the liturgies of Matin and the Eucharist are yardsticks to help the devotee in measuring his own worth, and are links in the drama of his spiritual rejuvenation.

In *Everyman*, these exhortations are provided in turn by Death, Good Deeds, and Knowledge. Death accosts Everyman with the provocative question, "Hast thou thy Maker forgot?"[25] The question unloosens trends of thought that change the entire course of Everyman's life. So far he has been unconscious of death. His mind beset by *fleshly lusts, and his treasure,* there is no conflict between the forces of good and evil in him; he is treading the "primrose path" of dalliance and is unconcerned with thoughts of heaven. He is shaken out of his complacency when told "Thy book of count with thee, thou bring."[26] "How thou hast spent they life, and in what wise."[27] The words are a challenge for retrospection. Everyman realizes that his life has not been what was expected of him, that the bad outweighs the good. The moment is both liturgical in its significance and highly dramatic in its revelation. The suddenness of the calamity is overwhelming, for Death has "no respite" for Everyman, yet Death allows him

19. *The Book of Common Prayer*, New York, 1945, p. 5.
20. *Ibid.*, p. 75.
21. *Ibid.*, p. 86.
22. *Ibid.*, p. 87.
23. *Ibid.*, p. 88.
24. *Ibid.*, p. 89.
25. Browne, "Everyman," *Religious Drama 2*, p. 269.
26. *Ibid.*, p. 270.
27. *Ibid.*, p. 271.

time to take stock of himself, exhorting him to penitence in the following words:

> Thou hast thy wits five
> And here on earth will not amend thy life,[28]

and leaves him to work out his own salvation. Like the priest, Death has led Everyman towards righteousness; Good Deeds and Knowledge show him the way further in their liturgical exhortations:

> Good Deeds: . . .go. . .Before the Blessed Trinity.[29]

Knowledge conducts Everyman to confession. He is adjured to "abstinence and perseverance in God's presence," and told:

> For your time draweth fast: and ye will saved be
> Ask God mercy and he will grant truly.[30]

The exhortation is for him to accept the pain of suffering patiently for then alone will God's mercy flow towards him in the Holy Sacrament and the Extreme Unction. His penance consists not only in suing for forgiveness and grace, but in mortifying the flesh by scourgings and the hairy shirt of contrition. He is told to proceed towards martyrdom, the last road to salvation. As Monsieur Saurat says of Samson,[31] the drama is set in Everyman's soul; it is as powerful in its homiletic quality as the Mass; it is a drama of the soul's progress.

The exhortations in *Samson Agonistes* reiterate self-examination and preparation for the moments of test. In the liturgy of the Mass, ". . .the intention [of the exhortation] is that priest and people should alike share in the preparation."[32] In *Samson Agonistes*, the protagonist, the Chorus, and Manoah all prepare themselves, though unwittingly, for the last sacrifice and

28. *Ibid.*, p. 272.
29. *Ibid.*, p. 287.
30. *Ibid.*, p. 289.
31. Denis Saurat, *Milton: Man and Thinker* (London: Dent, 1944), p. 236.
32. Clark and Harris, *Liturgy and Worship*, p. 310.

the acceptance of God's will. Manoah, in reproaching his son for his failure to serve God, gives him material for thought, and challenges Samson to a re-evaluation of his mission. Manoah emphasizes that due to his folly Dagon will be glorified while God is blasphemed:

> Which to have come to pass by means of thee
> Samson, of all thy sufferings think the heaviest,
> Of all reproach the most with shame that ever
> Could have befallen thee and thy father's house.[33]

In referring to Samson's misfortune and shame, he is helping his son to rekindle his desire for action and the destruction of God's and his enemies. Samson's faith in God's might and ascendancy is unshaken, and he is indignant and bemused that "Dagon hath presumed . . . to enter lists with God."[34] Manoah's exhortation, though couched in words of blame, has the desired effect on the hero; it cleans his doubts and strengthens his belief. Manoah goes on to say, in lyrical language, like the priest intoning the liturgical exhortations:

> Be penitent, and for thy fault contrite;
> But act not in thy own affliction, son.
> Repent the sin; but, if the punishment
> Thou canst avoid, self-preservation bids;
> Or the execution leave to high disposal,
> And let another hand, not thine, exact
> Thy penal forfeit from thyself.[35]

He feels that perhaps God wants Samson to return to his country and to serve God in the tabernacle with prayers and renewed vows. Manoah can not visualise an active life for his blind son, but everything he says, paradoxically enough, acts as a stimulus for Samson to use his physical prowess once more. He is "the chosen and dedicated servant of God, definitely conscious of his vocation, animated by faith and zeal."[36] Manoah is pitiless in goading Samson to action:

33. Milton, *Samson Agonistes*, p. 19, Line 445.
34. *Ibid.*, p. 20, Line 462.
35. *Ibid.*, p. 21, Lines 502 ff.
36. George Wesley Whiting, *Milton and This Pendant World* (Austin: University of Texas Press, 1958), p. 218.

Wilt thou then serve the Philistines with that gift
Which was expressly given thee to annoy them?
. . . . . .why else this strength
Miraculous yet remaining in these locks?
His might continues in thee not for naught,
Nor shall his wondrous gifts be frustrate thus.[37]

No priestly exhortation could be a better goad than these scathing remarks of Manoah, or his query as to the reason of Samson's returning strength. They do not miss their mark; nor does he let his son wallow in "the slough of despondency";

Believe not these suggestions, which proceed
From anguish of the mind, and humours black
That mingle with thy fancy.[38]

The Chorus takes the cue from Manoah and in liturgical passages exhorts Samson to a patience like Job's and to long suffering, asking him to sue for strength from above:

Some source of consolation from above
Secret refreshings that repair his strength
And fainting spirits uphold.[39]

The afflicted requires inner strength as does the sinner who comes to the altar for refreshment. Samson in the passage is pressed to draw his strength from Heaven.

The exhortation in *Murder in the Cathedral* is subtle and comes early in the play, as seen in the ominous words of the Chorus:

Here let us stand, close by the cathedral. Here let us wait
Are we drawn by danger? Is it the knowledge of safety that draws our feet
Towards the cathedral?[40]

37. Milton, *Samson Agonistes*, p. 23, L. 577 ff.
38. *Ibid.*, p. 23, Line 599.
39. *Ibid.*, p. 25, Line 664.
40. T.S. Eliot, "Murder in the Cathedral," *The Complete Poems and Plays*, p. 175.

The cathedral is the stronghold of hope and faith; security seems to lie in its shadow despite the conflict between the State and the Church. Through the years of unrest, the equilibrium of the rank and file had been shaken, yet their salvation lay in adherence to the Church. Like St. Peter, they vacillate between the material, warmth-giving fire, and the love for the Master; but their very presence near the Cathedral, as that of Christ to St. Peter, lends strength to themselves. Their exhortation to each other is to stand by the Cathedral, the symbol of their belief.

> . . .We wait, we wait
> And the saints and martyrs wait, for those who shall be martyrs and saints.[41]

Their waiting is impelling martyrdom, not the false martyrdom steeped in pride, but martyrdom for the cause, the glory of God. It is also to vindicate the Church as the home of the saint and the released sinner, and not that of the high-minded semi-politicians, semi-ecclesiasts. Becket's besetting sin had been evident:

> I know that the pride bred of sudden prosperity
> Was but confirmed by bitter adversity.[42]

The exhortations are for the exoneration of the sin of pride and an unmixed martyrdom.

"Fare forward, forward to the end,"[43] says the last Tempter, but his pointer to martyrdom is to the way of pride, "To do the right thing for the wrong reason."[44] The exhortation is there, but it is not till Becket leaves it to the direction of his "good Angel" that it turns effectively towards salvation. The exhortations given by the Chorus, the priests, and the tempters all point the way to martyrdom, but martyrdom without pride.

Confession and Petition

Confession presupposes guilt on the part of the individual and acceptance of its avowal on the part of the Confessor. Unlike

41. *Ibid.*, p. 176.
42. *Ibid.*, p. 178.
43. *Ibid.*, p. 191.
44. *Ibid.*, p. 196.

adoration, confession is not motiveless, for the one who confesses requires a return of some sort.

> Worship is essentially disinterested . . . but prayer is only in some of its aspects disinterested. One offers, the other asks. . . .[45]

The petition may be just a prayer for grace or mercy, but is closely allied to confession, for the former is the natural outcome of the latter.

The priest's exhortation in the *Morning Prayer* to "acknowledge and confess the manifold sins" is followed by a General Confession. The confession is repeated by the congregation "with a pure heart and humble voice, meekly kneeling."[46] The General Confession is one of the most compact and concise expressions of guilt and is charged with meaning. It confesses the waywardness of the worshippers, in the scriptural and symbolic language of the lost sheep leaving the fold and the paths of righteousness of God, the Good Shepherd. It acknowledges the wilfulness of man in following his own behests rather than God's laws. It confesses to sins of omission and commission, and to a state of degeneration and mental and spiritual imbalance; but it has provision for penitence and petition for God's grace, grace to live a "godly, righteous and sober life."[47]

The General Confession of the Eucharist is even more provocative, for in it man confesses his *manifold sins and wickedness* which have been committed from *time to time* and not only in action, but also in thoughts and words. In it, the timelessness of evil appears just as real as that of good, and man's tragedy lies as much in his mental attitude as in his speech or his actions. Dramatically, the penitent says,

> We do earnestly repent, And are heartily sorry for these our misdoings; The remembrance of them is grievous unto us; The burden of them is intolerable.[48]

45. Underhill, *Worship*, p. 9.
46. *The Book of Common Prayer*, p. 6.
47. *Ibid.*, p. 6.
48. *Ibid.*, p. 75.

In these short sentences lies the pith of the drama of life.

It is only when man becomes conscious of his failures and shortcomings and finds his sins overwhelming, that he tries to alleviate the pain and reach for help. Man is both a realist and a visionary, but often for him the vision of life lies obscured, till he himself becomes conscious of its obscurity and tries to seek reality. Reality is an awareness of himself, a lesson learnt in humility at the confessional or the altar. The penitent asks for mercy and forgiveness so that he can "Serve and please God in newness of life."[49] Regeneration is the reward. Confession is a voluntary catharsis, for it helps purge guilt psychologically.

The confessional element in *Everyman* is as liturgical as that of the Prayer Book. Everyman appears carefree, absorbed in the world and its pleasures; and full of self-reliance and self-love, he banks on his worldly goods and treasures. When Death accosts him, he asks falteringly, "What, sent to me?"[50] The words show a shock of recognition of both his end and his folly. He is made aware of the transitoriness of life, and with this awareness begins his regeneration. Death, on posing the question has awakened thought in him; thought which was latent and begrimed. He is troubled in mind:

> To give a reckoning longer leisure I crave
> This blind matter troubleth my wit.[51]

Death points out that his sins outweigh his righteous deeds, and tells him to examine his own past: "How thou hast spent thy life and in what wise."[52] Here comes in the element of retrospection and contemplation. Everyman is face to face with his situation; Death has told him that he himself has to be his attorney, for he is allowed no intermediaries; yet the obstinacy and obdurateness of the seasoned sinner keeps Everyman from accepting the inevitable:

> Full unready I am such a reckoning to give
> I know thee not. What messenger art thou?[53]

49. *Ibid.*
50. Browne, "*Everyman*," *Religious Drama 2*, p. 270.
51. *Ibid.*, p. 270.
52. *Ibid.*
53. *Ibid.*, p. 271.

The statement is a deliberate denial of reality; Everyman is deluding himself on purpose, the reality is too stark and poignant for him to accept. He needs time to orientate his mind to penitential preparation and the final act of worship, acquiesence to the will of God. His mind dwells on the world and his possessions, even to the extent of his offering a bribe to Death to avert the final blow. The sinner in him is vascillating between the world and God. Everyman finds the suddenness of the calamity overwhelming: "Alas, shall I have no longer respite?"[54] He is told that time and tide do not wait and that on account of his original sin, man must die. Convinced of the predicament Everyman's mental tragedy ripens into a stoic acceptance of any available respite, whether it be God's grace or his own repentance. He is troubled enough to desire companionship. Self-accusation, the hallmark of the penitent, is often on his lips in liturgical cries and reiterations of the Scriptural passages:

> O wretched caitiff, whither shall I flee
> That I might 'scape this endless sorrow![55]

His abjection and despair are complete for his friends abjure his company, and his book of accounts is "full unready."[56] He recalls events in his life that were pleasing; like Samson and Becket, he too has had good fellowship: "Been good friends in sport and play."[57] He wants friends to re-strengthen him in his jeopardy, but instead, he meets subtle temptation, as do his counterparts in the other two plays:

> My true friend, show to me your mind;
> I will not forsake thee to my life's end
> In the way of good company.[58]

Fellowship, like Delilah, feigns distress at Everyman's state, but empathizes with him more from curiosity than concern, and so he is prompted to say: "Show me your grief and say no

54. *Ibid.*
55. *Ibid.*
56. *Ibid.*, p. 272.
57. *Ibid.*, p. 273.
58. *Ibid.*, p. 274.

more."[59] Fellowship's evasions and excuses soon shake Everyman's credulity. His disillusionment is complete when he realizes that he can have companions in crime and lust, but not in adversity. He is left to his own devices in words that suggest Eliot's lyrics: "For you I will remember that parting is mourning."[60] The lyrical despair of the passage beginning, "Alack! Shall we thus depart indeed"[61] shows the conflict in the protagonist's mind. In preparing himself for the end, he acknowledges his sins of commission and omission:

> Also of ill deeds that I have used
> In my time sith life was me lent
> And of all virtues that I have refused.[62]

Yet it is difficult for him to uproot himself from the world, from his kith and kin and pleasures. He cannot accept the candid avowal and refusal of his cousin. The Cousin is as direct as the "straight-forward Englishman" of *Murder in the Cathedral* when he says:

> Trust not to me; for, so God me speed,
> I will deceive you in your most need.[63]

Everyman is tenacious. He attempts to hold his Cousin but is rebuffed and told that every individual is accountable for his own soul; a restatement of mediaeval theology. At this juncture Everyman's cry is Faustian in his despair: "Ah, Jesus, is all come hereto?"[64] Everyman seeks the comfort of friends, riches and goods; he is conscious of his diseased mental state, and requires sustenance from sources other than himself. The liturgy says, "For there is no health in us";[65] Everyman acknowledges: "It is another disease that grieveth me."[66] He knows the transitory nature of the world, but as he vacillates he sinks deeper into sin

59. *Ibid.*, p. 275.
60. *Ibid.*, p. 278.
61. *Ibid.*
62. *Ibid.*, p. 280.
63. *Ibid.*
64. *Ibid.*, p. 281.
65. *The Book of Common Prayer*, p. 6.
66. Browne, "Everyman," *Religious Drama* 2, p. 282.

and its ensnarement. He censures himself in blaming his treasures, as Samson does Delilah:

> Thou traitor to God that hast deceived me
> And caught me in thy snare![67]

But in the reply, aptly like that of Delilah to Samson: "Ere I to thee, thou to thyself was cruel,"[68] Everyman is told, "Marry, thou brought thyself in care."[69] These staments of allegorical characters as in *Everyman*, or of concrete Biblical personages in *Samson Agonistes*, reflect phases of the conflict in the protagonist's mind. Everyman perceives that life has nothing more to offer him, that he has to be reconciled, but he agonizes over all he loved and has to leave. His loneliness leads him to contrition, "O to whom shall I make my moan. . . ."[70] He is abashed at his folly and reorients his thinking when he decides to approach his Good Deeds. Everyman is a drama of man's soul; his mental pilgrimage in search of ultimate truth. Contrition and confession help him to discern the way:

> O glorious fountain, that all uncleanness doth clarify,
> Wash from me the spots of vice unclean,
> That on me no sin may be seen!
> I come, with *Knowledge*, for my redemption,
> Redempt with heart and full contribution.[71]

The confession is liturgical in tone and in significance. Everyman, accompanied by Knowledge, asks for Redemption. The playwright of *Everyman* is conscious that Knowledge, both subjective and objective, is the key to the understanding of God and salvation. Everyman seeks salvation not only by penance but by mortification of the flesh. He scourges himself and puts on the hairy shirt of contrition in preparation for sainthood; mortifying his flesh which, like Samson's, had been a cause of his unconcern and forgetfulness of things supra-mundane.

67. *Ibid.*, p. 284.
68. Milton, *Samson Agonistes*, p. 29, Line 784.
69. Browne, "Everyman," *Religious Drama 2*, p. 284.
70. *Ibid.*, p. 285.
71. *Ibid.*, p. 288.

Forgive me my grievous offence

. . . .

Hear my clamorous complaint though it late be.
Receive my prayers unworthy in this heavy life
Though I be a sinner most abominable
Yet let my name be written in Moses table.[72]

Everyman's anxiety for grace is intense in that passage, and it culminates in the cry, "O Jesus, help! All hath forsaken me!" Dramatically he is at the nadir of despair. Though Everyman has been progressing towards recovery, the moments of abjection never leave him. This last lamentation comes when he is passing through *the valley of the shadow of death*, in complete isolation, bereft of all aid. Beatty and Parks call the play "medieval in spirit and Catholic in doctrine."[73] It has Catholic and theological overtones in its successive themes of sin, awakening, contrition, and confession; and retribution. The mediaeval Everyman leaves all his worldly attachments; and is shriven for the end.

Samson Agonistes begins on a note of utter dejection and frustration. In it, confession is preceded by self-examination, self-accusation, and the conflict between pride and humility. Samson recalls past events, not subjectively, but in relation to the moot question asked by the Chorus: "God of our fathers! What is Man?"[74] Samson accepts his own part in the fall, which Whiting calls "his own lust and moral blindness,"[75] but reason fails him in comprehending how one elect of God and dedicated since birth to his service could be tempted and tried and humiliated as he was:

Why was my breeding ordered and prescribed
As of a person separate to God
Designed for great exploits, if I must die
Betrayed, captived, and both my eyes put out,
Made of my enemies the scorn and gaze,

72. *Ibid.*, p. 290.

73. Edd Winfield Parks and Richard Croom Beatty, eds, *The English Drama*. An Anthology 900-1642 (New York: W. W. Norton and Company, Inc., 1935), p. 57.

74. Milton, *Samson Agonistes*, p. 25, Line 667.

75. Whiting, *Milton and the Pendant World*, p. 213.

To grind in brazen fetters under task
With this heaven-gifted strength?[76]

He questions God's providence, yet tries to rationalize it, but without conviction.

God, when he gave me strength, to show withal
How slight the gift was, hung it in my hair
But peace! I must not quarrel with the will
Of highest dispensation, which herein
Haply had ends above my reach to know.[77]

This statement of acceptance of his calamities as God's dispensation is not convincing, and is followed by his most bitter complaint:

But chief of all
O loss of sight, of thee I most complain.[78]

Samson's suffering is mental and physical. Monsieur Saurat says that Milton "sets his drama in Samson's soul."[79] In reality, it is the drama of a man suffering mental agony as well as physical strain. Samson is going through the throes of self-inflicted penance of the sinner aspiring to sainthood. But Samson's aspiration is for no sainthood; his desire like Milton's, is to glorify God and justify His ways to idol worshippers, whether they are the followers of Dagon, or the lax court of the Restoration. In the beginning of the play, there seems no way out for Samson. Self-examination and contemplation lead to greater dejection and self-contempt. The thought that he was a stooge, a garrulous and gullible fool in the hands of an unscrupulous wanton is rasping: "But I God's counsel have not kept. . . ."[80] He goes through what Clark calls "the 'negative moment' of repentance [where] the sinner feels despair and horror of himself."[81] It becomes the

76. Milton, *Samson Agonistes*, p. 8, Line 30.
77. *Ibid.*, p. 9, Line 58.
78. *Ibid.*, p. 9, Line 66 ff.
79. Saurat, *Milton: Man and Thinker*, p. 236.
80. Milton, *Samson Agonistes*, p. 21, Line 497.
81. Clark and Harris, *Liturgy and Worship*, p. 33.

moment of nothingness; and can threaten annihiliation. Life loses its meaning:

> . . .as for life
> To what end should I seek it?[82]

The torment is mental and overweighs bodily suffering. The poignancy of his cry is real and savours of a tragic figure in a psychological play of today.

> Thoughts, my tormentors, armed with deadly stings
> Mangle my apprehensive tenderest parts,
> Exasperate, exulcerate and raise
> Dire inflammation. . . .[83]

Even *death's benumbing opium* does not come his way. He has reached the extreme *negative moment*, the nadir of despair and destitution, and like Christ's cry on Calvary, *Eli, Eli, Lama Sabachtani*, Samson feels a "Sense of Heaven's desertion."[84] But like the sinner at the altar, Samson rises out of this mood. With his returning strength and a sense of comfort, and the challenge from Manoah and the Danites, Samson gains self-confidence. He confesses his faults; accepts God's will, however irrational it seems, and moves on his way to regeneration. His words of confession and penitence are parallel to the liturgy of confession in the Prayer Book. These passionate expressions of grief in essence are poetic utterances of the liturgy. Samson confesses his faults and folly while bewailing his lot:

> What if all foretold
> Had been fulfilled but through my own default?
> . . .O yet more miserable!
> Myself my sepulchre, a moving grave;
> . . .confused with shame
> How could I once look up, or heave the head
> Who, like a foolish pilot, have shipwrecked
> My vessel trusted to me from above

82. Milton, *Samson Agonistes*, p. 21, Line 522.
83. *Ibid.*, p. 22, Line 623.
84. *Ibid.*, p. 22, Line 632.

. . .Tell me friends
Am I not sung and proverbed for a fool. . . .[85]

The witty, sarcastic remark about his strength and his wisdom, gives pith to the argument, "These two, proportioned ill, drove me transverse."[86] Samson feels that his marriage was ordered of God, but still he seems to have "offended against God's holy laws," and "done those things which he ought not to have done"[87] by giving himself license to marry a second time from among the Philistines: "I thought it lawful from my former act."[88] He realises though, that his suffering was not entirely Delilah's fault: "She was not the prime cause, but I myself."[89]

Proud of his prophetic birth, his Nazarite upbringing, his exploits in war, feats of arms and prodigious strength, he does not blame himself altogether either; he feels that Israel's governors were partly responsible for his failure. For him, as of Becket in *Murder in the Cathedral*, it can be said, his "fall seems to typify a human tendency to fall during life from the estate in which men find themselves, a natural perverseness . . . Samson's fall . . . was primarily due to pride, only secondarily to sensuality"[90] and it was "humility, intellectual clarity, and self-knowledge"[91] which brought him his regeneration. This dramatic situation is

> derived from the very essence of Greek tragedy . . . Milton's attempt to interpret Samson's tragic error as *hubris*, that overconfidence which leads men to trust too much to their own power and provokes an attack on them by the jealous gods.[92]

The Chorus stresses the idea of *hubris* as well as change in the tragedy:

Amidst their height of noon

85. *Ibid.*, p. 8, Line 44.
86. *Ibid.*, p. 13, Line 209.
87. *The Book of Common Prayer*, p. 6.
88. Milton, *Samson Agonistes*, p. 13, Line 231.
89. *Ibid.*. p. 13. Line 234.
90. E.M.W. Tillyard, *Milton* London: Chatlo and Windus, 1949) p. 350.
91. *Ibid.*, p. 351.
92. James Holly Hanford, *A Milton Handbook* (New York: Appleton-Century-Crofts, Inc.), 1954, p. 283.

Changest thy countenance and thy hand, with no regard
Of highest favours past
From thee for them or them to thee of service.[93]

Samson's tragic error was his pride, a pride which could not be countenanced even by his compatriots, partly due to their own fear of the Philistines, and also because of Samson's once unhappy alliance with the enemies. But Samson has learnt the lesson of humility; he acknowledges his guilt:

. . .I myself have brought them on;
Sole author I, sole cause
. . .traitor to myself.[94]

He suffers most as he recalls his base enthrallment; the blindness of his soul; and feels that his greatest failure has been Dagon's seeming triumph over God. Like the prodigal son, and the penitent in the confessional, he says:

Father, I do acknowledge and confess
That I this honor, I this pomp have brought
To Dagon . . . my chief affliction, shame and sorrow.[95]

Like the penitent at the altar, he has reached the stage when he cannot trust his own judgment. A power superior must control the situation. The conflict is between the God of Israel and Dagon, and Samson is confident that evil will not prevail; that connivance at evil is not God's forte, and that Dagon will have to stoop.

Samson is humble before God and acknowledges his own failure, but his self-respect is not impaired. He has no desire to sue for grace at the hands of his enemies; he cannot repeat the error of being led to the sacrifice like a meek, shorn lamb. No promise of a life of ease at the hands of his enemies is tempting enough, nor can Samson accept anything other than God's design for him; and nothing can assuage the prick of guilt and shame. Only before God can Samson be in the confessional; not before man. God

93. Milton, *Samson Agonistes*, p. 26, Line 683.
94. *Ibid.*, pp. 17 and 18, Lines 375 and 401.
95. *Ibid.*, p. 19, Line 448.

Whose ear is ever open, and His eyes
Gracious to re-admit the suppliant;[96]

His pride admits no humility before men like Harapha. He indulges in caustic wit while speaking to the Philistine giant:

    No man withholds thee; nothing from thy hand
Fear I incurable; bring up thy van;
My heels are fettered, but my fist is free.[97]

Like cowardly forces of evil, Harapha slinks away, and the Chorus announces: "His giantship is gone somewhat crestfallen."[98] Nor can Samson bend before the sovereign lords of the Philistines:

Can they think me so broken, so debased
With corporal servitude that my mind even
Will condescend to such absurd commands![99]

His contrition and penitence and petition have all led him to the apocalypse. He can accept God's will without demure; evil poses no challenge to him. His returning strength is an indication of God's re-acceptance of him. In confessing his faults, Samson has regenerated himself. In the lyrical chants of the Chorus and Manoah, we learn that Samson has acquitted himself honourably as the great deliverer. He bought his salvation through penitence and contemplative prayer, much before any action.

The elements of confession and petition in *Murder in the Cathedral* are masked under lyrical verbiage and chants. The Herald announces that the Archbishop has returned, but "He comes in pride and sorrow, affirming all he claims."[100] The seven years of exile made no difference in Becket's assertions, and his return is equated with Christ's triumphant entry into Jerusalem. Unlike Christ, who combined strength with humility, there is no humility in Becket. He is more like Samson, a man of strong convictions, but fallible.

96. *Ibid.*, p. 39, Line 1172.
97. *Ibid.*, p. 41, Line 1233.
98. *Ibid.*, p. 41, Line 1244.
99. *Ibid.*, p. 44, Line 1335.
100. Eliot, "Murder in the Cathedral," *The Complete Poems and Plays*, p. 178.

. . .The Lord Archbishop
Is not the man to cherish any illusions,
Or yet to diminish the least of his pretensions.[101]

Pride and obstinacy and tenacity are Becket's failings. Even as a Chancellor, he was misunderstood, for he was different; a man apart, conscious of being above the general run of men:

Despised and despising, always isolated
Never one among them, always insecure.[102]
. . . .
Wishing subjection to God alone.

Adulated as the hope of the people, the leader, the *rock*, the "head dispelling dismay and doubt,"[103] Becket had the onerous responsibility of living up to this expectation of himself; but he knew his shortcomings and had to dispel them. He was far from "Secure and assured of [his] fate,"[104] and voiced the reality of his own suffering when he confessed:

They know and do not know, that acting is suffering
And suffering is action.[105]

According to Eliot, all relationship is correlated, because it is patterned and is a part of the wheel of fortune; the wheel which repeats the cycle of life—birth, death and rebirth or resurrection. Eliot's is the patterned world of Donne and Sir Thomas Browne. "The early seventeenth-century poets were most interested in the little world of man,"[106] a patterned world, perfect in its globular form till marred by Sin. Man was the microcosm of the macrocosm, the universe, where perfection was symbolized by the circle. This prediction for Eliot is repeated in the cycle where action is suffering, and suffering is action; the two complement each other like two sectors of the same circle, the Chinese "yin" and

101. *Ibid.*, p. 179.
102. *Ibid.*, p. 181.
103. *Ibid.*
104. *Ibid.*, p. 182.
105. *Ibid.*
106. Marjorie Hope Nicolson, *The Breaking of the Circle* (Evanston Ill.: Northwestern University Press 1950), pp. 21 and 34.

"yang," to make life unified. This circle of perfection is completed in Becket only when he accepts the Will of God, through confession; suffering turns Becket's own cycle of being into "becoming," from sainthood he moves to spiritual perfection; his rebirth after death.

In *Samson Agonistes*, the protagonist had bewailed his state; patience was not his forte. The tone of the confessional element in *Murder in the Cathedral* is subdued and the moments seem fraught with expectation which involves waiting. Becket advocates waiting even though it is difficult to be patient. He knows the preliminary strife of subduing his pride and acknowledging it to himself and his Maker, is but the shadow of the great conflict that will end in martyrdom and reality:

> Meanwhile the substance of our first act
> Will be shadows, and the strife with shadows.
> Heavier the interval than the consummation.[107]

Becket is preparing himself to accept the inevitable and also God's Will, which for a proud man like him, is not easy.

The temptations that come to him are the epicycles of his own life—his youth, his early influence on the barons, his chancellorship, his life in the See. They tempt him with his own desires:

> This is a sentence not taught in schools.
> To set down the great, protect the poor,
> Beneath the throne of God can man do more?[108]

His zeal for social uplift is used as a bait to substitute his acquiescence to God's will. Becket's strength lay in his spiritual power, yet he is told, "Your spiritual power is earthy perdition";[109] as he is not wielding the power according to the direction of his desires. In confessing to this temptation, he has risen on the ladder of recovery; he has no mission to toy with things "Not controlled by the order of God."[110] It is not his sin that *soars sunward*, as the Tempter says, but his soul which is elevated towards God.

107. Eliot, "*Murder in the Cathedral*," *The Complete Poems and Plays*, p. 183.
108. *Ibid.*, p. 186.
109. *Ibid.*
110. *Ibid.*, p. 187.

Before he reaches complete transcendence, like Samson, Becket is seen searing his soul to overcome the temptations; he confesses that his mission is ". . .to trust none but God alone."[111] In this statement, Eliot has reiterated the attitudes of the protagonists of *Everyman*, and *Samson Agonistes*. Becket, like Samson, recalls his own glory;—he had ruled "like the royal bird over doves"; could he now stoop to be one with the pack against the king? It is a formal confession of his pride and arrogance, as well as his chagrin at being thought capable of doing anything wrong or unworthy. The temptation to accept the challenge of the Tempters is great for a man faced with failure and death.

> To make, then break, this thought has come before,
> The desperate exercise of failing power.[112]

Yet, in confessing it, he has saved his integrity.

The last temptation is Becket's alter-ego exhorting him aloud. He is faced with the immediate situation, not the past; his aspiration to sainthood through martyrdom. His martyrdom is argued from every angle, even from the crisp, lacerating angle of becoming just an event in the archives:

> And later is worse, when men will not hate you
> Enough to defame or to execrate you.
> But pondering the qualities that you lacked
> Will only try to find the historical fact.[113]

To this tirade, Thomas meekly confesses his desire for an "enduring crown" in God's kingdom, and the Tempter ends it in the climactic statement:

> Seek the way of martyrdom, make yourself the lowest
> On earth, to be high in heaven.[114]

It leads to a direct and penitential outburst of confession on Becket's part. The torment is just as real as in Samson's impassioned cries:

111. *Ibid.*, p. 189.
112. *Ibid.*
113. *Ibid.*, p. 192.
114. *Ibid.*

No!
Who are you, tempting with my own desires?
. . . .
Dreams to damnation
. . . .
Is there no way, in my soul's sickness,
Does not lead to damnation in pride?
I well know that these temptations
Mean present vanity and future torment.
Can sinful pride be driven out
Only by more sinful? Can I neither act nor suffer
Without perdition?[115]

Acknowledgement and realisation of his own folly are breaking the shackles that make Thomas desire martyrdom, though the chorus of Tempters goes on censuring him; and Becket's despair is great.

This man is obstinate, blind, intent
On self-destruction
. . . .
Lost in the wonder of his own greatness.[116]

As in *Everyman* and in *Samson Agonistes*, there comes the negative moment, the moment of desolation and utter despondency. Becket's anguish and a deep sense of loss are voiced by the Chorus:

God is leaving us, God is leaving us, more pang, more
pain than birth or death.[117]

But the very nadir has propelled Becket to victory, for it has revealed him to himself. Self-knowledge, as he confesses, has made the way clear to him:

Now is my way clear, now is the meaning plain:
The last temptation is the greatest treason.[118]

115. *Ibid.*, p. 193.
116. *Ibid.*, p. 194.
117. *Ibid.*, p. 195.
118. *Ibid.*, p. 196.

He recalls his entire life as he lays it bare before God. He points out his greatest temptation, that which can come to a man of God alone:

> For those who serve the greater cause may make the cause serve them. . . .[119]

Becket ends his speech with a prayer for protection from his own thoughts and desires; he is a saved man.

The confessional element is also present in the Archbishop's homily delivered on Christmas morning. It reiterates the cycle of birth and death, rejoicing and mourning, recovery and sin. Sainthood, he says, is not the result of any contriving and willing on the part of the individual, but an act of aligning man's will with that of God.

In a final outburst of agony, the Chorus asks for Thomas' supplication for them. At this point, his victory over self is almost at its zenith, he advises the Chorus that in the completion of God's purpose will lie the triumph. Patience and the perfection of the will in obedience to God is the reward of the penitent; it is here that the Church will rise "triumphant in adversity."[120]

The Chorus shares Becket's victory, but it emphasizes the liturgical element of the play in the last chant; the confessional element being as prominent as that of praise and thanksgiving. In words borrowed from the liturgy, it says:

> Forgive us, O Lord, we acknowledge ourselves as type of the common man.
>
> . . . .
>
> Who fear the injustice of men less than the justice of God.
>
> . . . .
>
> We acknowledge our trespass, our weakness, our fault.
>
> . . . .
>
> Lord, have mercy upon us. . . .[121]

And God forgives:

119. *Ibid.*
120. *Ibid.*, p. 219.
121. *Ibid.*, p. 221.

> Thus saith the high and lofty One that inhabiteth eternity, whose name is Holy; I dwell in the high and holy place, with him also that is of a contrite and humble spirit, to revive the spirit of the humble, and to revive the heart of the contrite ones. (Isaiah 57:17)

Absolution and the Priest

The Absolution in the Order of the Eucharist communicates to the worshipper the fact that God

> of his great mercy hath promised forgiveness
> of sins to all those who with hearty repentance and
> true faith turn unto him.[122]

The worshipper who has confessed his sins and is penitent already has God's promised grace. The priest, as His representative, has the authority to pronounce the words of benediction and absolution. In the liturgy, he asks God's mercy on the votary, asks for God's pardon and deliverance, and for the confirmation and the strengthening of the suppliant in righteousness preparatory to everlasting life. According to the Prayer Book, the ordained priest has to be "apt and meet, for his learning and godly conversation" and he has "to exercise his Ministry duly, to the honour of God, and the edifying of his Church."[123] He has to be replenished "with the truth of [God's] doctrine, and be adorned with innocency of life"[124] to serve God faithfully in word and deed. He is the shepherd, the labourer in God's fields, and his Office is one of dignity. He is the "Messenger, the Watchman, the Steward of the Lord; to teach, and to premonish, to feed and provide for the Lord's family. . . ."[125] He has the weighty charge of the welfare of God's entire people; and is responsible for bringing knowledge to them and confirming them in their faith; and above all, he has to be a "godly example and pattern for the people to follow."[126] These are some of the onerous duties of the

122. *The Book of Common Prayer*, p. 76.
123. *Ibid.*, p. 536.
124. *Ibid.*, p. 537.
125. *Ibid.*, p. 539.
126. *Ibid.*, p. 541.

priest, and it is only when he perfects the Will of God that he can truly represent Him on earth and be the medium of His grace. Ethically, the *Humanum Genus* is God's priesthood, for God has given it the rational faculty to choose right from wrong, and as such, in its moments of elation, of majesty, and sublimity, it should represent God, and like the priest, should be God's ordained agent.

In *Everyman*, priestly qualities can be ascribed to Death, to Knowledge, Good Deeds and Confession. Confession offers Everyman God's mercy, and the extreme unction. Knowledge absolves him of the past and its sins, and commits him to God's care, telling him to be joyful. Good Deeds commends Everyman's penance and blesses him, and Death points the way to him. Everyman himself is on his way to priesthood, for he can pray for others: "I pray God reward you in his heavenly sphere."[127] His Five Wits tell him that the least priest of God is greater than kings and statesmen:

> For of the blessed sacraments pure and benign
> He beareth the keys and thereof hath the cure
> For man's redemption.
> . . . .
> For priesthood exceedeth all other thing:
> To us holy scripture they do teach
> And converteth man from sin, heaven to reach;
> God hath to them more power given
> Than to any angel that is in heaven.
> . . . .
> The priest bindeth and unbindeth all bands,
> But in earth and in heaven.
> . . . .
> God gave priests that dignity
> And setteth them in his stead among us to be
> Thus they be above angels in degree.[128]

This eulogy of the priests shows the liturgical character of the drama more clearly, for the mediaeval age (as later the 17th century) was keenly interested in the church and its impact on

127. Browne, "Everyman," *Religious Drama* 2, p. 294.
128. *Ibid.*, p. 295.

the people. The Church was the center of life of mediaeval society, but abuses had crept in and made men distrust the pecuniary practices of the Church and other current evils, as Knowledge states in *Everyman*. The playwright lightly touches on the abuses of the Church and brings the unsavory argument to a close by making Five Wits say:

> I trust to God no such may we find
> Therefore let us priesthood honour,
> And follow their doctrine for our soul's succour.
> We be their sheep and they shepherds be
> By whom we all be kept in surety.[129]

Such was the standard the Mediaeval Church set for its priests, before they were considered equipped to administer the sacraments and lead the flock. Everyman is absolved of his sins after confession; Good Deeds says, like a priestly intermediary:

> Fear not. I will speak for thee
> . . . .
> Shorten our end and 'minish our pain![130]

And Knowledge affirms his faith in Everyman's salvation, "Thy *Good Deeds* shall make all sure!"[131] The abstractions play their part in helping Everyman's spiritual recovery, like the priest in the Church. Such, then, is a true act of worship both on the part of the votary and the priest, for "worship . . . has not only an expressive function but also a suggestive or impressive one."[132] "Liturgy not only expresses what we feel; it also teaches us what we ought to feel."[133] Liturgy and religious drama complement each other, in making man conscious of his spiritual need.

In *Samson Agonistes*, the priestly office is performed by the Chorus and by Manoah. In the very beginning, the Chorus exonerates Samson of full responsibility of his act:

> In seeking just occasion to provoke

129. *Ibid.*, p. 297.
130. *Ibid.*, p. 302.
131. *Ibid.*, p. 303.
132. Clark and Harris, *Liturgy and Worship*, p. 13.
133. *Ibid.*

The Philistine, thy country's enemy,
Thou never wast remiss, I bear thee witness.[134]

Even in his choice of a bride, it says, there was some motivating power behind him.

Manoah exhorts his son to repentance, but adds priestlike words of absolution as to the penitent:

Perhaps
God will relent, and quit thee all his debt;
Who evermore approves and more accepts
(Best pleased with humble and filial submission)
Him who, imploring mercy, sues for life. . . .[135]

The Chorus, while philosophizing on Stoicism and patience, realizes that the arguments cannot help a wounded soul like Samson's unless God sends down His grace on him:

Unless he feel within
Some source of consolation from above,
Secret refreshings that repair his strength
And fainting spirits uphold.[136]

Like the priest at the altar, the Chorus asks God:

. . .and turn
His labours, for Thou canst, to peaceful end.[137]

It absolves him of disloyalty and urges him to obey the behest of the Philistine Lords, not as a deserter of Israel, but as an act of policy, for matters were already strained between the Israelites and the Philistines. Samson is absolved because "Where the heart joins not, outward acts defile not."[138] As Samson leaves, the blessings of the Chorus follow him, with the liturgical and prophetic words that the Spirit "Be efficacious in thee now at

134. Milton, *Samson Agonistes*, p. 13, Line 237.
135. *Ibid.*, p. 21, Line 509
136. *Ibid.*, p. 25, Line 663.
137. *Ibid.*, p. 26, Line 708.
138. *Ibid.*, p. 45, Line 1368.

need!"[139] The Chorus and Manoah perform all the offices of the priest; exhortations, absolution, the sacrifical act, the benediction are all part of their priestly function in the play. Yet Milton has little time for unworthy ministers of God's law and God's word. As early as 1637, in "Lycidas," Milton had censured the hirelings of the Church as *Blind Mouths;* the episcopals or overseers who had degenerated into blindness, and the pastors, the feeders, who themselves had become receptacles; thus endangering the lives of all in their care. In *Samson Agonistes*, the same overtones are heard, even though the censure is directed at the false Philistine priests. Delilah states:

> . . .and the priest
> Was not behind, but ever at my ear,
> Preaching how meritorious with the gods
> It would be to ensnare an irreligious
> Dishonourer of Dagon.[140]

For Milton, who believed that a man dedicated to the service of the gods was a *vate*, a prophet, a seer, one whose lips were touched by the hallowed fire, any falsity was heinous. In the chaotic history of his time, Milton had seen political and state intrigues hatched within the Church and sponsored by it, so that the words have a more bitter reverberation than would a statement just censuring the false priests. For him, it was just the "upright heart and pure"[141] that could be a true temple or a priest of God. Manoah and the Choru's, though they rationally question the ways of God, embody in themselves the priestly concepts, and acquit themselves of all mundane trammels and concerns; they too are purified for the last act of worship and are in themselves both priest and votary.

The absolution in *Murder in the Cathedral* comes from Becket himself. His tempters provide the element of uncertainty in Becket's own mind, but in transcending those uncertainties he absolves himself of the temptation and desire to accept the earthly for the heavenly rectitude. Not tempted by love and beauty, he says he is twenty years too old to accept the offer, although there are:

139. *Ibid.*, p. 47, Line 1437.
140. *Ibid.*, p. 31, Line 857.
141. John Milton, *Paradise Lost*, edited by Merritt Y. Hughes (New York: The Odessey Press, 1935), Book I. Line 19.

Voices under sleep, waking a dead world
So that the mind may not be whole in the present.[142]

The lines are as significant in their concept as the liturgical lamentation, "We have sinned in thought, word and deed,"[143] and point to a disintegration of the personality, but the absolution clears the taint:

You were safer
Think of penitence and follow your master.[144]

Thomas is his own high priest; as he overcomes the temptations he absolves himself from the desire of succumbing to them. The temptation to be a secular leader again is great, to rule over the quibbling gentry and thus weaken the king's power, but as he thinks aloud, he knows that his mission is different: it is fulfilling God's will even to the death.

To make, then break, this thought has come before,
The desperate exercise of failing power.
Samson in Gaza did no more.
But if I break, I must break myself alone.[145]

Becket accepts the inevitable; obedience to the will of God, and emerges as a saint, though not yet as a martyr. He knows the danger he had faced as a priest.

Servant of God has chance of greater sin
. . . .
For those who serve the greater cause may make the cause serve them, still doing right.[146]

Eliot too, like Milton, has sardonic remarks to make of the unworthy priest:

142. Eliot, "Murder in the Cathedral," *The Complete Poems and Plays*, p. 185.
143. *The Book of Common Prayer*, p. 75.
144. Eliot, "Murder in the Cathedral," *The Complete Poems and Plays*, p. 184.
145. *Ibid.*, p. 190.
146. *Ibid.*, p. 196.

> Your spiritual power is earthly perdition
> Power is present, for him who will yield.[147]

He mentions that "pretence of priestly power" is "For the power and the glory," and like Milton's *Blind Mouths*, refers to the excommunicated bishops as "hungry hatred,"[148] hungry for power hating the man seeking leadership, as Becket is tempted to do. Priests, according to Eliot, should not only be the custodians of *the keys of heaven and hell*—but be able to submit to *the order of God* and eschew "temporal power, to build a good world,"[149] even though the latter seems a worthy cause.

> The theme of the conflict of the spiritual and the secular powers, the relation of Church and State, was topical, and is a subject on which Mr. Eliot has spoken much in prose.[150]

Words put into the mouths of twelfth-century characters voice current concerns and issues, one of which is Eliot's keen interest in the revival of religious thought and practices,

> His poetry has shifted from early evocation of the malaise of modern life to efforts in both reflective verse and poetic drama at re-establishing the Christian vision, so has his criticism . . . to a series of attempts at using the analysis of literature for a Christian critique of our culture.[151]

In portraying Becket as the high priest in his role of the protagonist, Eliot has fused the elements of absolution as a priestly office with that of the penitent searching for the ultimate reality through absolution. Becket in aligning his will with that of God is ready for the final sacrifice of praise and thanksgiving as are Samson and Everyman.

147. *Ibid.*, p. 186.
148. *Ibid.*, p. 187.
149. *Ibid.*
150. Helen Gardner, *The Art of T.S. Eliot*, p. 133.
151. Irving Howe, "Books and the Arts," Modern Criticism in America, *The Nation*, Vol. 184, Nov. 22, 1958, p. 388.

Anthems of Praise

The sinner once shriven is jubilant and anthems of praise fall involuntarily from his lips:

> Holy, Holy, Holy! Lord God of hosts,
> Heaven and earth are full of thy glory: Glory
> be to thee, O Lord Most High. [152]

In the liturgical adoration quoted is the quintessence of worship. True worship is an unadulterated adulation of the Deity, "for worship is essentially disinterested—it 'means only God'."[153] The Prayer Book, as the Scriptures, contains hymns of praise, which neither extol the Powers Above, as prefaces to the votary's requests, nor are used as palliatives to appease the wrath of God. They are just songs of praise, lyrical in their beauty, deeply emotional in their ardour, and can be equated with the adoration of the lover for the beloved.

Revelation 4:8 reiterates the words "Holv, holy, holy. Lord God Almighty which was, and is, and is to come,"[154] and it is in the same spirit of awe-inspired adoration that the Lord's Prayer begins, *Our Father, Who art in Heaven, Hallowed be Thy Name.* The versicles and responses, taken from the psalms; (Ps. 51:15 and Ps. 70) are the cantor's and the people's song of praise:

> O Lord, open Thou our lips
> And our mouths shall show forth Thy praise.
> . . . .
> Praise ye the Lord.
> The Lord's name be praised.

> The Versicle and Response seems to have been suggested by the parallel structure of the psalms, which from early times were frequently recited in this manner; either by cantor and choir, or by two groups of singers. It is a form which can be adapted to many purposes, both of praise and supplication.[155]

152. *The Book of Common Prayer*, p. 77.
153. Underhill, *Worship*, p. 9.
154. *The Book of Common Prayer* p. 5.
155. Underhill, *Worship* p. 103.

Historically, the versicle and response can be traced to the rule of St. Benedict and the concluding doxology to each psalm; the *Gloria Patri*, to a practice current in Gaul in the fourth century. These poems of praise are recited antiphonically, like the psalms, by the priest and the congregation, and embody the adoration and fervour of a worshipper who comes to praise and marvel at God's omnipotence and omniscence without petitioning aught for himself. They are

> the stylized form of that Biblical and non sacramental devotion which the infant Church took over from Judaism. Here God is praised in the ancient poetry of the psalms and canticles; and in the Scripture lessons, His nature and laws, and His gracious dealings with the children of men are brought to mind.[156]

In the lines quoted from the Prayer Book and in similar chants of praise in other parts of the Book, we find that the worshipper effaces his own personality and transcends all desires other than the praise of the Maker. It is at this point that worship becomes sublime. Lowther Clark calls worship "religious drama, a full expression and satisfaction of the aesthetic instincts,"[157] for it is at such a moment of sublimity that man has the closest view of the Ultimate Reality, which is also Ultimate Beauty and Ultimate Truth. Like St. Augustine's, the worshipper's prayer becomes an oft-repeated name of God and nothing more. These sighs for the Eternal are as far-reaching as the cadences of the *Venite*, "O Come, let us sing unto the Lord,"[158] or of the *Te Deum* which the Breviaries ascribe to St. Augustine and St. Ambrose—"We praise thee, O God; we acknowledge thee to be the Lord. . . ;"[159] they mirror the same feelings of awe and wonder and love.

Similar anthems of praise are still current among primitive societies, where, like the leader of the dithyramb, one man repeats words of praise, and his companions, join him in the repetition of the words. The Antiphony was

156. *Ibid.*, p. 120.
157. Clark and Harris, *Liturgy and Worship*. p. 31.
158. *The Book of Common Prayer*, p. 9.
159. *Ibid.*, p. 10.

> sung at first without words, then the vowel a was replaced by words . . . the tropes had their origin in the melismatic Alleluia, in the wordless lyrical chant of jubilation.[160]

These wordless chants were the true expression of worship, like bird songs, and they did not lose the essence of worship when words of praise for the Deity were formulated out of the sounds and made part of the vocal music.

> The appearance of dramatic dialogue in the services of the Church has been traced to the ninth century, where words were fitted to the additional melodies (at first sung only to vowel sounds). . . . Of these interpolations or "Tropes" as they were called, the most important in its dramatic influence was that sung on Easter-day.[161]

Samuel Fuller says:

> The voice greatly aids devotion. It is not only the outlet, but, to a great extent, the exciting cause of devotion . . . our voices arouse the sympathies of those near us, and the flame of holy fervour thus kindled spreads.[162]

Whether we agree with the latter half of the statement or not, it is a known fact that words have just as great a poignancy as any melody or dramatic silence; and that music and words together are the medium of worship.

In *Everyman*, there are many epithets used for God, which show His transcendent nature and man's awe of His glory. The playwright has used attributes in praise of the Almighty relating to God's majesty and righteousness, His might and celestial kingship, His relation to man as the Creator and "Maker,"[163] His lordship as "the chief Lord of Paradise,"[164] His graciousness, His

160. Cargill, *Drama and Liturgy*, p. 15.
161. Pollard, *English Miracle Plays, Moralities, and Interludes*, p. xiv.
162. Fuller, *Characteristic Excellences of the Liturgy*, p. 3.
163. Browne, "Everyman," *Religious Drama 2*, p. 271.
164. *Ibid.*, p. 287.

messianic quality, His purifying grace as the "glorious fountain, that all uncleanness doth clarify."[165] At the beginning of one of the most touching and dramatic prayers, Everyman praises God:

> O eternal God! O heavenly figure!
> O way of rightwiseness! O goodly vision,
> Which descended down in a virgin pure
> Because he would every man redeem,
> . . . .
> O blessed forhead elect and high divine,
> . . . .
> O ghostly treasure! O merciful redeemer!
> Of all the world hope and conductor!
> Mirror of joy and founder of mercy
> Which illumineth Heaven and earth thereby.[166]

The passage as a song of praise is liturgical, lyrical and theologically meaningful. Although the hero mixes his own motive of forgiveness with the praise, the playwright's piety and devotion to God are more than evident in the rhythmic outburst. It is on account of passages like this that T.S. Eliot classes *Everyman* as "a drama within the limitations of art,"[167] and uses its liturgical versification and rhythms as models for his own play, *Murder in the Cathedral.* When Everyman dramatically praises and blesses "Almighty God, loved may thou be!"[168] the office of Compline is called to mind, "Let us bless the Lord; Thanks be to God."[169] But it is in the wordless Allelujah of the chorus of the play that the liturgy has its culmination as an act of praise. The song is sung in motiveless purity of worship; and justifies the statement "a disinterested delight in the splendour of God is the highest and purest of . . . religious responses."[170]

Milton, in *Samson Agonistes*, praises God, but seldom in a direct epithet. The attributes of God are so woven into the fabric of the speeches that any reference to Him, however laudatory, follows the sequence of a character's thoughts and dialogue. It is

165. *Ibid.*, p. 288.
166. *Ibid.*, p. 289.
167. Parks and Beatty, *The English Drama*, p. 57, and T.S. Eliot, *On Poetry and Poets*, p. 85.
168. Browne, "Everyman," *Religious Drama 2*, p. 294.
169. *Ibid.*, p. 303.
170. Underhill, *Worship*, p. 104

only in two sections of the play that anything can be claimed near an anthem of praise in its liturgical sense. One is the ode sung by the Chorus in lines 293-325, following Samson's speech in which he "forgives his people for neglecting him, but reproaches them for forgetting the cause of God's deliverance of Israel."[171] The Chorus in reprimanding him, sings the song of praise:

> Just are the ways of God
> And justifiable to men.[172]

In it Milton reiterates Ps. 14:1, "The fool hath said in his heart, There is no God." He censures those who doubt God's ways, for, like the philosophical angels of *Paradise Lost* (Book II), they are also in "mazes lost" and ". . .never find self-satisfying solution." God, the interminable, cannot be confined nor can He be bound by Laws He made for His creatures. He is the Creator, the Architect of a patterned world, the adjudicator of all laws of nature, thus giving them order and precision. In Him is perfection, as known alone to the great advocates of perfection of 17th century England. Even Samson's non-Hebraic marriages were God's patterned plan. Thus says Milton, who can claim knowledge of God's intentions, for Reason itself fails before His Providence. This is one of the highest paeans of praise that Milton could raise to the Deity; for Milton Reason was man's most cherished birthright, alongside of liberty. In writing these lines, Milton accepts the numinous in God; the point where the world of sense has to resign itself to the acceptance of the world of spirit, and to make it even more difficult, without comprehension.

> The known fades into the unknown [and gives]. . .a thrill of mystery; . . . there seems complete discontinuity and the events appear to come from an unknowable sphere quite outside our experience.[173]

This, then, is the numinous, the mystery surrounding God, yet it is justifiable, for God is just though incomprehensible. It is a beautiful song of praise.

171. Merritt Y. Hughes, *John Milton: Paradise Regained, The Minor Poems and Samson Agonistes* (New York: The Odyessy Press, 1937) p. 556, Footnote 291.
172. Milton, *Samson Agonistes*, p. 15, Line 298.
173. Clark and Harris, *Liturgy and Worship*, p. 24.

The other passage that recommends itself as a hymn of praise in *Samson Agonistes,* is the last chorus beginning at line 1745:

> All is best, though we oft doubt,
> What th'unsearchable dispose
> Of Highest Wisdom brings about,
> And ever best found in the close
> Oft he seems to hide his face,
> But unexpectedly returns. . .

The paean here is to God's wisdom and His might in bringing to fruition "His uncontrolled intent."[174] He is a God who does not fail His elect, even though for a time "He seems to hide His face."[175] In writing these words, Milton may have recalled Christ's own cry at the Cross, *Eli, Eli lama sabachtiani,* as well as the psalmist's plea, "Hide not thy face far from me."[176] Earlier in the play (line 632) he mentioned a "sense of Heav'n's desertion." This is the negative moment of human experience; everything seems dark, even God's presence seems removed, but the praiseworthy fact is that God is omnipresent and the negative moment is in the votary's mind, not in God's relationship to him, for God "unexpectedly returns."[177]

Other terms of praise in *Samson Agonistes* are dispersed throughout the play. God is mentioned and praised in connection with strength (57), light and nature (70), Logos (the great Word, 83), His Will (210 and 374), His election of the choice few (227), His prowess through man, the medium (242), His graciousness (355), His uniqueness (440), His election of Abraham and Israel (465, 666), His wisdom and counsel (472-76), His fatherhood (510), His miraculous power (580), His incomprehensible capricousness (666 ff.), His Reality as the living God (1140), His grace and approachability (1172), His being inspiring and drawing adoration (1177), His Hebraic character as a jealous God (1376), His aloofness from all that is "impure, unworthy, dishonourable" (1423), His omnipotence (1528), and His awe-inspiring Reality as "Our living dread" (1670). In these various attributes, Milton gives his own idea of God while praising Him, but all that Milton says of God is part of the play and can not be considered doctri-

174. Milton, *Samson Agonistes*
p.56, Line 1754.
175. *Ibid,* p. 56, Line 1749.
176. Psalm 27: 9, *The Holy Bible.*
177. Milton, *Samson Agonistes,* p. 56, Line 1750.

nal theology; that he left for the *De Doctrina Christina.* Although the cloying ardour and verbosity of the *Gloria in Excelsis* is lacking in Milton's songs of praise, his language is essentially Biblical, some words and phrases being incorporated word for word from the Scriptures. This style was peculiar not only to his genius, but to his times:

> The seventeenth century, an era of enormous erudition almost wholly concerned with Biblical scholarship, following the twin *momenta* of Reformation and Humanism, stands in the history of Biblical study, the great age of Philosophy . . . fed by the period's precocious outburst of linguistic learning, a formidable complex and brilliant quest for a final, proved, and unrefutable rendition of the Bible, the religion of the Protestants.[178]

Milton's simple, pithy, concise and hauntingly beautiful style savours of the Bible, and his songs of praise are reminiscent of similar anthems incorporated in the *Book of Common Prayer* from the Scriptures.

Merritt J. Hughes, in his edition of *Samson Agonistes,* calls *Murder in the Cathedral* the "most Christian tragedy."[179] Its Christian character, though evident even in hallucinations of evil like "grey necks twisting, rat tails turning"[180] is brought more clearly to the forefront after the final sacrifice when on a quieter note of resignation, the anthem of praise is repeated chorally to the distant music of the *Te Deum.* The *Te Deum* in the *Book of Common Prayer,* and the final acceptance of the martyrdom in the play are parallel in more than the lyrical structure and the language. God is praised in the loftiest terms of adoration by all His creation, both animate and inanimate. Eliot, in his hymn, reaffirms the triumph of things spiritual over the secular, "only in Thy light, and Thy glory is declared even in that which denies Thee";[181] the triumph of good over evil, "the darkness declares the glory of light",[182] of life over death, "all things affirm Thee in

178. George Newton Conklin, *Biblical Criticism and Heresy in Milton* (New York: King's Crown Press, 1949), p. 2.
179. Hughes, ed., "Samson Agonistes," *John Milton,* p. 440.
180. Eliot, "Murder in the Cathedral," *The Complete Poems and Plays,* p. 207.
181. *Ibid.*, p. 220.
182. *Ibid.*

living."[183] He praises God for His omniscience, "For all things exist only as seen by Thee, only as known by Thee. . . ."[184] In the *Te Deum,* Christ's triumph over the *sharpness of death* is mentioned; Eliot thanks God for His *mercies of blood* and his redemption by it. Both the *Te Deum* and the Chorus dwell on martyrdom and sainthood, which are but steps in glorifying the Creator. It is the blood of martyrs that instills new life into the Church militant: "From such ground springs that which for ever renews the earth. . . ."[185] The two great hymns of praise end with the *Kyrie,* the *Te Deum* commits the votary into the hands of God, while the Choral song asks for the mediation of Thomas.

> Mr. Eliot's attempts to render . . . the horror and the glory of life in dramatic terms have given us the finest dramatic verse that has been written since the seventeenth century,[186]

and it is in sections like this glorious hymn of praise that Mr. Eliot's historic imagination seems at its height. He not only uses liturgical language and phrases, but captures the very spirit and atmosphere of the liturgy.

In the other sections of the play, no anthems of praise exist as such, but references to God and to Thomas, as the prototype of Christ, show the deep veneration the Anglo-Catholic playwright has for God. He mentions God as the God of an ordered world (pp. 176-186), the shaper of destiny (p. 176), one revealing Himself in the beauty of nature and in the wisdom of statesmen (p. 177), born in humility (p. 177), He is the rock which gives a "firm foothold" (p. 179). He is the God of grace (pp. 182, 192), but He pre-ordains man's life—the end is "God-given" (p. 183); even martyrdom is God's design for man, not man's for himself (p. 199), for death in the Lord renews life. By overcoming his own desire for martyrdom and suffering to keep the Holy Canon from being violated (pp. 209, 212), Becket was praising God; he had joined the *noble army of martyrs*: "the figure of God's purpose [was] made complete."[187]

183. *Ibid.*
184. *Ibid.*, p. 200.
185. *Ibid.*, p. 221.
186. Gardner, *The Art of T.S. Eliot*, p. 127.
187. Eliot, "Murder in the Cathedral," *The Complete Poems and Plays*, p. 208.

These hymns are symbols of praise; similar to the *Te Deum* and other anthems of the Prayer Book, where there is "a eucharistic preface uniting heaven and earth in praise,"[188] and blessing the name of the Lord.

Liturgical Silence

The sense of the numinous can be equated with "the hushed adoration of the Sanctus or the awestruck silence after the consecration."[189] The liturgical silence is punctuated between the *Sursum Corda* and the *Sanctus*, in the Prayer Book, and is the moment of mystical fear and of silent prayer. The priests and the deacons take a statuesque position around the altar, the people kneel in humble adoration, and a calm loaded with awe and expectation pervades. It is the dramatic moment when the angel appeared to Abraham as his hand was uplifted to strike the beloved son, the untainted paschal lamb, and averted the fatal blow; the moment of the final decision, and it may be called the point of no return. Although the playwrights in the three plays have given no such instruction for a lull in the proceedings, there are moments that could very well be considered the awestruck pondering of the soul before the sacrifice and the counterparts of liturgical silence.

After Five Wits has expounded the merits of the seven sacraments, there is a distinct break in the tone and the sequence of thought, before Everyman, in all humility like the Prodigal Son, states his decision:

> Fain would I receive that holy body,
> And meekly to my ghostly father I will go.[190]

This is the moment of silent prayer, when the pros and cons have been thoroughly weighed and the point of decision has been reached and is final. In the words of St. Cyril, it is "the hour of greatest trembling,"[191] the most fearful, for it anticipates suffering as well as consummation.

188. Shepherd, *The Liturgical Movement and the Prayer Book*, p. 21.
189. Clark and Harris, *Liturgy and Worship*, p. 14.
190. Browne, "Everyman," *Religious Drama 2*. p. 295.
191. Clark and Harris, *Liturgy and Worship*, p. 97.

The moment of silence in *Samson Agonistes* is described by the Hebrew messenger as he comes seeking safety from the calamity that has befallen the Philistine Lords. In describing the last moments of the tragedy, he says of Samson:

> . . .with head a while inclined.
> And eyes fast fixed, he stood, as one who prayed,
> Or some great matter in his mind revolved.[192]

The words are significant and convey all the implications of the liturgical silence and psychological decision. The element of awe is there, that of determination, and also that of exaltation and exultation. Samson has, in this moment of silence, justified himself in his own eyes and is ready to offer himself as the burnt offering.

In *Murder in the Cathedral,* when the Priests are urging that Becket should protect himself by taking sanctuary, Becket silences their concern, as did Christ the storm at sea, by saying:

> Peace! be quiet! remember where you are and what is happening.[193]

On the overwrought nerves of the Priests, the words hardly have the desired effect, but they help to confirm Becket in his own mission. He knows that death is in store for him, but the danger to his soul is past; the mental unrest is gone and the victory over self-aggrandizement is won. He is a saint. A calm pervades everything; it is the calm and peace of the darkened cathedral.

In moments of aloofness and short meditative silence, momentous decisions are often made; and the dramatists do not lag far behind the psychologists in giving prominence to the calm that leads men to the crux of heroism.

The Sacrifice of Thanksgiving

After the priest has pronounced the words of comfort from the Holy Scriptures, and turning to the altar has said:

192. Milton, *Samson Agonistes*, p. 52, Line 1636 ff.
193. Eliot, "Murder in the Cathedral," *The Complete Poems and Plays*, p. 209.

> It is very meet, right, and our bounden duty that we should at all times, and in all places, give Thanks unto Thee, O Lord, Holy Father, Almighty, Everlasting God,[194]

and the anthems of praise have been sung, he is ready to perform the final eucharistic sacrifice in offering the alms and oblations of all present as a gift of thanks to the Great Giver. The ritual of the eucharist seems a stylised religious practice for "ritual weaves speech, gesture, rhythm, and agreed ceremonial into the worhipping action of men,"[195] but it is the commemoration of God's greatest act of love and sacrifice. The ceremonial part of eucharistic worship can be considered essential, "aiding visualization and concentration,"[196] most of the dramatic practices of the ritual being symbolic. The genuflection shows humility and adoration, the incense the up-soaring sighs of the votaries, the "dim religious light"[197] from the stained glass and the vermilion glow of the sanctuary lamp, part of the mystery surrounding the numinous in God. Liturgy and drama in their symbolic content are close:

> . . .the connection between drama and worship is an old one. The Greek play was (in theory at least) a religious art, the altar smoked in the orchestra, and the High Priest of Dionysus presided on his throne. . . If there were movements on the stage by which the actors express a sense of solemnity and awe, they are surely the right movements for the public representatives of religion as they approach the altar; what Newman called "the sacred dance of the ministers" at High Mass. . . . After all both drama and worship have reference to life.[198]

Liturgy is symbolic and dramatic, but the element of drama is so merged with the spirit of adoration, that each is vital to the other in making worship possible. Unlike the dramatic performance, liturgy lacks the lure of entertainment; it is purely an act

194. *The Book of Common Prayer*, p. 76.
195. Underhill, *Worship*, p. 37.
196. *Ibid.*, p. 38.
197. Milton, "Il Penseroso," *John Milton*, ed. Hughes, p. 201, Line 160.
198. Clark and Harris, *Liturgy and Worship*, p. 29.

of thanksgiving and sacrifice on the part of both the individual and the group, and is communion with the Ultimate Truth and Reality.

> . . .The Eucharist (is) as something given and done, rather than as something seen or heard or felt. The early Christian said that he went "to offer," not "to receive communion" or "to hear Mass." To offer or to give over a thing unto God's possession is the essence of sacrifice. That giving may demand the very life of the giver, as it did that of the Son of Man.[199]

This sacrifice of thanksgiving provides a *life-force* or *libido*, an energy that can only be derived from a complete mental and spiritual surrender, and is the motivating factor in life.

The idea of sacrifice in Christian worship is derived from the Old Testament, where the Paschal lamb was sacrificed as a thanks offering in memory of the deliverance from Egypt and the Passover.

> In common with many peoples, the Hebrew believed that the life or soul of both men and animals resided in the blood. . . [200]

and life being the most treasured possesion, its gift was the supreme act of devotion. Christ's filial obedience in accepting the Cross is the occasion for the Eucharist:

> His Incarnate Work culminated in the Passion and Death of the Cross, which was voluntary and free. . . . The iterated emphasis on freely-willed obedience is significant; it is God's Will which is paramount and given to all men of the free acceptance and fulfillment of that Will. The climax of His Incarnate Work is in the Institution of the Eucharist, with its commemoration of the Body broken and the Blood shed, in sacrifice for men. . . . The Eucharistic rite is, however, rising to the climax in the memorial of the Institution. . . [201]

199. Shepherd, *The Liturgical Movement and the Prayer Book*, p. 29.
200. *Ibid.*, p. 41.
201. *Ibid.*, p. 100-103.

The Eucharist therefore gives final meaning to the whole gamut of life; starting with the Incarnation, the Epiphany, the Passion, the Sacrifice and the Resurrection, it reveals the cyclic destiny of man, as ordained by God. The three acts of salvation, that is, re-creation, redemption, and sanctification, are its guerdon. Man emerges as a demi-god, fit for things supra-mundane, which supposedly still remain in their pristine stage of perfection, and are a part of the cosmic drama.

The supermen of *Everyman*, *Samson Agonistes* and *Murder in the Cathedral* follow the same pattern of the Eucharistic sacrifice in their own drama of life. By the time they are ready to yield themselves on their crosses, they have sanctified themselves in obedience to God's will. Theirs has been the liberty of choice as that of Christ; each has had his Gethsemane, but the acceptance of the supreme sacrifice is volitional. As death is inevitable, the "idea of fatality"[202] is there, but the hero is not "a doomed man"[202] in the sense that his death is the final step in his salvation.

According to J.H. Muller, elements which arouse concern for man's suffering have the pith of tragedy in them. Melodrama and bloodcurdling tales are sensational, but do not savour of real tragedy; it is uncertainty, doubt, mystery, seemingly unsurpassable problems that make for tragedy. These are the aspects of life which are the trials of Man, Man in the generic sense of the word. In tragedy the problems and flaws may arise from the complexity of man's nature, his caprice or his folly, but they arouse anxiety and are a cause of concern, and make the spectator and listener suffer with the protagonist. The last sacrifice of Everyman, Samson, and Becket is excruciating in suffering, but the purgation is there, as of the resurrection; the ultimate value of the tragedy is triumph. The priest has uplifted to God the "full, perfect, and sufficient sacrifice"[203]—the *Body* and *Blood* of the New Testament as the last act of worship, and it is acceptable to God.

> Everyman has been shriven
> Peace! For yonder I see Everyman come,
> Which hath made true satisfaction.[204]

202. A.C. Bradley, *Shakespearean Tragedy* (New York: Meridian Books, 1957), p. 31.

203. *The Book of Common Prayer*, p. 80.

204. Browne, "Everyman," *Religious Drama* 2, p. 297.

In the words of the Prayer of Consecration, he has given a *full, perfect, and sufficient . . . satisfaction* in recompense for his own sins as did Christ *for the sins of the whole world,* and with the prayer in the Office of Compline, he goes to the sacrifice, his choice being made in the full liberty of action; "Into thy hands, Lord, my soul I commend."[205] For Milton:

> The "service" of God was "perfect" freedom. Conversely, perfect freedom was the service of God, and only in the spirit of perfect freedom could God be properly worshipped.[206]

It is with this freedom of choice that Samson proceeds to the arena of festivities. "There is a partial recognition in Samson's mind when he feels that he is tending to something great and mysterious,"[207] but the liberty of choice is his, and he goes forward knowing that God's strength is in him once more. In the words of the Chorus, he has fulfilled the mission for which he was appointed, and like the phoenix has risen from his own ashes, his union with God accomplished. Samson is *Agonistes*:

> Professor Parker has declared that Samson Agoniestes is "more than Samson the Wrestler". . . [he is] "an advocate, an actor, and a champion". . . when Milton used the epithet *Agonistes* he probably intended it both to denote a specific conception of Samson and to connote a view of life.[208]

He emerges the victor after the *good fight* like Christ:

> In *A Briefe ofthe Bible* (1596), Henoch Clapham said of Samson, "A Nazarite he was, and a figure of our Nazarite Anointed". . . The allegorical interpretation of Samson as a figure of Christ was, in the seventeenth century, one of the most prevalent connotations of the hero of Milton's tragedy. It is impossible to suppose that any of Milton's

205. *Ibid.*, p. 303.
206. E.H. Visiak, *The Portent of Milton* (London: Werner Laurie, 1958), p. 43.
207. Tillyard, *Milton*, p. 344.
208. F. Michael Krouse, *Milton's Samson and the Christian Tradition* (Princeton: Princeton University Press, 1949), 109.

literate contemporaries could have thought of Samson without thinking also of Christ.[209]

Once he is before the Philistine lords he is not slow to perform their behest, for he knows all is from God. His last feat is self-destruction for the Israelites and to vindicate the ways of God to Man. Donne in the *Biathanotos* calls the act suicide on the part of Samson. The point is controversial, but the reality of the sacrifice is "victory on the human level. Samson's story, paralleling as it does the story of *Christus Victor* reveals him as *Homo Victor*, a palpable exemplification of the meaning to Man of his Redemption."[210] "The final act stemming from the conquest destroys the universal doubt about the wisdom of God's Providence. . . ."[211] God is triumphant; in the saint and in the martyr, He has brought to perfection the cycle of being—death, atonement and rejuvenation.

E.M. Stephenson says of Becket that he belongs to that category of men who are "aliens in an alien world, they themselves presage their destiny."[212] The temptations of memory, of Chancellorship, of alliance with the Barons, and lastly the insidious suggestion of martyrdom have all been overcome, but Thomas, like Sydney Carten in *A Tale of Two Cities* can only claim death when he is worthy of it.

> All my life
> I have waited. Death will come only when I am worthy,
> And if I am worthy, there is no danger.
> I have therefore only to make perfect my will.
> . . . .
> And I am not in danger: only near to death.
> . . . .
> Go to vespers, remember me at your prayers.[213]

The end is as triumphant as that of a victor:

> I have had a tremor of bliss, a wink of heaven, a whisper,

209. *Ibid.*, p. 119.
210. *Ibid.*, p. 73.
211. *Ibid.*, p. 207.
212. E.M. Stephenson, *T.S. Eliot and the Lay Reader* (London: The Fortune Press, 1948), p. 70.
213. Eliot, "Murder in the Cathedral," *The Complete Poems and Plays*, p. 209.

And I would no longer be denied: all things
Proceed to a joyful consummation.[214]

Matthiessen writing on T.S. Eliot's plays says:

> But in our time of broken standards and beliefs he wanted to see what reinvigoration for drama might lie in a return to its source in liturgy. The structure of *Ash Wednesday* . . . draws upon the drama of the Mass.[215]

And to a great extent, that of *Murder in the Cathedral* is dependent on the Mass. It is a morality play; didactic, homilectic, culminating in Eucharistic catharsis; even "the prose of modern debate"[216] of the Tempters-cum-Knights does not arrogate from the solemnity and elation of the martyrdom, for in the last sacrifice of thanksgiving the cycle of death and rebirth is complete, the cult of the Year-Daemon iterated, the song of fertility and new life begun, and tragedy triumphant. Man has achieved his destiny; he is purified through suffering, has defeated evil, and order is restored. The spirit of tragedy is an "affirmation of positive values"; it is victorious.

The Benediction

The benediction at the end of the Eucharistic Mass has the sanctifying grace of sublime poetic utterance and a warmth-giving quality soothing to an acutely wakened consciousness. To the votary who has identified himself with Christ's Epiphany, Death and Resurrection, it supposedly gives complete peace of mind and renewed faith in God's grace. The priest enshrines the blessing in the august words:

> The peace of God, which passeth all understanding, keep your hearts and minds in the knowledge and love of God. . .[217]

The Eucharistic drama is thus enacted to

214. *Ibid.*, p. 209.
215. F.O. Matthiessen, *The Achievement of T.S. Eliot*, p. 161.
216. *Ibid.*, p. 164.
217. *The Book of Common Prayer*, p. 84.

> lead the creature out from his inveterate self-occupation to a knowledge of God, and ultimately to that union with God which is the beatitude of the soul. . . [218]

It is on this note of calm that the liturgy ends; its function to purify and enlighten being performed. The ritual is stylized but its sanctifying power is real for receptive minds.

Everyman, shriven of his sins and filled with sanctity, calls for God's blessing on himself as he commends his soul to God:

> In *manus tuas* of mightës most.
> For ever commends *spiritum meun.*[219]

He achieves the peace necessary for the acceptance of death. He has learnt the meaning of life, which can only be learnt through tragedy, but the calm that prevails is that of Man who has struggled and is reconciled. He is at peace with himself and is reaching towards the ultimate. In the words of the Doctor:

> Unto which place God bring us all thither
> That we may live body and soul together.[220]

In the statement there is an urge for the liberation of the psyche and the body so that man can attain perfect communion with God; the God of love, of peace, and of knowledge. In the play, the benediction of death silently paves the way for this union, and Everyman is at peace with God and himself.

Samson Agonistes began on a note of intense mental unrest, and the occurences in the play did not help to alleviate the struggle and the suffering of the protagonist. Samson continually battles with situations that seem to spell doom; the Chorus says:

> This Idol's day hath been to thee no day of rest,
> Labouring thy mind.[221]

Samson fights lassitude and "despair, sprouting from sin and

218. Underhill, *Worship,* p. 17.
219. Browne, "Everyman," *Religious Drama 2* p. 303.
220.*Ibid.*, p. 304.
221. Milton, *Samson Agonistes,* p. 43, Line 1297.

from a sense of unworthiness";[222] the Tempters in the shape of his aged father, the erring wife, and the vaunting enemy; and above all, the loss of intellectual integrity which caused him to blame God for his sorrows. The intensity of Samson's mental struggles points towards disaster, but the play ends on a note of calm and purges the mind of all unrest. It is "significant in its feeling of peace after tragic storm,"[223] and breathes a benediction in the Recessional as the Chorus chants:

> Go, and the Holy One
> Of Israel be thy guide.
> . . . .
> Send thee the Angel of they birth, to stand
> Fast by thy side,
> . . . . . . .that Spirit
> Be efficacious in thee now at need![224]

Also in the last song of the Chorus, where God's purpose is fully revealed and His ways are justified:

> His servants He with new acquist
> Of true experience from this great event,
> With peace and consolation hath dismissed,
> And calm of mind, all passion spent.[225]

The beatific triumph is complete; Samson has redeemed his spiritual tragedy; order and peace reign once again in the soul.

Becket's arrogance is symbolized in the play by words such as "Peace, but not the kiss of peace."[226] The danger seems imminent to his soul as the Chorus repeats, "O late, late, late is the time."[227] in the same rhythmic spondees as Samson's lamentation, "O dark, dark, dark, amid the blaze of noon."[228] There is little hope of recovery from the sin of pride, but the purgation

222. Don Cameron Allen, *The Harmonious Vision, Studies in Milton's Poetry* (Baltimore: The Johns Hopkins Press, 1954), p. 81.
223. Visiak, *The Portent oj Milton*, p. 337.
224. Milton, *Samson Agonistes*, Lines 1427 ff.
225. *Ibid.*, Lines 1755 ff.
225. Eliot, "Murder in the Cathedral," *The Complete Poems and Plays*, p. 178.
227. *Ibid.*, p. 180.
228. Milton, *Samson Agonistes*, Line 80.

comes through desire for peace and acquiescence to God's will, for "The peace of this world is always uncertain, unless men keep the peace of God."[229] The Chorus recognizes the fact that God's benediction will descend on Man only when Man's faith in God is fully realized; not when Man's actions are coloured by the fear of his fellow men. The Chorus says that in itself it symbolizes:

> The type of the common man . . .
>
> . . . .
>
> Who fear the blessing of God, the loneliness of the night
> of God, the surrender required, the deprivation inflicted:
> Who fear the injustice of men less than the justice of God.[230]

Eliot makes it clear that it is God's relationship to man which leads to redemption and the final benediction.

The approach to the *Book of Common Prayer* is the same as to the three religious plavs Milton, "though favouring the Puritan wing of the Anglican church,"[231] it is steeped

> in the hermeneutic and homiletic literature of Christianity. From the biblical commentaries, the sermons, the *exempla*, and other writings of the Fathers of the early Church, the Schoolmen of the late Middle Ages, and the learned divines of the Renaissance, we can descry and reconstruct the Samson tradition which lies behind and between the lines of Milton's tragedy, the attitudes towards the hero which Milton expected his "fit audience" to have.[232]

If Milton belongs to the left wing of the Anglican Church, T.S. Eliot is very much in the right wing, and *Everyman* is Catholic in every sense of the word. The three tragedies are moralities where man is trying to free himself from the trammels of the world. When *Samson Agonistes*

229. *Ibid.*, p. 221.
230. Eliot, "Murder in the Cathedral," *The Complete Poems and Plays*, p. 201.
231. E.M.W. Tillyard, *The Metaphysicals and Milton* (London: Chatto and Windus, 1956), p. 63.
232. Krouse, *Milton's Samson and the Christian Tradition*, p. 17.

> has been read to the end, Samson, even more clearly than Archbishop Thomas à Becket in *Murder in the Cathedral*, has vindicated himself of the sin which Mr. Eliot makes the last chorus in that most Christian tragedy confess, both for itself and for the other actors—the sin of fearing the injustice of men more than the justice of God. Professor Clyde Curry has good reason to rank *Samson* among the tragedies which revolve "about the central idea of the Christian religion, namely sin and its inevitable ravages in the human heart, purification and reconciliation through repentance, self-sacrifice and atonement." For that very reason, *Samson* has seemed to many readers untragic.[233]

Everyman and *Murder in the Cathedral* are also tragedy triumphant; so is the death on the Cross. Everyman, Samson and Thomas à Becket enact the drama of salvation in their own lives, as the Eucharistic Mass does that of Christ. In their theme, their atmosphere, and their diction, the plays are as significant and didactic as the liturgy of the *Book of Common Prayer*. Like the formal, visible aspects of worship, they point the way to a deeper participation in and a greater realization of spiritual values and in them lies the seed of man's greatest heroic deeds.

233. Hughes, *John Milton, Paradise Regained, Minor Poems and Samson Agonistes*, p. 440.

Chapter III

The Liturgical Aspect of the Plays

In a provocative article entitled "The Modern Playwright and the Absolute," Charles I. Glicksberg shows his concern for the trends in modern drama:

> In its beginnings, the drama was closely related to the communal worship of the Gods, the religious aspirations of a people. But today the playwright is compelled to come to grips with the ultimate issues at a time when traditional religion has fallen apart and can no longer command universal assent. In an age of rampant disbelief, an age of anxiety and crisis, he looks out on life which has lost both its spontaneity and its certitude, not to speak of its supernatural sanction. His divided state of being, his metaphysical homelessness and hopelessness, his spiritual alienation—these are the symptoms of a "disease" afflicting his generation.
>
> How can modern man take his fate seriously when he regards himself primarily as a biological accident, a conditioned product, no longer the special concern of God? . . . Realistic drama is confined to the study of the commonplace or the exploration of the abnormal, and it presents . . . a hero who has been reduced to nullity, a pathetic embodiment of helplessness . . . [Science has led] man to suspect that his struggle on earth is without ultimate significance.[1]

If this statement has validity and this is an age of disbelief, the religious drama has not only a special significance, but it has

1. Charles I. Glicksberg, "The Modern Playwright and the Absolute." *Queen's Quarterly*, A Canadian Review, LXV, No. 3 (Autumn 1958) pp. 460-461.

a great contribution to make. Archibald MacLeish in *J.B.* has tried to recapture the message and content of the book of Job for a modern audience in a modern setting, bringing half-forgotten values to the forefront. Eliot in his *Family Reunion* tries to give meaning to existence. Dorothy L. Sayers, Christopher Fry, Lawrence Housman, Arthur Miller, W.H. Auden, Charles Williams, John Masefield are some of the other names which come to mind in relation to a revival of interest in religious plays. These playwrights all seek to reveal man to himself in the light of great ethical and religious truths. Religious plays are a medium whereby the disturbing nihilistic attitude of the modern age can be seen in a different perspective. The Existentialist theory need not be disturbing, if man can once again believe in the patterned cycle of life. Death seems a negation of existence, but rebirth suggests continuation of life, as in the plays under discussion. Justice, retribution, belief in the indistructability of the psyche and in the dignity of man are some of the values that make the hero rise to tragic heights, otherwise there can be no conflict, no real tragedy.

We know from the earliest times of written records and specially from those of dramatic performances, that drama was part of the religious rites. Conversely, all serious drama can be considered religious because it deals with human nature and human values. The main actors in every play portray and affect the emotions and actions of man in problematic situations. In the sequence of events, the homelessness of man's spirit is made evident, and the pursuit of God's love is revealed—herein lies the seed of Christian mystery and the religious plays. A tragedy is usually the physical embodiment of an inner torment, stemming from guilt or responsibility, but its catharsis is often effected by the religious awakening of a soul that is degenerate, thereby affirming and justifying existence.

The poet works through the material of communication, words; but faith in his material, his characters, and his theme and thought must precede all expression. The Church uses the same vocabulary as the poet. As for the dramatist, so for the Church, hope is never dead, and the element of change is always challenging. Nothing can be more painful than rebirth for the terrified spirit; for man is part of an unredeemable past, and the experiences of the past colour most expectancy for the future; as T.S. Eliot says in the "Four Quartets," time present and time past are both present in time future. The world of reality is not important enough, for both the cautious and the reckless have been known to fail, and suffering, therefore, becomes a means, not an end. It is the belief in man's ordination and mission in life, as that of the highest created being, which is of importance. The emphasis in religious plays is often on sin and expiation, and the idea of annihilation is non-existent. The religious dramatist's function is liturgical; in his art he tried to give meaning to life, and his service to epochs like the present is of vital importance.

Eliot at the Canterbury festival, like Milton in the seventeenth century and the playwright of *Everyman* in the mediaeval times, wrote for the period, the place, and the people that were of special interest to him. Each of the three plays is topical both in its significance and its homiletic quality.

Everyman, one of the greatest moralities, shows a purity and unity in the conception of the world of mediaeval drama, an enormous depth of Biblical knowledge, and a satisfaction and delight in things religious. There is a symmetrical pattern about the play which is in keeping with the unified Christian civilization of the period, a civilization that believed in order and symmetry, the Church being the pivotal point around which society revolved:

> It was characteristic of the Middle Ages to arrange events in patterns. Order was the foundation of life. In a time of insecurity this was natural, but furthermore, it was the conception which grew from the international Christian society of the Church. And so when they dramatized the history of the world, it was as the working of God's plan.[2]

For the mediaeval man, the turmoils and transitions were all resolved by adherences to faith in God; life was a pilgrimage, and God's mercy if it chastened also subdued and deflected from sin and suffering. Although the *Dãnce of Death* figured widely in all mediaeval art, it was not the motif of annihiliation, but just a *memento mori*, a reminder of a further step towards the ultimate goal; and the example of the Cross was always there.

Farnham writes of the morality as the author's "choral com-

2. Browne, *Religious Drama 2*, p. 9.

ment upon human destiny; . . . [an] implicit comment upon life . . [for] the moral drama enforced the doctrine preached from the pulpit and made the preacher, in whatever guise, its chorus."[3] The morality shows man's allegorical fight with the mediaeval conception of evil, embodied in the world, the flesh and the devil, and the Seven Deadly Sins. The mediaeval man was stoically resigned to events and acts believed as pre-ordained, but in the moralities there is a definite advance from the unquestioned acceptance of things pre-ordained. The recurring conflict of good and evil in *Everyman* is a progressive and critical attitude in the conception of the way-faring, war-faring life of the individual, and shows a considerable advance in dramatic technique from the earlier mystery plays. Thus it appeals to the modern man. The bi-polarity of good and evil has the germ of all human experience and all human drama. *Everyman* stresses the pre-eminence of God, a fact most vital to the mediaeval mind, but points out that union with God can best be achieved after the struggle. The way to salvation is a militant way. There is no physical suffering as such in *Everyman* but the spiritual and mental conflict is great and gives the play its intensely psychological character. The dramatic element is intensified and enhanced by the shortness of time for preparation that Everyman is allowed; and the comicality of allegorical figures and abstractions, like Fellowship, Goods, Beauty, and Strength, heightens the tragic effect and the liturgical aspect of the play. The emphasis throughout is not so much on sin as on man's folly and his deliberate occupation with the world. He is oblivious of things supra-mundane till he is actually faced by Death: "mortal life by its very nature is an insidious blindness and a heady drunkenness to the ordinary human soul, no matter how clear his vision may be . . . "[4] To a society essentially based on religion, a play like *Everyman* must have been didactic, yet had a special appeal, for it deals with basic truths that were pertinent to the time, and to all times. Though regarded as a translation of the Dutch play, *Elckerlijk*, *Everyman* has its roots in the Greco-Roman tradition and can be considered as the "truly logical manifestation of Neo-Platonic, Augustan Christianity,"[5] of the Middle Ages. Liturgical in concept, it has come down as one of the most powerful plays of

3. Farnham, *The Medieval Heritage of Elizabethan Tragedy*, p. 176.
4. *Ibid.*, p. 189.
5. *Ibid.*, p. 210.

the mediaeval Church. In language simple but dramatic, and lyrical in certain passages. *Everyman* holds up the mirror of life to the man in the street; making him realize that life and its values are just as realistic and important to creative artists and men of literature who seek the ultimate as it is to theologians.

The seventeenth century, vibrant with the *new philosophy*, had challenged religious values as it did the existing philosophy and astronomy, and the limitations of scholasticism. The quest was for truth and reason, for scientific explanations of natural phenomena in the State, for a government that would spell controlled liberty of action and thought; and in religion, for a rational God. Religious values were changing, God had been conceived as perfect; His "symbol [being] the circle,"[6] but now He seemed distant; "Seeking God in a new universe that had grown beyond comprehension, the religious poet sometimes thought Him lost."[7] The questioning mind was in "mazes lost"[8] yet the century was a time of great output of religious literature, both in prose and in poetry.

Milton, like many of his contemporaries, had delved deeply into all available knowledge of his day, and his views on religion are enshrined in poems and pamphlets that have been jealously preserved, the longest and most provocative religious treatise being the *De Doctrina Christina*. *Samson Agonistes*, religious in theme, ethical in concept, liturgical in purpose, can be called a realistic play, for it reveals the stark horror of life. Yet unlike many modern dramas, it redeems itself by adhering to all the religious and ethical truths that count. Written at a time of scepticism when religion was not of special interest to the elite of the English society, it has captured in its perfect form and rhythm, theme and diction, the eternal verities and beauty, that outshine all the plays of the period, and give the drama its special didactic and liturgical significance.

Samson, whether a mythical figure or a historical person, had been considered a national hero in Hebrew literature. By the seventeenth century a long tradition had grown round him:

> Here, as according to the Pauline doctrine of the election of believers, Samson was set down as one of the chosen

6. Nicolson, *The Breaking of the Circle*, p. 35.
7. *Ibid.*, p. 36.
8. Milton, *Paradise Lost*, Book II, p. 59, Line 561.

(electi) of the Old Testament. Later Christian writers made *electus* synonomous with *sanctus.*[9]

Samson was considered a saint of the Church and, according to the Alexandrian school, a figure of Christ. Milton knew these traditions, and chose the subject as befitting a great tragedy. "Humanism, that deep and searching study of the nature of man, as revealed in his thoughts and his works, both past and present,"[10] was a subject of great interest to the age. Milton made his study of Samson humanistic, for the play deals with Samson the vanquished, who psychologically rose to be the triumphant martyr, not the herculean hero of the Israelites. Like a well-versed psychiatrist, Milton had explored the recesses of the protagonist's mind and helped this child of his creation to greatness step by step, always keeping God and His purpose for Samson in view. The fall of Samson may have been due to his pride, *hubris,* or the disloyalty of a vain woman, but Milton voices the dictum of his age on Samson when he makes Samson say that his adversity was due to his own frailty and folly and his forgetfulness of his election and ordination. Helen Darbishire in *Milton's Paradise Lost* says that Milton shows man's "littleness and his greatness, his frailty and his supreme responsibility. Man is nothing in himself, everything in his spiritual destiny . . . in his relation to God."[11] The words can be applied to Samson as to Adam. Samson's drama was built on his frailty and his strength. Samson has been called the prototype of Christ, the God-man, his mission being the salvation of the Israelites as Christ's of the whole world, but Samson's appeal, like that of Everyman, is greater, for his failings are human as his triumphs god-like. In his drama there is a tragic justification of life. As for the seventeenth century, so for the modern age, the play has its liturgical message, that values need not crumble if man keeps the ultimate reality in view. Milton has justified God's ways to man and affirmed his confidence in human nature and life.

In the modern theatre it is not easy to make the dichotomy,

9. Krouse, *Milton's Samson and the Christian Tradition, p. 30.*

10. Helen C. White, Ruth C. Wallerstein, and Ricardo Quintana, eds., *Seventeenth-Century Verse and Prose* (New York: The Macmillan Company, 1951), p. p. 13.

11. Helen Darbishire, *Milton's Paradise Lost* (London: Oxford University Press, 1951), p. 5.

religious and secular. The plays either affirm ethical values or they are nihilistic. It is the realistic drama which is of interest to the modern age.

Murder in the Cathedral can be classed as a realistic play, not in its social aspect, but psychologically, for in it Eliot has depicted

> . . .human personality in highly dynamic terms, with the self becoming a kind of battlefield upon which fierce struggles rage between impulse and regulation, desire and convention—a vision . . . close to the scrutiny of inner motives that is so frequent in nineteenth- and twentieth-century writings.[12]

Eliot presupposes a saint to be a sinner. His cross is the perennial human struggle, though rational Christianity affirms that man is never defeated, but always triumphant; if there is ultimate extinction, a Stoic affirmation of life makes existence meaningful; for life itself is a paradox, what matters is *to do the right thing for the right reason*. Eliot has sought to wed the exalted ritual of the Church to the everyday life of man, to see divine revelation in things prosaic and mundane, to convey religious dimensions through poetic drama, to re-establish the Christian vision.

Unlike *Samson Agonistes*, *Murder in the Cathedral* can leave a bitter taste in the mouth. Eliot, for all its liturgical characteristics, has made the play ironic in the *monolithism* of the protagonist. Becket renounces the world, but seems so occupied with his own salvation that he is not convincing as a prototype of Christ. The Celtic incantations of the Chorus, the superstitious symbols, are far from liturgical; and the rapid association of ideas and transitions in diction seem a poor imitation of the metaphysicals, and alien to the religious character of the play. Yet the use of poetic devices as the lilting cadences, the prosaic outbursts, use of *stichomythia*, the verbal quips and turns, the hauntingly lyrical lines, make *Murder in the Cathedral* a powerful drama in the modern theatre. Eliot has perfected his art by trying to make it a mode of salvation. He has made the play realistic in bringing out contrasts; the juxtaposition of the serious and the trite adds reality to the historical play and makes it alive.

12. Irving Howe, "Books and the Arts," Modern Criticism in America, *The Nation*, November 22, 1958, p. 286.

Liturgically the play is a great success. In portraying Becket, Eliot has shown:

> that the distinguishing feature of human life consists in the occasions on which the individual most fully reveals his character and that those are the moments of intense "moral and spiritual" struggle.[13]

The protagonist emerges triumphant when he gives his life *to the law of God above the law of Men,* with his mission in life fulfilled and God glorified above man.

Everyman, Samson Agonistes, and *Murder in the Cathedral* are liturgical. They celebrate all those ethical and religious values that have proved a talisman and a catalyst in alleviating man's doubts and despair. They are the true embodiment of art, for they purge the soul of all dross and uplift it heavenwards and reaffirm the beatitude of eternity. After studying the three plays, one can claim with Glicksberg:

> So long as art flourishes, the writer will oppose the deathward drive and ritualistically exalt the miracle of rebirth, the resurrection of the dead god, the mysterious, unbroken continuity of life.[14]

13. Mattiessen, *The Achievement of T. S. Eliot,* p. 21.
14. Glicksberg *Queen's Quarterly,* p. 471.

BIBLIOGRAPHY

I. *LITURGY*

1. *The Book of Common Prayer*. New York, 1945.
2. Cargill, Oscar. *Drama and Liturgy*. New York: Columbia University Press, 1930.
3. Clark, W.K. Lowther, and Harris, Charles, eds. *Liturgy and Worship*. London: S.P.C.K., 1933.
4. Dowden, John. *The Workmanship of the Prayer Book*. London: Churchman's Library, 1898.
5. Fuller, Samuel. *Characteristic Excellences of the Liturgy*. Boston, 1845.
6. Heiler, F. *The Spirit of Worship*, translated by W. Montgomery. London: Hodder and Stoughton, 1926.
7. Hislop, David Hall. *Our Heritage in Public Worship*. Glasgow: Trinity College, Scribner, 1935.
8. *Holy Bible, The*. Cambridge: Printed at the University Press (King James' Version).
9. Liddell, Henry George and Scott, Robert. eds. *A Greek-English Lexicon*. New York: American Book Company, 1897.
10. Shepherd, Massey Hamilton. *The Liturgical Movement and the Prayer Book*. Evanston, IL. Seabury-Western Theological Seminary, 1946.
11. Underhill, Evelyn. *Worship*. New York and London: Harper and Brothers, 1937.

II. *EARLY MORALITY PLAYS AND TRAGEDY*

1. Adams, Henry Hitch. *English Domestic or Homiletic Tragedy*, 1575 to 1654. New York: Columbia University Press, 1943.
2. Bradley, A.C. *Shakespearean Tragedy*. New York: Meridian Books, 1957.
3. Brooke, C.F. Tucker. *The Tudor Drama*. Boston: Houghton Mifflin, 1911.
4. Browne, E. Martin, ed. *Religious Drama 2*. New York: Meridian Books, 1958.

5. Chambers, Sir Edmund Kerchever. *The Mediaeval Stage*. Oxford: The Clarendon Press, 1903.
6. ———. *English Literature at the Close of the Middle Ages*. Oxford: The Clarendon Press, 1947.
7. Cunliffe, John W., ed. *Early English Classical Tragedies*. Oxford: The Clarendon Press, 1912.
8. Farnham, Willard. *The Medieval Heritage of Elizabethan Tragedy*. New York: Barnes and Noble, 1956.
9. Halverson, Marvin. *Religious Drama 1*. New York: Meridian Books, Inc., 1957.
10. Herrick, Marvin Theodore. *Tragicomedy*. Urbana: University of Illinois Press, 1955.
11. Lewis, C.S. *English Literature in the Sixteenth Century Excluding Drama*. Oxford: At the Clarendon Press, 1954.
12. Livingston, James C., ed. *Dialogue*. Issued occasionally, The Protestant Office, Columbia University, Autumn 1958, Number 3.
13. Muller, Herbert. *The Spirit of Tragedy*. New York: Knopf, 1956.
14. Parks, Edd Winfield, and Beatty, Richard Croom, ess. *The English Drama*, An Anthology 900-1642. New York: W.W. Norton and Company, Inc., 1935.
15. Pollard, Alfred W., ed. *English Miracle Plays, Moralities and Interludes*. Oxford: At the Clarendon Press, 1954.

III. *MILTON AND THE SEVENTEENTH CENTURY*

1. Allen, Don Cameron. *The Harmonious Vision, Studies in Milton's Poetry*. Baltimore: The John's Hopkins Press, 1954.
2. Bush, Douglas. *English Literature in the Earlier Seventeenth Century*, 1600-1660. New York: Oxford University Press, 1952.
3. Banks, Theodore Howard. *Milton's Imagery*. New York: Columbia University Press, 1950.
4. Clark, Donald Lemen. *John Milton at St. Paul's School*. New York: Columbia University Press, 1948.
5. Conklin, George Newton. *Biblical Criticism and Heresy in Milton*. New York: King's Crown Press, 1949.
6. Daiches, David. *Milton*. London: Hutchinson University Library, 1957.
7. Darbishire, Helen. *Milton's Paradise Lost*, Geoffrey Cumberlege. London, New York and Toronto: Oxford University Press, 1951.
8. French, J. Milton. "Milton's Family Bible." *PMLA*, LIII (June 1938): 363-366.
9. Grierson, Sir Herbert J.C. *Milton and Wordsworth, Poets and Prophets*. London: Chatto and Windus, 1950.

10. Hanford, James Holly. *A Milton Handbook*. New York: Appleton-Century-Crofts, Inc., 1954.
11. Highet, Gilbert. *The Classical Tradition*. New York: Oxford University Press, 1957.
12. Hughes, Merritt Y. ed. *John Milton, Paradise Regained The Minor Poems and Samson Agonistes*. New York: The Odyssey Press, 1937.
13. ———. *John Milton, Prose Seletions*. New York: The Odyssey Press, 1947.
14. Hutchinson, Francis Ernest. *Milton and the English Mind*. London: Hoddar and Stoughton, 1947.
15. Krouse, F. Michael. *Milton's Samson and the Christian Tradition*. Princeton: Princeton University Press, for University of Cincinnati, 1949.
16. LeComte, Edward. *Yet Once More: Verbal and Psychological Patterns in Milton*. New York: Liberal Arts Press, 1953.
17. Lewis, C.S. *A Preface to Paradise Lost*. London: Geoffrey Cumberlege, Oxford University Press, 1956.
18. Lovejoy, Arthur O. *The Great Chain of Being*. Cambridge, MA: Harvard University Press, 1953.
19. Milton, John. *Samson Agonistes*, Introduced by H.M. Percival. London: Macmillan and Company, 1916.
20. Nicolson, Marjorie Hope, *The Breaking of the Circle*. Evanston, IL: Northwestern University Press, 1950.
21. Rajan, B. *Paradise Lost and the Seventeenth Century Reader*. New York, London: Chatto and Windus, 1947.
22. Saurat, Denis. *Milton: Man and Thinker*. London: Dent, 1944.
23. Senior, H. *John Milton Supreme Englishman*. London: W.H. Allen and Co., Ltd., 1944.
24. Sprott, S. Ernest. *Milton's Art of Prosody*. Oxford: Basil Blackwell, 1953.
25. Thorpe, James. *Milton Criticism*. New York: Rinehart, 1950.
26. Tillyard, Eustace Mandeville Wetenhall: i. *The Miltonic Setting*, Cambridge: at the University Press, 1938; ii. *Milton*. London: Chatto and Windus, 1949; iii. *The Metaphysicals and Milton*. London: Chatto and Windus, 1956; iv. *The Elizabethan World Picture*. London: Chatto and Windus, 1948.
27. Tuve, Rosamund: *Elizabethan and Metaphysical Imagery*. Chicago; The University of Chicago Press, 1947; *ii. Images and Themes in Five Poems of Milton*. Cambridge, MA: Harvard University Press, 1957.
28. Visiak, E.H. *The Portent of Milton*. London: Werner Laurie, 1958.
29. White, Helen C., Wallerstein, Ruth C., and Quintana, Ricardo, eds. *Seventeenth Century Verse and Prose*, Volume One:

1600-1660. New York: The MacMillan Company, 1951.
30. Whiting, George Wesley. *Milton and This Pendant World*. Austin: University of Texas Press, 1958.
31. Willey, Basil. *The Seventeenth Century Background*. London: Chatto and Windus, 1949.
32. Wolfe, Don M., ed. *Complete Prose Works of John Milton*. Volume I. New Haven: Yale University Press, 1953.

IV. *T.S. ELIOT AND CONTEMPORARY CRITICISM*
1. Drew, Elizabeth A. *T.S. Eliot, The Design of His Poetry*. New York: Charles Scribner's Sons, 1949.
2. Eliot, Thomas Stearns. *The Complete Poems and Plays*, 1909-1950. New York: Harcourt Brace & Co., 1952.
3. ——— *On Poetry and Poets*. New York: Farrar, Straus and Cudahy, 1957.
4. Gardner, Helen. *The Art of T.S. Eliot*. London and Hertford: E.P. Dutton & Co., Inc., 1950.
5. Glicksberg, Charles T. "The Modern Playwright and the Absolute." *Queen's Quarterly*, A Canadian Review, LXV, No. 3 (Autumn 1958), pp. 459-471.
6. Howe, Irving. "Books and the Arts." Modern Criticism in America, *The Nation*, Vol. 184, p. 386, Nov. 22, 1958.
7. March, Richard, and Tambimuttu,eds. *T.S. Eliot, A Symposium*. London: PL Editions Poetry, 1948.
8. Matthiessen, F.D. *The Achievement of T.S. Eliot, An Essay on the Nature of Poetry*. New York and London: Oxford University Press, 1947.
9. Morris, David. *The Poetry of Gerard Manley Hopkins and T.S. Eliot in the Light of the Donne Traditions*. Berne, 1953.
10. Maxwell, Desmond Ernest Stewart. *The Poetry of T.S. Eliot*. London: Routledge and Paul, 1952.
11. Stephenson, E.M. *T.S. Eliot and the Lay Reader*. London: The Fortune Press, 21 Belgrave Road, S.W.I, 1948.